Deep Purple, Vienna, 2017

Spain, 1987

...ekatekas and Turners, Lesotho, 1965

Ming Tombs, 1996

UNITED KINGDOM   UN, 2017

Turkmenistan, 1994

My daughter, Anna, 1994

Yorkshire, 1974

'There are diplomats for whom the word "luck" means quiet work in a calm country. Leigh Turner's diplomatic career can be called successful from the opposite point of view. He was lucky to regularly find himself in the middle of crisis situations with poorly predictable endings. This book is not only a fascinating read, but also a valuable source for understanding the recent past in world politics.'
Andrey Kurkov, novelist

'Insightful and compelling ... Ambassador Turner is an extraordinary raconteur whose book is a masterclass in diplomacy.'
Ayesha Riyaz, former ambassador of Pakistan

'A highly entertaining picture of a varied career – with real human insights both for diplomats and leaders more generally.'
Neil McMillan CMG, ex-diplomat and public servant

'Diplomacy is badly misunderstood and undervalued. Leigh Turner's book not only entertains and surprises – it also challenges your preconceptions.'
Catherine Royle, NATO political adviser and former ambassador

'A gifted writer, Leigh Turner has provided a vivid account of his impressive diplomatic career in the service of the Foreign Office.'
Oliver Rathkolb, Universität Wien

'This brilliant book shatters any doubt about the necessity of diplomats. A must-read for anyone seeking insight into the complexities of international relations.'
Maria-Pia Kothbauer, Princess of Liechtenstein, Liechtenstein ambassador in Vienna

'Interested in the nuts and bolts (and steely screwdrivers and painful pliers) of diplomacy? Try Leigh Turner's subtle, sharp exploration of the diplomatic toolbox.'
Charles Crawford CMG, former HM ambassador in Sarajevo, Belgrade and Warsaw

'It is said that diplomats think twice before saying nothing. Leigh Turner is luckily an exception: he thought twice and has written a highly entertaining guide to what diplomats really do – or what they wish they could do.'
Alexander Schallenberg, foreign minister of Austria

'Entertaining, instructive and absorbing: an excellent insight into the professional and personal challenges and excitements of being a diplomat.'
Stephen Wall, former ambassador to the European Union

'Entertaining insights into decades of diplomacy, from the 20th to the 21st centuries, in hotspots ranging from Moscow and Kyiv to Hong Kong and Shanghai.'
Marc Elsberg, author of international bestselling novel *Blackout*

'An engagingly self-deprecating, witty and well-written collection of diplomatic tips and tales.'
Nicola Brewer DCMG, former British diplomat

'"Diplomats are all hopeless. You'd be mad to do it." Having ignored this advice, Leigh Turner now unpacks, with a huge dose of British humour, what diplomats can make out of hopelessness.'
Ulrike Guérot, founder and director of the European Democracy Lab, Berlin

LESSONS IN DIPLOMACY
Politics, Power and Parties

Leigh Turner

First published as *The Hitchhiker's Guide to Diplomacy: Wie Diplomatie die Welt erklärt*
in German in 2023 by Czernin Verlag

This edition published in Great Britain in 2024 by

Policy Press, an imprint of
Bristol University Press
University of Bristol
1-9 Old Park Hill
Bristol
BS2 8BB
UK
+44 (0)117 374 6645
bup-info@bristol.ac.uk

Details of international sales and distribution partners are available at
policy.bristoluniversitypress.co.uk

British Library Cataloguing in Publication Data
A catalogue record for this book is available from the British Library

ISBN 978-1-4473-7392-6 hardcover
ISBN 978-1-4473-7394-0 ePub
ISBN 978-1-4473-7395-7 ePdf

Cover design: Keenan Design
Front cover image: Leigh Turner © 2024

Bristol University Press and Policy Press use environmentally
responsible print partners.

Printed in and bound in Great Britain by CPI Group (UK) Ltd,
Croydon CR40 4YY

FSC
www.fsc.org
MIX
Paper from
responsible sources
FSC® C013604

To the many brilliant diplomats from whom
I learned the lessons in this book.

Contents

Acknowledgements

Diplomacy, particularly overseas, has a way of forging intense relationships, mostly in the positive sense. I was fortunate in having colleagues in the Foreign Office, in posts including but not only Vienna (twice), Moscow, Berlin, Kyiv and Istanbul, and in the Departments of the Environment and Transport and HM Treasury, who consistently staved off chaos and kept me on the right track. Thanks to the lot of you. I have name-checked a few people in the text. Many other stellar figures, inevitably, remain anonymous and unsung.[1]

As I hope this book makes clear, any diplomatic career relies on contacts and connections from all walks of society, from cleaners and security guards to presidents and prime ministers, in dozens of countries. Many become friends; many you never see again, once you leave a job or post. Thanks to all of you, too. What a ride it's been.

I first wrote this book, in English, for Czernin Verlag in Austria, who published it in German under the title *The Hitchhiker's Guide to Diplomacy: Wie Diplomatie die Welt erklärt*.[2] The brilliant Benedikt Föger at Czernin came up with both the idea and the title. Hannah Wüstinger guided the book to publication; Karl Bichler masterminded the publicity. Translator Lisa Strausz did a superb job capturing the spirit of the English text.

For the English edition, special thanks are due to all the team at Bristol University Press. I am particularly grateful to Ginny Mills for her excellent and thoughtful editorial input, and her enthusiasm. Kathryn King has shown me the ropes on marketing, and Ellen Mitchell has provided all-round support.

---

[1] I once mentioned to maverick diplomat and colleague Charles Crawford that a certain valued but low-key official in the Moscow embassy was somewhat unsung. "No," he replied, "I think he's pretty sung."

[2] The subtitle means 'how diplomacy explains the world'.

I am grateful to Caradoc King and Becky Percival at United Agents, for their fiery belief in this project and for helping me develop the English version. Their advice and friendship have been wondrous. I look forward to working together on further projects.

Early readers whose insightful comments, often on numerous versions, helped me cut to the good stuff included Alison Cawley, Stephen Turner and others who are too shy to be named.

Pamela Major accompanied and supported me through the early years including London, Moscow, Berlin and Kyiv. I am so grateful for all of it. Thanks too for the thoughtful input from Pamela and from Anna and Owen Turner-Major on the text.

I have pestered some colleagues to try and patch my leaking memory. Special mentions to Duncan Allan for advice on support for the Russian Unity Party in Crimea in 2010, and to Mark Bertram for help with the history of the British embassy in Vienna.

My parents, John and Susan Turner, gave me an international mindset, starting with my conception in Nigeria and early years there aged zero to three, and later in Lesotho and Swaziland aged six to twelve. Perhaps a faint smattering of their qualities as great educationalists rubbed off on me.

Some of my language exchange partners and hosts over the years became lifelong friends. Without you, I would have remained a language duffer. Thank you, Luc de Belloy and Christian Fivaz (French); Rüdiger Borstel, Karin and Gerhard Klaus, Gudrun Mende, and Georg Wimmer and Barbara Wimmer-Stöllinger (German); Elena and Sergei (Russian); Mariya and Mykhaylo (Ukrainian); and Akın Bayraktaroğlu (Turkish).

The friendly staff of the Flowers and Fire Yoga Garden, in Gili Air, Lombok, provided a fine environment to work on late drafts of this book in 2023.

Finally, special thanks to Gözde Eren for supporting *Lessons in Diplomacy* so passionately from start to finish, for putting up with me writing it 23 hours a day, and for everything else.

Prologue:
Diplomacy in flux

These, however, are parsimonious days ... The telegraph has made a difference in the position of Ambassadors. When men can and do receive instructions hourly about the smallest details, and, indeed, ask for them as if anxious to escape responsibility, it is easy to conceive that the Foreign Office will not again insist on the Treasury behaving with boundless liberality.

The Times, reporting on the debate about
rebuilding Pera House, British embassy
in Istanbul, after the fire of 1870.

Diplomacy has been in flux for centuries. Are diplomats and their tradecraft redundant in today's world? Or are they more vital than ever for humanity's survival?

When I started this book, the simmering Russia–Ukraine conflict, launched in 2014 by President Vladimir Putin's invasion of Russia's peaceful neighbour, had already claimed 14,000 lives. Yet it seemed remote and obscure to many in Britain, the European Union, and the United States. Putin's decision in February 2022 to launch a full-scale war of annihilation against a sovereign country larger than France with a pre-war population of over 40 million transformed the world and upended diplomacy.

This book explores the background to the conflict: what the world did wrong, what it did right and what Vladimir Putin does not understand. It puts 21st-century diplomacy in context by digging into the Berlin Wall, the rusting of the Iron Curtain, terrorism, espionage, and how British politics prepared for Brexit – from 1987 onwards.

How, where and why does diplomacy happen, and what can it teach the rest of us? What can Jonathan the tortoise on St Helena tell us about institutional stability? Why is diplomatic immunity a necessary evil? I explain why you can't cure international terrorism and what to do if you find broken glass in your fruit salad at a banquet at the Argentine Foreign Ministry. On the way, we meet extraordinary people, from Queen Elizabeth, Vivienne Westwood and Jane Goodall through Paul McCartney and the wisdom of Deep Purple to US former C-17 pilot Brigadier General Lyn D. Sherlock – and Satan, whom I met one night in Russia. More on him later.

Moscow 1993

On Sunday 3 October 1993, a group of expats gathered at the British embassy *dacha*[1] in north-west Moscow for a child's fifth birthday party. Families huddled around tables in a garden of pale autumn sunshine, sipping Tuborg and munching crisps. Well-wrapped toddlers stuffed with jelly, scones and chocolate cake played hide and seek.

I was helping the birthday boy and his friends assemble a pirate ship when a diplomatic colleague strode up. Shooting had broken out at the Russian Parliament,[2] where riot police had for days hemmed in armed rebels seeking the overthrow of President Yeltsin. Our party included journalists and diplomats. As children played football and ate more cake, adults agonised about what to do.

Reports grew of killings, militias heading for the TV centre at Ostankino, and armoured vehicles joining the demonstrators. We decided to form a convoy, led by the flag car of a Latin American ambassador, and drive into town. If we saw violence or crowds, we would turn back.

As fighting raged elsewhere, our rag-tag convoy nosed through suburban Moscow. People queued as normal outside shops, women stood at metro stations selling household goods, kiosks advertised imported vodka. Only when we reached the city centre did we discover that a rebel convoy had crossed a flyover

---

[1] Traditionally a simple Russian country cottage, in recent decades often a palatial villa. The embassy dacha, long since lost, was the former.

[2] The confusingly named White House or Supreme Soviet of the Russian Federation.

on the inner ring as we passed under it. That night, we watched every Russian TV channel blink into blackness as fighters stormed Ostankino. 'Latest news', I wrote to my parents[3] that night, as tracer bullets lit up the sky to the north, 'is that tanks, presumed to be pro-Yeltsin, are moving into town.'

In the morning, I climbed into my chilly Lada Niva, put my gloved hands on the plastic steering wheel, and switched on the radio to accompany me on the drive to work. The traffic news came on, with the usual list of roadworks and broken-down vehicles. "You should also avoid the area around the Defence Ministry," the presenter quipped. "Armoured vehicles are massing there."

On the morning of 4 October, tanks of the Taman Division loyal to Yeltsin began shelling the White House and the coup collapsed.

The two Russian putsches, of August 1991 against Soviet leader Mikhail Gorbachev and October 1993 against Russian President Yeltsin, reflected the same tensions within Russian society that led to Putin's invasions of Ukraine in 2014 and 2022. The suffering of Russians in the chaotic 1990s helps explain why they put up with Putin for so long.

Diplomatic lessons

Who, as *The Times* thundered in 1870, needs diplomats when you have the telegraph/the television/the internet? That morning in the embassy, as tanks crushed the uprising against Yeltsin, we tuned in to CNN to find out what was going on.

Like most work, diplomacy is about making the best possible decisions based on the best possible understanding of the issues. Priorities will evolve. But, I will argue, the need to have diplomats who understand countries, multilateral organisations and the people who make them tick remains. We can apply lessons from diplomacy to careers, family life, politics, friendship and burying – or displaying – dead bodies. Is a diplomat's life as glamorous as a royal visit or as dramatic as a *coup d'état* in Turkey? Let's find out.

---

[3] Most quotes in this book are from my private correspondence, dated for clarity when needed. I have not quoted from official sources except where indicated.

This is not your standard manual on diplomacy. If you seek an explanation of the Vienna Convention on Diplomatic Relations or the theory of diplomatic etiquette, please look elsewhere. But if you're after concrete examples of how diplomats really work with spies, how immunity allows killers to escape justice, how Russia broke up the Soviet Union then nursed its resentment at the consequences, or what we can learn from a good diplomat or ambassador – read on.

Hitchhiking and diplomacy

In 1983, I told my boss in the Department of the Environment that the Foreign Office[4] had accepted my application.

"Diplomats are all hopeless," he said. "You'd be mad to do it."

"That's what they told me in New York in 1979," I said, "when I set off to hitchhike around the United States. They said I'd be raped, castrated and sold for medical research before I reached New Jersey. But I made it home."

The same hitchhiking skills that helped me get home safely in the summer of '79 proved invaluable in diplomatic life. Take, for example, my ride with Ray, a shambling, swarthy, sunken-eyed bear of a man who picked me up outside Durango, Colorado.

The first thing I saw when I peered into the cab was his butcher's arms: broad and sheened with sweat. Next, I took in his tattoos and his square jaw, thick with stubble, set in a sullen half-smile. A broken six-pack of Schlitz was wedged between his thighs.

Schlitz – the beer that made Milwaukee famous. *What's made Milwaukee famous has made a loser out of me.*[5]

Was it dangerous to enter the old Ford pick-up? Standing by the roadside in the cooling evening, I had seconds to decide.

---

4   The Foreign Office, founded in 1782, became the Foreign and Commonwealth Office (FCO) in 1968. In 2020 it became the Foreign, Commonwealth and Development Office (FCDO). In theory this suggests the next rebrand is due around 2034, but it may come sooner: in April 2024, with elections looming in the UK, experts convened by University College London and Hertford College Oxford proposed a further round of institutional reforms including a new name. Let's see. In this book, I use Foreign Office or FCO unless common sense suggests something else.

5   Jerry Lee Lewis.

"Where are you heading?" I asked.

"Cortez," he replied. The next town. I nodded and climbed in.

"Here you go." The driver nudged me with a beer. "The name's Ray. The seat belt's broken."

"Thanks," I said. The cab smelled of camphor. I wound down my window and took a sip. "Long trip?"

"No." He tossed an empty bottle on the floor. I heard a clinking sound. "Just out of prison. On parole."

"What were you in for?" It seemed polite to ask.

"Killed a man with a pool cue. Judge said it wasn't premeditated. Sure wasn't. Just kinda happened."

I gazed ahead and took another sip of my beer.[6]

Both hitchhiking and diplomacy require tolerance of uncertainty. Both rely on building relationships, earning goodwill and influencing people. In both, you have to take the measure of others, make quick decisions and act on them.

In hitchhiking, you stand by a roadside not knowing if anyone will ever stop – or where any ride may take you. In diplomacy, you may live and work anywhere in the world in five years' time. You'll have new colleagues, a new culture and perhaps speak a new language.

They say good generals make bad admirals. At sea, everything is more uncertain than on dry land. Leaders need to react quickly, and flexibly, as maritime conditions change. Are diplomats good admirals, or all at sea?

In my final diplomatic job, as British ambassador to Austria and permanent representative to the UN and other international organisations in Vienna,[7] people suggested I should share my experience and 'give something back'. Few jobs offer such a stimulating career. Some of the diplomatic lessons in this book may, to use civil service parlance, be STBO.[8] Others may, I hope, offer some insights into diplomacy – and life in general.

Welcome to the world of real diplomacy.

---

[6] More of this story is on rleighturner.com.

[7] No relationship, direct or inverse, exists between the length of diplomatic titles and the importance of the job.

[8] Stating the Bleeding Obvious.

Introduction:
How to become an ambassador

My 42-year mostly diplomatic career began in 1979, shortly after Margaret Thatcher became prime minister in May of that year. She was to have a baleful impact on my future.

That spring, I sat the civil service exams and attended a two-day assessment centre in London. I did well enough to be invited to a final selection board at the Old Admiralty Building in London, on the eve of the election. My goal was to join the Foreign Office.

Before the interview, I gathered every scrap of available intelligence about its format. Several people told me the FSB was a formality: by the time you had passed the earlier phases, you were as good as in. Relax and enjoy it, they said.

This was bad advice.

The first question of the grim-faced all-male panel was: 'Imagine it is 4 May, and Margaret Thatcher has been elected prime minister. You are sent to No. 10 Downing Street to brief her on Britain's top foreign policy priorities. What would you tell her?'

I responded with an answer so poor that I have blotted it from my memory. It may be unfair to blame Mrs Thatcher for this.

London: learning the basics

Thus it was that on 3 October 1979, with a heavy heart, I approached 2 Marsham Street, the since-demolished HQ of the Departments of the Environment and Transport. I had spent the summer hitchhiking around 27 states of the continental US. Having been rejected by the Foreign Office, I was about to start work in a three-towered monstrosity that architectural historian Nikolaus Pevsner had labelled 'the very image of faceless bureaucracy'.

"You've come to the wrong building," the receptionist said. "Go to Lambeth Bridge House."

I plodded across the river to a grim red 1940s office block – also since demolished, and described by Pevsner as 'brick, utilitarian and indifferent'. Within, the corridors grew narrower and gloomier.

I was beginning to have doubts about my career choice.[1]

At last, I reached a door marked 'Personnel, Management and Training Department'. Two women, half-concealed by a haze of cigarette smoke, smiled and waved me in, transforming my perceptions of my new job in an instant.

In the next four years, before a friend said "Why don't you try for the Foreign Office again?" I worked in four government departments. In the Department of Transport, I handled legislation to 'denationalise'[2] the National Freight Corporation, a state-owned trucking business. I would pass my policy efforts, in longhand, to my boss across the desk then watch, at length, as he improved them.

In 1980, I moved to the Property Services Agency, based at the headquarters of the NATO Northern Army Group and the British Army of the Rhine in Rheindahlen, Germany. We joked that our 'joint HQ' would be the first target of any Soviet nuclear attack.

In 1981 I returned to London, to work on housing policy. We introduced the 'assured tenancy' and looked after houseboats and 'mobile homes', that is, residential caravans. Mobile homes are about as mobile as a dead elephant.

In 1982 I moved to HM Treasury to help implement Thatcher's 'supply-side policies'. These were meant to enhance the efficiency of the UK economy through measures such as promoting cashless pay. The economy would surge ahead through less need for tough blokes in body armour transporting cash in vans.

I supported ministers in debates in the Houses of Parliament; travelled with a long-distance truck from Lincoln to Clermont-Ferrand and back; went through Checkpoint Charlie with

---

[1] The word 'choice' is an exaggeration. Others who turned me down included Thomas Cook, British Airways and J. Walter Thompson.

[2] The word 'privatisation' had not yet been invented.

a cavalry colonel in West Berlin; and met the head of the Residential Boat Owners' Association, the Earl Grey.

Bureaucratic grunt work taught me the basics of politics, economics and getting stuff done. My civil service colleagues were second to none – including the two women in the personnel department on the first day who rescued my hope.

Vienna: the first post

In 1983, I reapplied to the Foreign Office. Luckily, the interview panel asked me about Welsh devolution, which I had discussed with a friend passionate about the subject in a pub the night before.

When the FCO called to offer me the job, I was in an economics course at the Civil Service College where the speaker was David 'Two Brains' Willetts,[3] then a Treasury official. I waited until the end of the lecture to learn my fate.

The switch initially seemed a blunder. My first job in London was desk officer (responsible expert) for El Salvador and Nicaragua. I had to answer thousands of identical complaints sent to Members of Parliament by the public about UK support for US policy on El Salvador (where Washington was propping up a right-wing regime) and Nicaragua (where the US was undermining a left-wing one). We received reports from the region by letter on air-mail paper in the diplomatic bag.[4]

One day in 1984, Judith Macgregor, my personnel officer, put her head around the door and beckoned. Someone had resigned as second secretary political and press officer at the British embassy in Vienna. They needed a German speaker, fast. Was I interested?

Having grown up in Nigeria and Lesotho, I yearned for a first posting to Africa or Latin America. Vienna – not so much. I consulted colleagues. One, Alison Cawley, sent me a note scrawled with the words 'This means nothing to me.'[5] Another, Louise Kroll, said 'Vienna? You'd be mad not to.'

---

[3] Famed for his mighty intellect.

[4] The bags, closed with a tamper-proof seal, were transported by Queen's Messengers, official Foreign Office couriers equipped with special super-thick passports marked '*Courrier Diplomatique*'.

[5] The chorus of 'Vienna', a 1981 song by Ultravox.

I went by train. Travelling overland, you witness the rivers, mountains and forests that shape history and culture.[6] Fly, and you see the departure lounge. In 1984, the rail route still ran along the Rhine. As night fell, I gazed out as one illuminated castle after another marked the path into a continent riven by centuries of strife. I arrived at the Westbahnhof to be met by my colleague James Dunlop, a canny Scot with a sense of occasion. I recognised him, by his upright bearing and the rolled-up copy of *The Times* he had promised to carry, as he walked straight past. It was an inauspicious start to diplomatic life overseas.

Vienna was turbulent. In 1984 I met Green Party politician Kaspanaze Simma at an anti-dam protest in the Hainburger Au. The Austrian wine scandal, whereby antifreeze was added to wines to make them sweeter, came to light in 1985. In 1986, former Wehrmacht officer Kurt Waldheim[7] was elected president. The same year, in Innsbruck, I watched young right-winger Jörg Haider take over the Freedom Party.

But work did not dominate my life in Vienna.

The Austrian capital, jammed against the Iron Curtain east of Prague, appeared dour. Road signs to Bratislava and Budapest seemed laced with irony. Yet beneath the surface throbbed the beating heart of a party town. Vienna's *joie de vivre* took as its origin myth the city's role as a Cold War entrepôt, portrayed in Carol Reed's seminal movie *The Third Man*. It was fuelled by the opening of the 'UN City' on the banks of the Danube in 1979 and the 'Bermuda Triangle' of bars and restaurants in the city centre, famed for being hard to leave.

My head of Chancery, Tony Morgan, told me to have fun. "Your first posting is your best," he said. "No family. No responsibilities. Make the most of it."

I followed this advice. As a German speaker, I was designated to open the door to the Vienna police when they arrived at parties to turn the music down. One night, two cops barged in and advanced towards the stereo. A young US woman, possibly

---

[6] Some say that the soul can only travel at the pace of a camel.

[7] Waldheim's campaign slogan majored on his job from 1972–81 as UN secretary-general in New York. Against a Manhattan skyline were the words: 'An Austrian whom the world trusts' (*Ein Österreicher, dem die Welt vertraut*).

having enjoyed a drink, approached the grim-faced senior officer, seized the walkie-talkie from his lapel, and yelled "Beam me up, Scottie." This was poor diplomacy.

One morning, groggy and unshaven after an event at my attic flat, I shrugged on my leather jacket to lug four carrier bags of empties to the bottle bank. A neighbour passed me as I left. As I returned, a police car, sirens wailing, screeched up onto the pavement ahead of me. Two officers jumped out and demanded ID. I convinced them of my *bona fides*. Why, I asked, had they stopped me? "An anonymous complaint," one said. "One of your neighbours reported a possible burglary."

At another party, at 3 a.m., a session of 'Flap the Kipper' grew competitive as people seized telephone books and whacked the wooden floor to lend their fishes urgency. When the doorbell rang, it fell to me to assuage a quivering, white-haired neighbour in his dressing gown, who stared at me goggle-eyed. "*Sind Sie verrückt?*"[8] he said. We decided to play something else.

Forged in the furnace

I left Vienna by train on 24 October 1987, arriving in the UK by ferry. A once-in-two centuries hurricane had raged through London and the Home Counties nine days earlier: I saw devastation as my train trundled through Kent. It was an apt metaphor for the turbulent political climate into which I was heading.

The day I started my job as desk officer for budget and finance in the European Community Department (Internal) of the Foreign Office was a long one.

That night I sat in Room E121[9] of the FCO and watched the moon rise. My predecessor, Mark Lyall-Grant, had become private secretary to Lynda Chalker, minister for Europe. Stephen Wall, the head of ECD(I), had picked me to fill what he described as 'one of the most crucial desks in the FCO during the autumn'.

As the moon shone down, the door opened and Chalker herself walked in. "You must be Leigh Turner," she said. She urged me never to hesitate to seek advice from Mark in the weeks ahead.

---

[8] Are you insane?

[9] Later converted to a gents' lavatory.

"That shows", my colleague Ralph Publicover observed after she had left, "what you've let yourself in for."

He was not the first to warn me. My letter to my parents that weekend records that on arrival that morning 'I was met with numerous expressions of sympathy and condolence at my having to assume such a fearsome range of tasks.'

First up was preparing a European Council in December 1987 on the future financing of the European Community. The outcome would affect UK contributions to the EC[10] by billions of pounds. This was a subject to which Prime Minister Margaret Thatcher attached importance.[11] I also covered Economic and Monetary Union – a subject of political debate in the UK.[12]

Why did I apply for the job? Because I thought working on European Community issues would be central to UK interests, might be fun, and could help my career. All were true. Returning from the office as a chorus of birds announced the dawn was commonplace. I learned how to work to the highest quality at the utmost speed on the most complex subjects.

Important work meant stellar colleagues. My line management chain of Nigel Sheinwald, Stephen Wall and John Kerr gave me a crash course in hard work and excellence.[13] Several of my talented fellow desk officers became lifelong friends.

In 1989 I joined the Security Co-ordination Department, dealing with counter-terrorism. As 'head of ops', I led on the British government's response to terrorist attacks overseas, or the FCO element of a domestic incident. We ran exercises to test UK police forces, and after the fall of the Berlin Wall in 1989 explored counter-terrorism cooperation with dodgy spooks in former Warsaw Pact countries.

Working in SCD swelled my respect for the UK security and intelligence agencies and elements of the armed forces

---

[10] It became the European Union in 1993.

[11] British understatement.

[12] More British understatement.

[13] I once discussed with Kerr whether a speech should refer to the UK joining the Exchange Rate Mechanism of the European Monetary System when the time was 'right' or 'ripe'. He insisted on the latter, to imply a greater sense of inevitability.

with whom we worked closely. It also taught me lessons about delegation and operational crisis work that served me well later.

Moscow: coping with chaos

In 1990 I met Pamela, an FCO colleague. We sought a joint posting. Only three missions had two suitable vacancies: Washington (too much like Whitehall), Brussels (too close to London) and Moscow.

She already spoke Russian (and Chinese). I'd have to learn, having been officially classified as having zero language skills. We applied, and were successful.

Then everything changed.

On 19 August 1991, days before I started Russian language training,[14] we woke to the news that Communist hard-liners had launched a coup against Soviet leader Mikhail Gorbachev. The first words we heard were an 'expert' saying: "Gorbachev – if indeed he is still alive ..."

The speaker was Robert Maxwell, former British Member of Parliament, publishing tycoon and suspected spy, whose naked body would be found floating in the Atlantic near his yacht 11 weeks later.

Gorbachev survived. But the putsch was terminal for Soviet power. On 8 December 1991, the leaders of Russia, Ukraine and Belarus signed the Belovezha Accords, dissolving the Soviet Union.

I had started my course learning Russian phrases such as 'the inevitable collapse of capitalism'. By 1992 it was 'the transition to a market economy'.

On my first day at work in Moscow in December 1992 I watched from our 13th-floor flat as a blood-red sun rose from a murky horizon, then set off to walk to the metro station through the snow. Our offices were in portacabins at the back of the embassy, opposite the Kremlin.

I was responsible for reporting on economic reform. Petrol stations stood empty: we bought fuel from roadside bowsers

---

[14] A nine-month, full-time course that took me to the C1 level of language aptitude ('a level of ability that can be used in academic and professional contacts').

run by Chechens. Our first meal was a scraggy chicken bought from a shabbily dressed pensioner outside a metro station. For many Russians, inflation wiped out savings. In 1992 a Metro token cost 5 kopeks. By 1995 the price rose to 5,000 roubles: 100,000 times more.

People told the story of a manager summoning engineers at a ballistic missile factory and presenting them with a modern washing machine. "Here you go, lads," the manager said. "Make that." In November 1994 the manager of an oil trading company showed me the Makarov pistol he had bought to protect himself, ejecting the clip to show it was loaded. 'He seemed genuinely worried about the risk organised crime posed to him personally,' I wrote, 'I shall aim to call on him again in 1995.' I never did; he was murdered a few months later.

Russian business people took such perils in their stride. 'Despite the death threats,' I wrote after visiting a factory in Yekaterinburg, '[Mr X] seemed more relaxed than on my previous visit.' In 1993, according to police figures, 37 entrepreneurs were assassinated in Moscow.

That year, a Russian game called 'Business' went on sale. I bought a set, only to find a rip-off of 'Monopoly'. The main difference was that instead of going to jail, the player was taken hostage by the mafia – the picture showed a gagged man in a bow tie with a gun to his head. The title of the game may have reflected the fact that, for many Russians, the difference between a business and a monopoly remained blurred.

The Russians kept going. I saw pensioners dancing in the open air in minus five degrees Celsius in the snow at Dzerzhinsky Park; youths erecting barricades on Tverskaya Street to resist the 3 October 1993 anti-Yeltsin putsch; and locals fishing from jagged ice floes on the coast of Sakhalin Island.

"We have to adapt to the situation," a scientist said when I visited the Akademgorodok science park in Siberia. "If I drive 200 kilometres to pick mushrooms in the forest and my car breaks down, I can fix it. My US colleague going to the supermarket has to call a tow-truck."[15]

---

[15] Another scientist at Akademgorodok told me: "We can breed you any colour of mink."

Hong Kong: making a difference

I returned to London in 1995 to work on the handover of Hong Kong to China in 1997. "It really matters," someone told me. "You can make a difference."

The UK and China had begun talks on the future of Hong Kong in 1979. After Margaret Thatcher and Deng Xiaoping met in Beijing in 1982, intense negotiations led to the signing of the Sino-British Joint Declaration in December 1984. This set out principles for Hong Kong after the handover to China on 30 June 1997. 'One country, two systems' meant Hong Kong would retain a high degree of autonomy, except for defence and foreign affairs, and maintain its existing governance and economic systems, for 50 years after 1997.

When I started as deputy head of Hong Kong Department in November 1995, my top task was to complete the issue of new British National (Overseas) passports to 3.5 million eligible residents of Hong Kong and the construction of the new consulate-general, in Admiralty.

As the handover drew closer, tempers frayed, and pressure grew. The eight-hour time difference meant that the end of the working day in Hong Kong coincided with our arrival at the office in London, placing a premium on turning work around within the day – a kind of virtuous treadmill of policy formation.

I travelled regularly to Hong Kong and Beijing, working with the dedicated officials of the Hong Kong government, led by Chief Secretary Anson Chan, and the governor's office, led by Governor Chris Patten. Policy was intensely debated on the British side[16] – particularly whether holders of British National (Overseas) passports should be given the right to live in the UK. Both main British political parties rejected such a move.

On 30 June 1997 I ran a reception at the Banqueting House in London hosted by Deputy Prime Minister John Prescott. A big screen showed the handover ceremony in Hong Kong. As midnight ticked closer in Wan Chai, the first soldiers of the People's Liberation Army marched into the Convention and Exhibition Centre carrying the Chinese flag. A hush fell. As the

---

[16] Translation: there were constant blazing rows.

9

Union Jack came down, a waiter in London dropped her tray of drinks.

On 3 July I was promoted to head of Hong Kong Department. We introduced six-monthly reports to Parliament on the implementation of the Joint Declaration. Beijing said they were otiose: what happened in Hong Kong was none of Britain's business.

Becoming a bigger cog in the system meant contact with more senior people. It was around this time that a British diplomat who had been awarded an honour told me "I am about as senior a diplomat as you can get, you know." This was good coaching in humility.

China did not fulfil its obligations under the Joint Declaration. On 1 July 2020, in response to events in Hong Kong, the government of Prime Minister Boris Johnson overturned UK policy by announcing a new immigration route for British Nationals (Overseas) and immediate family dependants. Over 100,000 applied in the first year. The figures suggest the impact could eclipse that – already significant – of the roughly 30,000 Ugandan Asians who settled in the UK after their expulsion by Idi Amin in 1972.

The UK continues to publish six-monthly reports on Hong Kong. China continues to criticise them.

Bonn and Berlin: Euroscepticism rising

After Hong Kong, I applied for jobs that would have meant a fresh start. Having two young children made posts as consul-general in Melbourne or high commissioner in Swaziland tempting. But the job for which my application was successful, in 1998, was as counsellor (EU and economic) in Bonn.

Bonn, the 'federal village' immortalised in John le Carré's *A Small Town in Germany* 30 years earlier, was sinking back into provinciality. The fall of the Iron Curtain had led to the relocation of government organs to Berlin. French, US and British military formations whose presence had shaped local communities since 1945, and which I had helped maintain from Rheindahlen in 1980–81, had disappeared. They left behind ghostly 1950s officers' clubs and NAAFI stores across the former West Germany.

The British embassy in Bonn, built in 1953 to an austere design with a view to being converted to commercial use should the embassy ever return to Berlin, closed in 1999 and was promptly demolished. We moved eastwards in a convoy of removal vans.

The British embassy in Berlin resumed operations on 3 September 1999. After war, division and reunification, the shattered city was feeling its way to a vibrant new identity with its Love Parade, open-air movies and techno scene. 'Enjoyed a curious café in a tent', I wrote, 'featuring a cage full of rats, a free-range rabbit, and biker types playing billiards in an atmosphere thick with cigarette smoke and fumes from the deeply suspect plumbing.'

From the German-Russian Museum[17] at Karlshorst in the east to the Glienicke Bridge in the west, the Sachsenhausen concentration camp in the north and the remains of the Berlin Wall all around, the new capital was steeped in Germany's 20th-century history. Our local supermarket was on the site of Spandau Prison, where Rudolf Hess had been incarcerated from 1947 until his death, aged 93, in 1987. The prison was demolished the same year.[18]

With Euroscepticism rising in the UK, I gave countless talks on 'The UK and the EU' to reassure sceptical German business types that the United Kingdom remained a reliable partner. We engaged with the European Central Bank in Frankfurt, and with companies such as Volkswagen (investing in the UK) and Vodafone (investing in Germany).

But the evolution of the European Union in ways uncomfortable to the UK was evident. More EU members signed up to the Schengen Agreement, abolishing internal border controls and introducing a common visa policy. On 1 January 1999, the euro was introduced. On 1 January 2002, I walked through the snow to an ATM on the island of Hiddensee in the Baltic to take a look at the new notes as the euro became legal tender.

---

[17] Now the Museum Berlin-Karlshorst.

[18] According to one source, the supermarket built on the prison site was known as Hessco's, rhyming with Tesco's, but I never heard it used.

Both steps changed the functioning of, and life in, the EU. The UK – for a range of practical and political reasons – did not participate in either.

My job, too, was about to change radically.

Work isn't everything

In October 2002 I took over as chief carer for our children, Owen (then 10) and Anna (8). Pamela, in turn, took over my job at the embassy. Someone said it was like a reality TV show, only it was real, and it wasn't on TV.

One of the first mornings I dropped the kids off at school, I ran into an embassy colleague. "How the mighty have fallen," he said. I couldn't think of a witty response.

The Foreign Office calls taking a career break to do something specific, such as looking after your children, 'special unpaid leave'. US friends tell me it sounds as if you've been fired.

One bonus was that back in 2002, giving up a reasonably senior Foreign Office job to care for my children attracted some interest. An editor at the *Financial Times* remarked "Man at home: rich source of copy." Would I like to write an article about how it felt?

'From Herr to Maternity',[19] in the FT of 9 May 2003, kicked off my short career in journalism. I went on to write several dozen pieces for the FT, the *Boston Globe* and other newspapers.

Most of my writing was about travel, from comparing German and French holiday camps to New Zealand eco-tourism. A few were on gender issues, including a piece about how a British colleague became a senior diplomat having started as a secretary, without a university degree – unthinkable in Germany's stratified labour market. I also wrote two novels.

The hardest thing about stopping paid employment was dealing with other blokes. The idea there's something weird about a man who is not the main breadwinner in a relationship is tenacious. Men poured scorn on my choice. I couldn't care about my career, they said. I'd regret it. My wife must wear the trousers.

My German friend Bernd Becker had a similar experience. "Everyone said it was a mistake," he told me. "Most men said

---

[19] Sub-editors, not journalists, decide the headlines in newspapers.

they would do it like a shot, if they could. Then they would give 20 reasons why they couldn't."

Women sometimes struggled too. One said to me: "So you're the house-boy now, are you?" Bernd had a better experience. "Most women wished they had a man like me. But a few thought I must be looking after the children because I had to. They asked when my wife died."

An embassy colleague whose husband accompanied her on a posting took a different approach. "People say to me, 'And what does your husband do?'" she told me. "I can see them thinking, 'What kind of bloke would put up with trailing round the world after a woman? Must be a right drip.' So I tell them the sex is mind-blowing. That usually shuts 'em up."

The biggest benefit of taking four years out of the office was that I developed a stronger, life-long bond with the children than could have happened otherwise. I'm not claiming to have uncovered some magical relationship fairy dust. But the fact of spending more time together, and taking more responsibility for them for four years, gave me a different connection. I remain grateful to this day, and commend the model to any male anxious about dipping a toe in the water.

Re-entry to the Foreign Office was a challenge. When I started applying on promotion[20] for jobs in London for which I had been told I was qualified four years earlier, I was not even shortlisted. I applied for jobs in my grade, without success. As I was getting desperate, Denise Holt, a wise colleague, called. "I wondered if you might like to apply for one of the most unusual jobs in the Foreign Office," she said. "It's in the Overseas Territories Department."

Overseas territories: maximum responsibility

Those dealing with the overseas territories, or OTs, of the UK must have attention to detail, a powerful sense of duty and a long memory. Events that happened or promises made decades ago may seem remote to bureaucrats in London. In the territories, they are existential.

---

[20] In FCO-speak, applying for jobs at the next most senior level up.

My time as director of Overseas Territories[21] from 2006–08 was both rewarding and scary. When storms damaged the jetty at Edinburgh of the Seven Seas, and threatened the rock lobster industry of Tristan da Cunha, we had to fix it pronto. When an iceberg holed a cruise ship in Antarctica, we fought to improve safety standards.[22] When Caribbean territories wanted to borrow more to fund economic development, we had to assess the liabilities if things went wrong.

Visiting the territories was an education in their remoteness. To reach St Helena you flew to Johannesburg, took a connecting flight to Walvis Bay in Namibia, then boarded the RMS *St Helena* for the four-day voyage to the island capital, Jamestown.[23] For the Falkland Islands, I flew from RAF Brize Norton on a snow-white 747 with Tagalog[24] signage for 16 hours, stopping to refuel at Ascension Island.

Most of the territories are modest in size[25] with populations ranging from around 50 (Pitcairn) to 70,000 (Cayman Islands). But the small numbers belie the complexity of the policy issues they generate. Several, notably the Falklands, Gibraltar and the British Indian Ocean Territory or BIOT, are subject to long-running legal disputes or territorial claims.

When we negotiated with OT governments on constitutional reform, any attempt to adjust the balance of power generated tensions. 'Constitutional talks with [the territory] …' I wrote after one exchange, 'more or less reached agreement by Wednesday lunchtime, when we were due to have a celebratory dinner; but since the talks as always went on much longer than expected, and since one or two members of the [territory] delegation were very outraged about various things, the mood was not that celebratory …'

The people of the OTs were as diverse and engaging a group as one could wish for. The key, as in all diplomacy, was never to

---

[21] The Overseas Territories Department became a directorate soon after I arrived.

[22] The MV *Explorer* sank on 23 November 2007. All 154 passengers and crew were rescued.

[23] In 2017 St Helena's airport opened and the RMS *St Helena* retired.

[24] A previous lessee had used the aircraft in the Philippines.

[25] The exception is the British Antarctic Territory, whose 1.7 million square kilometres make it seven times the size of the UK.

underestimate them. When I toured a prison on Anguilla, the inmates had much to tell me. Many callers to my interview on a radio station in Montserrat wanted more local powers, although few wanted independence. Falkland Islanders never ceased to explain how the Foreign Office could better represent their interests. 'Saints', or island residents, took me on a sponsored walk across St Helena, past dramatic rock formations such as Lot's Wife and the Gates of Chaos.

The reason most OTs have not become independent is that they are tiny islands, or remote; or remote, tiny islands. This makes them vulnerable to disasters from hurricanes to conflicts and COVID-19. Many OTs have unique flora and fauna; conservation initiatives there can help preserve biodiversity worldwide.

I wrote in my handover notes to my successor: 'Welcome to one of the most challenging, unpredictable and (on a good day) fascinating jobs in the FCO. You will have a great deal of autonomy and may find yourself taking decisions of a kind you have never faced before. Never sign anything – especially a legal document – in a hurry. The maxim that it is the quiet OTs, from which you have not heard much recently, where the biggest problem is brewing, has some validity. Good luck.'

Kyiv: trusty and well-beloved

In January 2008 I attended a conference in Miami on my way to Anguilla. The head of FCO personnel told me that our ambassador to Ukraine, Tim Barrow, was leaving the post early. "How would you feel about applying for HMA[26] Kyiv?" she asked. "We need a Russian or Ukrainian speaker, fast."

After long family discussions, I went to Kyiv unaccompanied and my wife Pamela continued her job in London. We later, as with many long-distance diplomatic relationships, decided to separate but remained good friends.

If you are in any doubt as to the responsibilities of being a British ambassador, the audience you receive with your head of state before leaving sets things straight. I was one of four ambassadors calling on HM The Queen on 13 June 2008.

---

[26] At the time, Her Majesty's Ambassador.

The person seeing Her Majesty before me was Ban Ki-moon, secretary-general of the United Nations.

I would like to think that my ten-minute chat with Her Majesty that day influenced the choice of words in my letter of credence, signed by her, which I handed to Ukrainian President Yushchenko ten days later. 'We have made choice of Our Trusty and Well-beloved Leigh Turner, Esquire, to reside with You in the character of Our Ambassador Extraordinary and Plenipotentiary.'

Any person being thus described will want to be sure that he or she is on peak performance.

Then, as now, Ukraine was a country key to the security of Europe. It had become independent from the Soviet Union following a referendum on 1 December 1991 in which 92.3 per cent of citizens voted for independence.[27] People quoted Zbigniew Brzezinski, former US national security adviser: 'Without Ukraine, Russia ceases to be an empire.'

Political and economic crises dominated my time in Kyiv. My team pointed me towards opposition leaders as well as government bigwigs. I met Party of the Regions leader Viktor Yanukovych (later president, ousted in 2014) and Mykola Azarov, with whom I lunched regularly when he later became prime minister.[28] Crises included Russia cutting off gas supplies to Ukraine in January 2009. In all my travels, from Lviv in the west to Donetsk in the east and Crimea and Odesa in the south, I never met anyone who said they wished their town or region could be part of Russia.

What many people in Ukraine wanted to do was join the EU. Brussels briefed President Putin about progress at regular meetings. In 2009 a senior Russian diplomat in Moscow told me Russia was entirely relaxed about Ukraine moving closer to Brussels. Subsequent Russian outrage that they had not been informed was 100 per cent synthetic.

Few people can spend time in Kyiv without developing an affection for Ukraine and its people. I learned Ukrainian – about as different from Russian as Dutch from German – including

---

[27] Including 83.9 per cent of citizens in Luhansk and Donetsk and 54.2 per cent in Crimea.

[28] The way my embassy colleague Duncan Allan urged me to build a relationship with Azarov in opposition was a fine example of proactive contact building.

language immersion in Lviv in a former monk's cell at a school for the performing arts where violin music seeped under the door. Although Ukrainian was the main language of discourse in politics, many business folk spoke Russian. I never detected any friction around language: it was commonplace to hear a conversation or a radio interview in which one person spoke Russian, the other Ukrainian.

My time as ambassador in Kyiv saw four years of relative stability in a country that, like Poland, suffered a grim 20th century. Chapter 5, 'How to understand Putin's war on Ukraine' explores what happened in the 21st.

Istanbul: can-do and conspiracies

Before starting my posting to Turkey in 2012 as Her Majesty's Consul General Istanbul and Director General for Trade and Investment for Turkey, South Caucasus and Central Asia, I read a history of Turkey.

Only halfway through the book did we reach the year zero.

Turkish history and culture are beyond ancient. The monumental statues of Mount Nemrut, built in 62 BC to mark the tomb of King Antiochus, should be on every bucket list. But the Neolithic steles of Göbekli Tepe, decorated with vultures, foxes and boars thousands of years older than the pyramids or Stonehenge, challenge our whole conception of history.

The turbulent metropolis of Istanbul, perched on the Bosphorus between Europe and Asia, was home to Pera House, the UK's palatial consulate-general. I had been sold on the job the moment someone told me that my flat in the building looked out over the Golden Horn. In 2011 the *Financial Times*, critical of surveys that ranked safe, quiet cities such as Zurich, Melbourne and Vancouver the best places to live, instead polled FT readers. They voted Istanbul the greatest city on Earth.

I threw myself into Turkish. Wikipedia notes that 'classification of the Turkic languages is complicated', due to similarities with everything from Japanese and Korean (Altaic languages) to Hungarian and Finnish (Ural Altaic). It is rich in proverbs, including such gems as *Bal tutan parmağını yalar* (he who handles honey, licks his fingers).

Turkish culture includes a passion for conspiracy theories. One weekend in Istanbul, I was invited with my partner Gözde, a Turkish hotel general manager whom I had met in Kyiv, to visit the Greek Orthodox seminary at the summit of the island of Heybeliada in the Sea of Marmara. On arrival, a cool breeze lured us to climb on foot, through fragrant pine woods, to our appointment. We arrived at the back door of the compound and strolled in. The place seemed deserted.

At last, we tracked down our host, waiting for us at the imposing front gate.

"Ah," he said. "The English always come from the other side."

Turkey faced challenges during my four years in Istanbul. I became familiar with tear gas during the Gezi Park protests of 2013. Plotters launched an attempted coup against the government on 15 July 2016 – the night of my farewell party. But the can-do attitude of Turkish entrepreneurs was breathtaking. I became a fan of Turkey's culture and people – from the bent-backed pensioner who offered me tea in his home in a back street in Urfa to my brilliant, mostly young, colleagues in Istanbul and Ankara.

Beyond Turkey, I visited the South Caucasus and Central Asia, working with local British embassies to realise opportunities arising from economies that varied in size, sophistication and potential. The fact flights to Central Asia invariably seemed to arrive at 3.45 a.m. lent a surreal air of caffeine-fuelled light-headedness to many visits.

In Tajikistan, the ambassador, Robin Ord-Smith, took me to visit Khujand, in the far north – a spectacular mountain route transiting the Anzob Tunnel, known as the 'Tunnel of Doom' for its giant potholes, protruding steel reinforcing rods, flooding and lack of ventilation. Even here, we found a local Brit, working to reclaim silver from mine tailings of excavations dating back centuries. In some countries of Central Asia, Russian remained a lingua franca; in others, English was spreading. All were, as now, adapting to the competing pulls of China, Russia and the rest of the world.

When I left Istanbul to take up my post as ambassador to Vienna in July 2016, staff threw water after me – supposedly to encourage an early, safe return. I do so with pleasure.

Vienna: the last post

My posting as ambassador to Austria began with Brexit and ended with COVID-19. Neither was an unmixed blessing.

I arrived in Vienna three months after the 23 June 2016 referendum on the UK's EU membership. My first guest was Foreign Secretary (later prime minister) Boris Johnson, who visited to call on 30-year-old *Wunderkind*, Foreign and Integration Minister (later chancellor) Sebastian Kurz.

Throughout my posting, my main job was to explain and promote UK positions on Brexit. That challenging task continued through the UK's departure on 31 January 2020, the interim period to 31 December 2020, and into post-Brexit issues such as the Northern Ireland Protocol and Gibraltar. We reached out to the roughly 11,000 British citizens living in Austria – about half of whom I met personally as we travelled the country – explaining how EU Exit would affect their position and what they needed to do.[29]

My position as UK permanent representative to the international organisations in Vienna gave me responsibility until 2017 for the work of the International Atomic Energy Agency, including the Joint Comprehensive Plan of Action on Iran; and until 2018 for the Comprehensive Nuclear-Test-Ban Treaty Organization. I chaired the Vienna-based Wassenaar Arrangement on conventional arms control and led UK participation in the UN Office on Drugs and Crime and other Vienna-based agencies.

Interaction with multilateral ambassadors in tackling and occasionally solving intractable issues at the UN was a revelation. As UK–Russia relations slumped post Vladimir Putin's invasion of Ukraine in 2014 and the poisoning of Sergei Skripal in Salisbury in 2018, nuclear arms control was a rare area where London and Moscow – then, at least – had compatible goals. I visited Ground

---

[29] I felt sorry for expat Brits in Austria who had voted against Brexit or had not been able to vote at all, but whose lives were turned upside down by the outcome. Many were anxious about healthcare, social security and other practical matters. I was grateful to colleagues from the Austrian interior and social security ministries who travelled with us, answering tricky technical questions. They hadn't voted for Brexit either.

Zero in Nevada and held half a kilo of heroin in my hand at the UNODC labs in Vienna. To sit in your national seat at the UN is an honour and a thrill.

When moving to a new country, a single contact can change everything. Old friends from my time in Vienna in the 1980s helped me get to grips with 21st-century Austria – repositioned at the heart of Europe by the lifting of the Iron Curtain. Visits to Austria's nine provinces enriched the mix; when I briefed Prime Minister Johnson before a meeting with Chancellor Kurz in Downing Street in February 2020 and he – bizarrely – asked me what the longest tunnel in Austria was, and then its length, I had just been down it.

From March 2020, COVID-19 rendered impossible the face-to-face meetings that are the lifeblood of diplomatic relationship building. More remote UK missions suffered greater practical problems than our comparatively comfortable European post. But the inability of staff to see families or partners for months at a time and drastic restrictions on meeting other human beings presented leadership challenges.

More positively, the COVID-19-accelerated explosion of online working helped me mentor colleagues around the world, give online speeches, and hold best-practice sessions on diplomatic tradecraft for staff in Vienna and beyond.

It's open to debate whether four decades working for the government makes you any wiser, but it certainly gives you a lot to talk about. The seeds of this book were planted in discussions with friends over whether a wider audience might like to hear about it.

I'll leave you to decide.

1

How to survive a crisis

Sunday 13 March 2016 was my birthday. To celebrate, my partner Gözde and I spent the weekend in Agva, a small resort on the Black Sea coast. As we drove back over the Bosphorus Bridge into Istanbul, my phone rang.

"A bomb has exploded in Ankara. A big one. City centre." My colleague from the British embassy in the capital of Turkey, five hours' drive to the east, sounded shaken. "Should we declare a crisis?"

Beneath the bridge spanning Europe and Asia, waves sparkled in the dusk. A sense of calm descended on me. I was chargé d'affaires in Turkey. It was my responsibility to decide what to do. But we had all trained for this, and I had managed crises before. A 'first 15 minutes' crisis plan lived in my wallet for precisely such occasions.

"Yes," I said. "Declare a crisis. Call the core team in to the embassy." I listed some people. "Check everyone is accounted for. We'll hold a crisis meeting in an hour."

Few of us face crises every day. But all of us sometimes have to cope with disaster. It's important to be prepared. That means having the training and experience to know when to swing into action – as we did that day in 2016 – and when to take a deep breath and adopt a policy of masterly inactivity.

When to act and when to freeze

When the putsch against Yeltsin kicked off in October 1993 or when the bomb exploded in Ankara in March 2016, all of us caught up in the crisis knew we must act quickly. Doing nothing was not an option. The same was true four months after the Ankara attack, when a new emergency struck Turkey.

On 15 July 2016, four days before the end of my posting to Istanbul, we planned to mark my departure at the annual British Chamber of Commerce summer party, complete with food stalls, music and, later, dancing, at which I would DJ. The evening began with speeches, networking and Pimm's. As guests chatted and swapped business cards in the balmy evening, the buzz of the city rose around the walled compound of Pera House.

Those sounds included helicopters. Istanbul is tumultuous 24/7, and no one paid them much attention. At 9.30 we moved inside and I started up the music: 'This was all excellent,' I wrote later, 'and we succeeded in getting a large group of people dancing in the Palm Court. Unfortunately, during this time news began to come through that something strange was happening on the Bosphorus bridges, or that a coup might be taking place.'

The initial response of party guests to the reports of a coup d'état was incredulity. President Erdoğan had led Turkey since 2003, and had purged the armed forces. How could they lead a coup against him? Then, at 11 p.m., Prime Minister Yildirim announced that the military were trying to seize power.

Ambassador Richard Moore, in Istanbul for the event, at once stopped the party and declared a crisis, setting up arrangements to report back to London and to establish if any British citizens were affected. The experienced crisis team moved smoothly into operation and worked in shifts throughout the next three days.

The coup leaders sought to foment uprisings in cities across the country. They tried to seize Erdoğan, who was on holiday in Marmaris. Tanks and soldiers occupied key locations in Istanbul, including Taksim Square, a few hundred metres from Pera House. When the authorities declared a curfew, dozens of party guests were trapped in the building overnight. Most kipped on the floor in designated safe zones away from doors and windows. Sonic booms from low-flying military jets rang out like explosions in the night. In Ankara, aircraft bombed the parliament and police headquarters. Three hundred people were killed and many more were injured.

Among the guests at the consulate was a journalist, Laura Pitel, who later published a piece in *The Mail on Sunday* headlined 'Diplomats danced as putsch began'. The subtitle, 'Turner played

DJ until coup began and staff went into crisis mode' was accurate. The tenor of the piece was that we had responded well in difficult circumstances. The fact that all our staff knew exactly what they had to do and were ready to do it – even in the middle of a party – made all the difference.

WHAT IF YOU get the balance between action and inaction wrong? In May 2013, environmentalists set up camp in the tiny wooded area of Gezi Park, near the Consulate in Istanbul. Developers wanted to build on the park, destroying hundreds of trees. Protestors resisted. Gradually a major anti-government protest built up, complaining about the government's religious bent, pro-business policies, lack of transparency and other grievances.

The Gezi protests started out localised, with much of the country carrying on as normal. Then things escalated. 'I spent much of Saturday [1 June] inside the building observing the battles outside, in the course of which our compound suffered some damage with all our CCTV cameras being smashed and various other things,' I wrote to my parents. 'I have to be careful as I want to show we're taking an interest without appearing to criticize the authorities or side with the protestors, many of whom are not cuddly tree-huggers (though many are) but wild hard leftists bent on barking anarchist destructive agendas.'

As violence flared, toxic fumes enveloped Pera House, where I lived alone in my flat in the Consulate-General. 'Tear-gas canister over wall of #British Consulate #Istanbul – all here OK,' I tweeted. 'Grateful if all concerned can try to avoid gassing us if poss.' The next morning, I collected dozens of spent tear gas canisters from inside the grounds.

On Monday, we closed the consulate and set up at our emergency fall-back location. We went into a 'battle rhythm' of regular twice-daily meetings to take stock of what was going on and to decide whether it was safe to open.

The Gezi protests lasted for months. In July, I wrote: 'When everything was quiet I decided to go out for a stroll, only to discover that the tear gas was still pretty fierce and the police were still chasing everything that moved, so I returned to the compound swiftly.' In September, we held a 'Sport is GREAT' Olympic countdown reception on the lawn to support potential business opportunities arising from Istanbul's bid for the 2020 Olympics. Unfortunately, Tokyo rather than Istanbul won on the night. As guests mingled, drifting clouds of tear gas from police actions nearby made our eyes sting.

When street protests or violence engulf a diplomatic mission, you face tough decisions on whether to evacuate or to stay. In the weeks following the Iraqi invasion of Kuwait in 1990, foreign embassies remained open. Most ambassadors were keen to stay as long as possible in what was dubbed a 'slow bicycle race' to see who could last longest. The British ambassador was eventually ordered home. Similarly, during the 1993 Moscow putsch, some colleagues showed bravery or recklessness in leaving the embassy to witness tanks shelling the White House across town. Being swept up in dramatic events in a country not your own may or may not be the correct response, either from a security or a political point of view.

'By Saturday evening', I wrote from Istanbul, 'the police suddenly gave up trying to keep demonstrators away from Taksim Square and the protesters occupied the whole area, including Gezi Park. I slightly boldly walked down there through the vast crowds with a colleague, tweeting out pictures en route.'

With hindsight, the apparent normality of much of Istanbul during the protests meant I took unnecessary risks – and several times swung into action when I should have sat tight.

Focusing on what matters

Even when no tear gas or tanks are involved, the 24-hour news cycle and frenetic pace of social media often generate a destructive drive to respond instantly to everything.

Working in the FCO on Hong Kong policy from 1995 to 1998, I often had meetings with Foreign Secretary Robin Cook. I sometimes saw there Gaynor Regan, one of his staff. She came across as self-effacing and friendly.

On 1 August 1997, as Cook sat in a car on the way to Heathrow Airport for a holiday with his wife Margaret a month after the handover of Hong Kong, he received a call from Downing Street press secretary Alastair Campbell. Campbell said that the *News of the World*, a tabloid newspaper, would publish a story the following Sunday revealing that Cook was having an affair with Gaynor.

Campbell's diaries, published in 2008, set out the exchanges that followed in excruciating detail. For hours, Prime Minister Tony Blair, Campbell, Cook and the *News of the World* were in constant communication about how to present the story. Downing Street demanded that Cook choose, fast, between Margaret and Gaynor, 'for clarity'. Margaret Cook also published an account of the day, ten years later, in the *Daily Mail*.

The incident is a perfect example of the strains that the ever-faster news cycle puts on both decision-making and relationships. The need to feed the media required Robin Cook to decide within hours on something that would affect the rest of his life and those of several other people – *in order to minimise damage to the government.*

Before making decisions at break-neck speed, consider whether you actually need to do so. Perceived time pressures that seem to oblige politicians, diplomats and others to make snap judgements may be self-generated. French master diplomat Talleyrand told young French diplomats '*Surtout, pas trop de zèle*' ('above all, not too much zeal'): his point was that important decisions should be based on careful consideration. With hindsight, the rush to force Cook to decide was unnecessary and cruel.

Gaynor was with Robin Cook when he died of a heart attack, walking in the Scottish Highlands, in August 2005.

IN SOME CRISIS situations, neither freezing nor moving will help. But training and preparation will maximise your chances of making the right decisions.

On Sunday 7 May 2017, I attended as ambassador to Austria an event marking the 1945 liberation of the Mauthausen concentration camp, near Linz. Back in Vienna, I decided to go for a walk in the Lainzer Tiergarten, a hilly, wooded park on the edge of town. I was due to walk part of the Pennine Way, in northern England, that summer and was getting in training.

Halfway through my walk, the heavens opened. I had Pennine Way-quality waterproofs, so carried on in what was now a deserted, sodden landscape. The absence of people encouraged the park's wild boar – usually notoriously shy – to emerge in quantity. I walked around a corner straight into a group of around 20 adults and piglets – which in German enjoy the exotic name of *Frischlinge*.

One of the females, a gigantic beast, decided I was threatening her offspring and charged me. I escaped by scaling at speed a pile of slippery logs, but damaged both hands to the extent that I could hardly hold a pen or type.

The following Tuesday I was due to give a TV interview about Brexit. Since by then my hand had been set in a spectacular splint, I judged that they were bound to ask what had happened. So I wrote up my version of events in a post on my official FCO blog, in a humorous, self-deprecatory tone.

The story of 'British ambassador attacked by wild boar' went viral around the world, including on the BBC's 'News Quiz'. Perhaps because I had sent myself up in the blog, the tenor of reports was generally kind.

What could I have done differently? Researching after the event, I found little advice on what to do if you accidentally confronted a wild boar. My favourite, and also the most practical, was a German website that urged you to climb a tree, or onto some rocks. 'You will be surprised at your climbing skills', they said, 'if a boar is chasing you.'

Had I been better prepared, I would have checked immediately where I might take refuge as soon as I glimpsed my sounder of heavyweight swine – in case one of them felt threatened.

As 31 DECEMBER 1999 loomed at the British embassy in Berlin, we faced a different kind of crisis. Tech experts warned that a 'millennium bug', the inability of computers to distinguish between the dates 1900 and 2000, would cause a global collapse of infrastructure from banking to energy, water, transport and, basically, all that kept humankind going.

Companies and governments spent vast sums trying to tackle the problem. IT experts earned squillions selling their services. Airlines grounded aircraft lest systems malfunction.

The Foreign Office told embassies to take precautions to ensure they could continue to operate. After numerous meetings on contingency planning, embassy staff in Berlin received instructions from management officer Martin Ryder.

'The Embassy's answer to the Millennium Bug', the message read, 'is Eric Fearne. He will be on duty as one millennium becomes the next (or as the purists would say 12 months before). The disasters that may befall all of us are therefore Eric's responsibility. He hands this responsibility over to Susannah Simon at 09.00 on 1 January 2000. So if the four horsemen start galloping across the land after that time please refer them to Susannah.'

'Personally,' the message continued, '(and this may be apparent to the more discerning of you from the tenor of this circular) I think that the biggest problem we will face is the long holidays when the shops are shut. It may make sense to stock up. If Armageddon is around the corner, then a good stock of drinking water might just see you through the torment to come.'

The millennium bug turned out to be a damp squib. We did what we could to prepare. But with hindsight, Martin Ryder's common sense and humour hit precisely the right note.

Putting your own oxygen mask on first

How can you prepare yourself, personally, for potential crises? One key lesson is displayed on passenger safety cards in aircraft: 'Put your own oxygen mask on first before helping others.'

When a crisis strikes, you will only be able to act, or lead, if you are fit and well. That means making sure that your mind and body are in the best shape you can manage.

One time when I failed to learn this lesson was when I arrived in Kyiv in my first ambassadorial post.

In November 2008, five months after arriving, I experienced ghastly chest pains, for which I was prescribed various drugs. Facial paralysis, disorientation and nausea followed. One snowy morning I was rushed to hospital for an MRI scan and other tests lest I might be having a stroke or heart attack.[1] A sympathetic embassy colleague[2] accompanied me.

---

[1] My excellent Colombian doctor said "I'm going to hospitalise you urgently," which in the UK would have meant she was about to cause me grievous bodily harm.

[2] The community liaison officer or CLO – a post, often filled by an embassy spouse or partner, designed to help expat staff integrate into local communities.

'I had a few moments on the way to the hospital', I wrote, 'wondering if I was about to die, but reflected that I'd had a pretty excellent life so could have nothing to complain about.'

I'd had a busy few months. Nothing extraordinary by the standards of newly appointed ambassadors, but countless meetings and evening engagements, the Russia–Georgia war, much travel, including to Lviv and Crimea, getting stuck into Ukrainian and so on. In the early weeks, I made a point of not learning how to lock up the embassy at night so as to discourage myself from staying late. But I found racing not to be the last to leave stressful in itself. So I learned to lock up, and strove to clear my desk.

One icy night I locked and left the entrance – in those days in the courtyard at the rear of the building – and made my way towards the street through the vehicle arch. I planned to walk home, a journey of about an hour, and was listening to Green Day on my headphones. Stumbling across the uneven, frozen surface in the darkness between the inner and outer vehicle gates, I was pleased to see a strip of what looked like freshly laid tarmac along the wall. That would be better underfoot, I thought.

At the last moment, I hesitated. I had been about to step into a two-metre deep trench, dug during the day during renovation work on the wall. I pictured myself lying in the bottom of the pit at midnight, leg broken, waiting for help as temperatures plunged.

I do not know whether my health issues in Kyiv were stress-related. But I did write later: 'The MRI was the highlight. The CLO had told me she'd needed a general anaesthetic to have one the previous week, she'd been so panic-stricken. I was prepared for the worst; but actually found the hour in the tube relaxing, since I wasn't tempted to get on with any work.'

In retrospect, I overdid it in those early months in Kyiv – to the detriment of myself and my team.

KYIV WAS WHERE I first met a global religious leader who made taking decisions slowly seem natural.

In 2008–12, religion in Ukraine was bitterly divided between clerics loyal to the breakaway Kyiv Patriarchate and those looking to Moscow. The Moscow Patriarch tended then, as now, to adopt a line spookily close to the Russian government. But since 1686 the Ukrainian Church had been subservient to Moscow. This rankled with Ukrainians who (rightly) saw the church as a tool of Russian influence.

In August 2008 the pro-western Ukrainian president, Yushchenko, invited to Kyiv Bartholomew I, Archbishop of Istanbul, Ecumenical Patriarch and spiritual leader of Orthodox Christians. Yushchenko urged Bartholomew to grant autocephaly (independence) to the Ukrainian Church.

This was exotic stuff, scarcely fathomable for a humble diplomat. 'It seems that in the hierarchy of the Orthodox Church, Bartholomew ranks at No. 1, whereas the Patriarch of Moscow, Aleksei, comes in only at No. 6,' I wrote. This reflected the fact that whereas Aleksei was part of a line that, at best, went back to Jonah of Moscow in 1448, Bartholomew was the 269th Archbishop of Constantinople since St Andrew in AD 38.

On a baking hot day rich in robes and elaborate headgear, Bartholomew sat politely through an interminable ceremony but did not, to Yushchenko's disappointment, opine either way on the dispute between Kyiv and Moscow.

Ten years later, Bartholomew acted. In 2018, four years after Russia's 2014 invasion of Crimea and eastern Ukraine, Bartholomew granted autocephaly to the Ukrainian church. In response, the Orthodox Church in Moscow broke communion with the Ecumenical Patriarchate – a bit like the Church of England breaking away from Rome in the 16th century. The historic implications of Moscow's move are not yet clear.

In November 2012 I had the privilege of an audience with Bartholomew in Istanbul. Learning more about the rocky road Orthodox patriarchs had travelled made it clear why he took the long view.

'I [...] went for an official call on the Greek Patriarch', I wrote, 'who is in theory the head of the entire Orthodox church including Russia and Ukraine [...] There are only about 2,000 members of the Greek Orthodox Church still in Istanbul, and the patriarchate has obviously been through immense difficulties in the last thousand years including a previous patriarch, Gregory V, being hanged outside the present building in 1821 by demonstrators – never encouraging. The door the demonstrators came through has been closed ever since.'

Over a cup of tea, Patriarch Bartholomew radiated calm and wisdom. He chatted amiably with me in Turkish, English and German about political, religious and environmental issues. Despite having rubbed shoulders with everyone from Barack Obama to Pope Francis, he seemed fully engaged and in no hurry, urging me to return for another chat at an early date.

Foolishly, I never did.

CRISIS RESPONSE IS something you can learn, and train for. That way you'll be as well prepared as possible to respond when problems arise – or, as Patriarch Bartholomew reminds us, to recall that sometimes, doing nothing can be the best option.

2

How to tackle terrorism

On 20 November 2003, terrorists detonated a truck bomb at the gatehouse of the British consulate general in Istanbul. Twelve people died inside, including Consul General Roger Short, and many more outside.

In response, the British government turned the complex into a fortress. Turkey provided armed protection for the new consul general and her successors – including me. 'I find that my new car is an armoured BMW weighing almost five tons,' I wrote when I arrived in Istanbul in 2012. 'A bit tank-like.'

You can reduce the impact of terrorism through training, mitigation and hard work. Whatever the rhetoric about a 'war on terror', however, you cannot stop it altogether. For diplomats, that means preparing for and living with a constant threat of attack: low-key in many countries, immediate in a few.

Diplomats keeping safe – or looking for trouble

Risk comes with the job. The IRA assassinated Christopher Ewart-Biggs in 1976 in Dublin because he was the British ambassador to Ireland. Militants killed the US ambassador to Libya Chris Stevens in Benghazi, Libya in 2012 because of who he was – the sixth US ambassador killed in office as the result of an armed attack. The same applied when an off-duty Turkish police officer assassinated Andrei Karlov, the Russian ambassador to Turkey, in 2016. Other diplomats fall victim to random acts of terrorism or crime in other high-risk environments – including in countries their home governments advise other citizens it is too dangerous to visit.

Bad luck can strike. When Turkish protesters surged down Istiklal Street in Istanbul towards the well-protected Russian consulate general during a period of tension between the two countries over the war in Syria in 2015, hot-heads initially scaled the gate of the less heavily fortified Dutch consulate general – the Dutch and Russian flags are similar. Dutch security officials politely pointed out their mistake.

Most of my postings were in low-threat environments. Moscow was a hotbed of business-linked assassinations during my posting from 1992–95. But the risk to a diplomat who was not personally engaged in organised crime was small. Omnipresent surveillance by organs of state security also provided a degree of protection.

In Istanbul, being constantly accompanied by an armed police bodyguard was less onerous than one might imagine: Deniz[1] provided constant support, from smuggling me through a back door at a football match to keeping me safe during police action against a banned Istanbul Pride demonstration. I am full of admiration for the many diplomats who work for months or years in countries riven by war or overshadowed by terrorism.

For those in high-risk environments, mitigation may include drills and training to prepare for anything from a mob to a bombing or a lone shooter, keeping itineraries secret, and avoiding crowded places and trouble-spots. The trouble is, crowded places and trouble-spots may be exactly where you want to be.

DIPLOMATIC JOB TITLES are often misleading, if not outright mendacious. The name of the FCO team I joined in December 1989, Security Co-ordination Department or SCD, was deliberately vague, to avoid drawing terrorists' attention to the existence of an outfit designed to thwart their efforts. But the disadvantages of this cloak-and-dagger approach outweighed any security benefits. It was renamed Counter-Terrorism Department a few years later.

When I started in SCD I asked around for primers on terrorism. A senior female colleague in the Security Service[2] lent me Alistair Horne's *A Savage War of Peace*, about the 1954–62 Algerian War of Independence. The motivation of the leader of the far-right

---

[1] Name changed.

[2] The UK's domestic security agency, sometimes called MI5.

terror group Organisation Armée Secrète, Sergent, quoted by Horne, is one every politician fighting terrorism should learn by heart. 'Our only chance,' Sergent said, 'is to create a situation obliging the regime to react violently and discredit itself.'

Democracies usually outlast terrorist organisations. But the latter have short-term strengths. De Gaulle, Horne wrote, 'suffered from the lesson that ... he who lasts longest, wins; that ... with the impatience of democracies and their volatile voters committed to electoral contortions every four or five years, the extremist generally triumphs over the moderate.'

This sounds eerily contemporary.

Much of the work we did to tackle terrorism was painstaking and bureaucratic. 'Delayed at work by a cocktail party to entertain the delegates at a conference on the marking of plastic explosives ...' I wrote. 'I'm concentrating on aviation security – how to stop people being blown up, mainly.'

The dull but worthy goal of the conference was to persuade manufacturers of substances such as Semtex to bake into the recipe ingredients to enable law enforcement to trace the origin of any given batch. Aviation security meant trying to get governments around the world to make it harder for people to board aircraft with weapons or bombs.

The events of 11 September 2001 showed the inadequacy of security at US airports a decade later.

CT work took me regularly for talks to a famously violent city. A joke at the time listed 'NRA[3] Dream Vacations' as including 'Beirut, Haiti and Washington, DC.' The drug liaison officer at the British embassy was said to offer officials seeking to understand the scale of the challenges facing law enforcement the chance to accompany local police on a night-time patrol in Anacostia, a deprived urban district of the nation's 'drug capital'.

Some of the issues we dealt with in SCD, including the kidnapping and holding hostage of British citizens such as John McCarthy and Terry Waite in Beirut, drew to a close. Washington cleaned up much of its criminality. Terror groups such as Abu Nidal and the Red Army Faction have faded into history. Yet worldwide deaths from terrorism soared after 2003, mainly due to killings in

---

[3] The National Rifle Association, a US 'gun rights' advocacy group.

Iraq, Afghanistan and Syria. Few people today would argue that terrorism is less serious in the 2020s than it was in the 1980s.

Knowing your enemies

The Beirut hostage crisis of 1982 to 1992 posed 'Western'[4] governments with a baffling diplomatic and negotiation challenge.

Countless militias and terrorist organisations claimed to be responsible for kidnapping dozens of American, French, British and other citizens in Lebanon and holding them for years in captivity. Hostages ranged from teachers and aid workers to military personnel. No one knew for sure if the hostages were alive or who held them, or even what the motivations of those holding them might be.[5]

Some governments, including the UK, refused to make concessions to get prisoners released. The logic was that paying ransoms could encourage more hostage-taking. But families and friends of those taken hostage, reasonably enough, pressured governments to do more – Jill Morrell, girlfriend of British hostage John McCarthy, campaigned actively for his release. A cartoon of the time showed a lazy Foreign Office mandarin perusing a newspaper headline saying 'FO inaction on hostages' and commenting 'I'd sue for libel, but I can't be bothered.'

As years passed without progress, and shadowy intermediaries emerged promising to secure the release of hostages, the principle of 'no concessions' was eroded. Governments unable to engage meaningfully with the hostage-takers on one side while trying to demonstrate activism on the other, made missteps such as the Iran-Contra affair.[6]

---

[4] I am sceptical about the term ' Western'. Everywhere is west of somewhere else. And where do Japanese, Australians or Brazilians fit in? But it's hard to avoid sometimes.

[5] Hostage-takers seem to have seized many individuals in the hope that they might prove useful or valuable, rather than with concrete goals.

[6] The US government secretly sold arms to Iran – despite an embargo – to secure money to fund Nicaraguan rebels – which was illegal – while pretending the arms shipments were to help secure the release of US hostages in Lebanon. Seriously.

With hindsight, most hostages were released, some after more than six years in captivity, simply because the hostage takers no longer found keeping them useful. The fog of information chaos around the hostages was a prelude to the post-truth free-for-all of the 21st-century internet. But the centuries-old asymmetric power of hostage taking remains as alive and well now as in the 1980s.[7]

FIGHTING TERRORISM INCLUDES finding out all you can about terrorist groups and their capabilities.

On 2 August 1990, Iraqi forces invaded Kuwait. As coalition forces gathered to launch a counter-invasion, CT experts fretted that groups sympathetic to or allied with Iraq might launch terror attacks in Western capitals, including London. News stories and intelligence, suggesting terrorists might have access to chemical and biological warfare (CBW) agents, stoked fears. I sat in meetings where anxious boffins argued the threat was real, explaining how the right kind of CBW device, correctly deployed, could cause hundreds of thousands of deaths in the British capital.

We concluded that evidence of an imminent CBW attack on London was not compelling. But we couldn't be sure.

On the night of 17 January 1991, as coalition forces launched the recapture of Kuwait with an air and sea bombardment in Operation Desert Storm, I gazed out of the window of my flat in London[8] and hoped our assessment had been correct. In the event, nothing happened. But the CT community remained on edge.

Three weeks later, 11 February 1991 was a snowy day. I was sitting in the morning briefing in SCD when a colossal explosion shook the building. "I hope that's the IRA," I said.

It later transpired that the IRA had launched three mortars from the back of a van close to the Ministry of Defence, targeting

---

[7] In a new development, 21st-century authoritarian governments increasingly arrest and imprison foreign nationals on flimsy charges with a view to swapping them for their own nationals convicted of espionage or terrorism.

[8] The opposite of what you should do if you fear an act of terrorism. If a bomb ever goes off near you or if there is a warning of a potential attack, stay away from the window.

the war cabinet, meeting in No. 10 Downing Street to discuss Desert Storm. One charge exploded in the garden of No. 10, with shrapnel breaking windows in the next-door Foreign Office. The other two did not explode.

Why was my initial hope that the attack was the IRA?

Set in the context of the nebulous Middle Eastern terrorist threat for which CT experts were bracing themselves, the IRA seemed the lesser of two evils. They had launched previous attacks on the British mainland; we had some idea what we were dealing with. Their activities were, in the phrase popularised later by US Secretary of Defense Donald Rumsfeld, a 'known unknown'. Had the explosion that morning been the first act of some new international terror group revealing hitherto unexpected capabilities, we would have been confronting an 'unknown unknown' – a far scarier prospect.

KNOWING YOUR ENEMIES includes not over-estimating them.

Before the 1991 Gulf War, analysts argued that Iraq might launch CBW attacks on Saudi Arabia, Israel or other nearby states supporting Operation Desert Storm.[9] The UK Foreign Office and Ministry of Defence negotiated about protective suits for UK citizens in the Gulf and who should pay for them.

Before the operation to free Kuwait started in mid-January 1991, the mood in the UK was edgy. The BBC banned certain songs.[10] Saddam was depicted as a brilliant, Machiavellian strategist. A friend asked me as late as February "Can we win?"

One detail that persuaded me Saddam was not an evil genius was the aftermath of the capture by Iraqi forces of over 800 US, British and other civilians during the invasion of Kuwait in August 1990. These included hundreds of Britons who landed

---

[9]   Iraq had repeatedly deployed chemical weapons in the 1980s, including an attack on the Kurdish city of Halabja in Iraqi Kurdistan.

[10]   They ranged from 'Billie Don't Be a Hero' by Paper Lace to 'We've Got to Get Out of This Place' by the Animals. In 2006, at RAF Mount Pleasant in the Falkland Islands, I witnessed the ground crew of the departing trooping flight to the UK, equipped with fluorescent jackets and high visibility paddles, doing a choreographed dance number to the latter song as passengers boarded the plane.

on British Airways flight 149 from London, en route to India and Malaysia, as the invasion took place.

The hostages were treated badly. Many were taken to strategic military locations in Iraq, to deter coalition forces from bombing those sites. When Saddam launched a PR offensive to show that the hostages were being treated well, by appearing with his arm around the shoulder of five-year-old Stuart Lockwood, he triggered a wave of revulsion. Who could sympathise with a dictator who used hostages as human shields, in contravention of the Geneva Conventions?

For coalition military planners and politicians, the presence of hundreds of their own citizens at critical military targets posed a dilemma. "I don't suspect many Brits stay up at night worrying about the future of the Al-Sabah dynasty," a senior official told me. "But if British bombs kill British hostages, they will be incensed."

The UN passed resolutions condemning the hostage taking. Some argued that the captives became a greater *casus belli*[11] than the invasion of Kuwait.

What went on in Saddam's mind we may never know. But on 6 December, Iraq announced that all foreign hostages could depart immediately. Sighs of relief were audible across Whitehall and Washington DC. Desert Storm – due six weeks later – could go ahead.

Saddam's decision may have been a humanitarian gesture or a calculated move made in the belief that releasing the hostages would reduce, rather than increase, the risk of war. But taken together with the earlier PR missteps it gave the impression of a leader floundering – and it certainly removed an obstacle to Western military action.

Saddam's hostage bungling was a reminder that while authoritarian leaders cultivate an 'evil genius' image for domestic and international consumption, in reality, they are no more all-knowing than the rest of us. The same is true of the terrorist groups they support, who are often as chaotic, faction-ridden and muddled as the democratic governments they seek to influence. While we should never underestimate them, we shouldn't big them up, either.

---

[11] An action justifying or causing a war.

Training, training and training

Three key elements of blunting the impact of actual terror attacks are training, training and training. As 'head of ops' in the Security Co-Ordination Department from 1989–91, one of my tasks was to accompany experts from Scotland Yard, the Home Office, the agencies and other organisations involved in counter-terrorism (CT) on their regular visits to provincial police forces such as Edinburgh, Durham and Cleveland. We ran exercises to test how such forces would handle a large-scale terrorist incident.

Exercises were split between the 'players' – those being tested, who participated in a scenario not knowing how it would turn out – and the directing staff, or DiStaff, who ran the exercise from behind the scenes trying to make things as realistic, and difficult, as possible. In this case, the main players were the local police force, whose training was the object of the exercise, plus volunteers representing the Home Office, FCO, hostages and so on.

A military element,[12] to be used to release hostages by force if all else failed, was invariably part of the exercise – in order to test them, too, in action under maximum pressure.

During exercises, I felt particularly sorry for the people playing hostages. They were often trapped in cramped accommodation, such as an aircraft or a basement, for hours or days while negotiators tested out tactics such as not emptying the toilets to put pressure on the 'terrorists' to make concessions. If and when a rescue was attempted, armed police or military units treated hostages – and manhandled them – as potential terrorists until they had proved their innocence.[13]

DiStaff running such exercises had immense experience, while the local police faced the stress and chaos of a scenario designed to force them to take tough decisions on the basis of inadequate information. Organisers took a sadistic pleasure in delivering to

---

[12] The 22nd Special Air Service Regiment, known as the SAS, came to prominence in 1980 when they freed prisoners taken hostage by terrorists at the Iranian embassy in London.

[13] At the end of the Iranian embassy siege, two terrorists tried to conceal themselves among the liberated hostages.

the players unexpected twists, such as the following imaginary diplomatic telegram from the British ambassador in Riyadh during an exercise in Cleveland:

EXERCISE EXERCISE EXERCISE
THE KING REQUESTED A PERSONAL AUDIENCE WITH ME AT 1145Z. HE EMPHASISED HIS CONCERN FOR THE SAUDI HOSTAGES, AND ASKED WHETHER IT WAS TRUE THAT SEVERAL DEAD HOSTAGES HAD NOT YET BEEN IDENTIFIED. SAUDI SUN FRONT PAGE THIS MORNING READS QUOTE TYNE-TEES TERROR AS CORPSES CARPET CLEVELAND UNQUOTE.

CAMEL-HUMPINGTON

New players would appear at the most inopportune moment – a top US politician wanting to assume control, angry relatives of hostages, or – a favourite – pushy journalists who would ask to borrow laptops or other equipment and walk off with them.

Training transforms people's ability to respond to pressure. Just as, at the Moscow State Linguistic University in 1992, instructors drilled us for hours on how to open a conversation on the telephone, and teachers at the Royal Academy of Dramatic Arts made diplomats practise public speaking in front of live video cameras, so CT exercises worked to mould the muscle memory of police officers the length and breadth of the UK.

Should you ever get a chance to take part in a CT exercise, step forward. My training as head of ops was invaluable when I later handled crisis work in the British Overseas Territories (mostly hurricanes), Ukraine (Russian invasion), and Turkey and Austria (terrorist attacks).

But never volunteer to be a hostage.

MY FINAL ACT in SCD was to head the advance party[14] for a major counter-terrorist exercise in Penang, Malaysia. It was my first visit either to the Far East or to RAF Brize Norton in Oxfordshire: 'endless concrete and vast hangars lit by lighting towers … damp

---

[14] About ten people, including representatives of, as I wrote to my parents at the time, 'various organisations too secret to name here'.

air hazy in the distance,' I wrote. My task was to negotiate the arrival of a larger team from the UK, headed by a minister, with the personnel and equipment to 'resolve' the imaginary terrorist incident we faced.

All ran smoothly: the main party arrived in a second RAF Tristar several days later. 'The exercise concluded on Thursday morning', I wrote, 'with the terrorists, in time-honoured fashion, getting the worse end of the deal.'

Three incidents stood out.

On the first night at the exercise site, a police barracks formerly a British Army base for fighting communist insurgents, the British and Malaysian exercise participants sat down for dinner. The Brigadier leading the Malaysian team came across to me. "All you chaps are sitting together," he said, "and so are my chaps. We should mix it up."

He was right. At his instigation, we redistributed the British and Malaysian teams across several tables – accelerating the bonding essential to cooperation over the difficult days ahead.

Early in the exercise, I and my team were invited to an urgent meeting in the middle of the night with the Malaysian side. We drove off at haste. But a check-point manned by armed soldiers blocked our route. They ignored our paperwork and sent us back.

"We should have planned for that," my military adviser told me.

After the close of the exercise, the Malaysians gave a party in a cavernous hall. The atmosphere was stiff. Things began to relax as the Malaysian chief negotiator went on stage to croon some Elvis ballads. In response, the Scotland Yard representative invited all the Brits up on stage. About fifty of us sat on two rows of chairs and sang 'My Bonnie Lies Over the Ocean', standing up and sitting down each time the letter 'b' came up in the song. By the end of the two performances, the atmosphere was cracking.

Most of us, thankfully, never have close contact with special forces units or senior police officers. The former are often smaller and wirier than you expect ('try getting a big bloke through a small hole', one told me). The latter often have a 'seen it all' Zen calm about them. Both are invaluable in dealing with the sharp end of a terrorist incident. More surprisingly, they are also champions at breaking the ice and bonding – just as diplomats should be.

TERRORISM, DESPITE THE best efforts of the military, police, diplomats and others, shows no sign of diminishing over time. That in turn means that continued action both to make life as difficult as possible for terrorists, and to tackle the causes that drive people to support them, remain as important as ever.

3

How to fail at geopolitical change: Brexit

British politics has been in chaos since 23 June 2016, when the UK electorate voted to leave the European Union.

What went wrong after that is a lesson in how efforts to tackle geopolitical change and exert influence internationally can only succeed if you take your people with you. 'Your people' means both your political allies and the electorate. Brexit was a fail on both.

Origins of Brexit: 1987 onwards

Brexit was already in the air when I joined the European Community Department of the Foreign Office in 1987. The day I arrived, my boss, Stephen Wall, shook his head. The coming months would be difficult for me, he said. I had come at a bad time. Minutes later his boss, Under-Secretary John Kerr, told me I would have a lot of fun: mine was "the best job in the Foreign Office right now".

Both were right.

My first task was renegotiation of the European Community's financing and budget system – 'Future Financing', nowadays known as the Multiannual Financial Framework or MFF. This included a so-called Fourth Resource, based on the wealth of each country, to make the budget fairer.[1]

---

[1] i.e. it would reduce UK payments.

Future Financing included UK demands to retain the 'rebate' negotiated by Prime Minister Margaret Thatcher at the Fontainebleau European Council of June 1984. This cut the UK's net contribution – the difference between what a member state paid into the EC budget and what it received – by two-thirds. Despite this, the UK in 1987 remained the second largest net contributor to the budget, after West Germany.

Mrs Thatcher applied the same passion to retaining the rebate she had in 1982 to retaining the Falkland Islands. This time, her opponents were not a military *junta* but other member states and the European Commission, which claimed the whole concept of net contributions was *non-communautaire*.[2]

The second bit of my job was UK policy on Economic and Monetary Union, or EMU – what later created the euro. This was a core project for those, such as European Commission President Jacques Delors, who wanted more European integration to build an economic and political counterweight to the US.

To achieve optimum results, Mrs Thatcher would ideally have formed an ironclad negotiating triumvirate with her foreign secretary, Geoffrey Howe, and chancellor of the exchequer, Nigel Lawson. Unfortunately, both believed the UK should join the exchange rate mechanism of the European Monetary System, a preparatory step towards EMU, which she opposed. Her sense that the two men were ganging up on her – which they were, along with much of the rest of the British establishment – led to political turmoil, bruising battles,[3] and a chasm of distrust and dysfunctionality at the heart of UK policy on Europe that persists to this day.

In April 1989, the Delors Report proposed a three-stage path to EMU. The UK opposed it.

'Busy getting the Chancellor's paper on alternatives to Economic and Monetary Union ready for publication, and whizzing copies of it to our posts around Europe,' I wrote in November 1989.

---

[2]   The readiness of the commission to talk about net contributions evolved as more states joined the EU and more, including France, became net contributors.

[3]   Howe left office in July 1989; Lawson in October.

Who remembers those alternatives? 'Look on my works, ye mighty, and despair.'[4] A divided UK government did not prevail on the international stage.

The hysteria that accompanied UK political and media debate on European integration and EMU, typified by *The Sun*'s famous 1990 headline 'Up Yours, Delors', was a foretaste of the polarisation of the UK – and both major parties – over Brexit. Practically the only voice of calm amid the frenzy, as so often, was the satirical magazine *Private Eye*, which in its Gnome Bore Awards of Christmas 1989 presented the Bore of the Year Award to 'The Exchange Rate Mechanism of the European Monetary System'.

TWENTY-FIVE YEARS LATER, when Foreign Secretary Boris Johnson flew into Vienna in September 2016, the British government was still in disarray over EU policy.

I was intrigued to meet Johnson, the object of loathing from opponents of Brexit for arguably doing more than anyone else to bring it about. He came across as focused on what people thought of him, peering at you from under his fringe to gauge your response as he produced a stream of witticisms.

'BJ is very similar in the flesh to his public image', I wrote, 'and undoubtedly has much charisma, even if you can't help feeling that he was a bit surprised to find that his participation had led to the UK leaving the European Union and, possibly, the end of civilisation as we know it.'

As Johnson flew in, the embassy received instructions from No. 10 Downing Street that the foreign secretary should on no account hold a joint press conference with Sebastian Kurz, the foreign and integration minister, after their meeting. This was tricky: a press conference was already in the programme. When we proposed removing it, the Austrians demurred. Kurz, they said, wanted a press conference. They asked what the problem was. It was hard to say.

We compromised on a joint press statement, without questions. Johnson quipped about a cow bell he had been given by Doppelmayr, the Austrian company that had built a cable car

---

[4]   Shelley, 'Ozymandias'.

across the Thames when he was mayor of London. As we drove away, his phone rang. It was Fiona Hill, Downing Street joint chief of staff with Nick Timothy,[5] giving Johnson an earful for appearing in public contrary to instructions.

I was surprised to find a political adviser telling off a senior cabinet minister in this way. I was even more surprised when Johnson ate humble pie, apologising profusely even though it was not really his fault. The incident chilled me. If No. 10 had so little trust in members of the cabinet, how could they possibly achieve UK goals on the forthcoming Brexit negotiations? My fears were borne out in the chaotic years that followed.

FACTIONS WITHIN THE British government were still squabbling over fundamental tenets of Brexit policy when Prime Minister Theresa May came to Austria in the second half of 2018, over two years after the June 2016 referendum.

Austria held the rotating Presidency of the European Council and was trying to drive forward Brexit negotiations. Chancellor Sebastian Kurz visited London in July, and May came to Austria in July and September, the latter for a Salzburg informal gathering of EU leaders at a critical juncture in the talks.

I liked May, who treated me politely when I first met her in London in July and deployed arguments I had suggested.[6]

'After the dinner between Kurz and May', I wrote, 'we returned to the hall of No. 10 for goodbyes. At this point, charmingly, Kurz's main adviser, a bloke called Alexander Schallenberg[7] who I know well, came up to May, who was standing next to me, and proceeded to praise me as an exceptionally brilliant ambassador ("He is everywhere in town." "You mean he is at all the parties?" May said. "He is giving all the parties," Schallenberg said ...).

---

[5] In 2016, British media forecast a Brexit clash of the titans between Hill and Timothy on the one hand and Martin Selmayr, chief of staff to European Commission President Jean-Claude Juncker, on the other. In the event, Hill and Timothy resigned after the 2017 UK general election. Selmayr stayed on until 2019, when he became the EU's permanent representative to Austria.

[6] Politicians vary in their likeliness to deploy points suggested to them by officials. Some grasp at them gratefully, others make a point of not using them.

[7] Later foreign minister and, briefly, chancellor of Austria.

This would be wonderful if the PM had any influence over my career or my pay, but unfortunately this is not the case.'

By the second half of 2018, May faced the impossible task of negotiating a Brexit deal without political support at home. At the September Salzburg meeting, she presented to EU leaders her 'Chequers plan', agreed by the British government in July. This called for the UK to stay in the EU Single Market for goods only. The plan had already led Boris Johnson, and Brexit Secretary David Davis, to resign from May's cabinet.

EU leaders then rejected it, too.

The strains on May were visible in Salzburg when I stood waiting for her in the hotel lobby to depart for a function. The lift opened, and French President Emmanuel Macron appeared. Like a turbo-charged bee flitting between flowers, he rushed to everyone in the lobby, grinning at and shaking the hands of baffled bell-boys, receptionists, photographers and even myself, wishing us all well. Then he steamed out of the door.

A few minutes later, Theresa May emerged from the lift. She peered around, and was guided by officials towards the exit. Her brow furrowed, she left the hotel and climbed into the waiting car without engaging with anyone.

Was Brexit inevitable?

Anarchy in the UK political establishment over Brexit was only half the problem. The other half was a population split down the middle on all things Brussels.

On 11 June 2016, 12 days before the Brexit referendum, I was pleased to run into a high-flying FCO EU expert in the main courtyard of the Foreign Office in London. We sat down on a bench in the sun and I quizzed him about EU priorities for my forthcoming ambassadorial job in Vienna. He set out a range of meaty issues, from financing to defence and EU expansion. I nodded, as if to imply that I was thoroughly conversant with UK aims and objectives in all these areas.

"But what about the referendum?" I asked. "What if people vote to leave?"

"It can't happen," he said. "It will be a minimum of 55 per cent in favour of 'remain'."

On 24 June 2016, I awoke in Istanbul at 05.30, clicked on the TV, and sat down on the sofa. I had not shared the confidence of my colleague in the outcome: referendums are unpredictable.[8] The 'remain' campaign had been clueless, and the fact the 20th century was kinder to the UK than to the rest of the continent fortified the Brits with an 'it'll be all right on the night' insouciance, baffling elsewhere, when it came to taking a leap into the dark. But friends and family were devastated – one described feeling 'bereaved'.

Speaking to my dismayed grown-up children, I opined that if Brexit went badly, the UK would grow at a rate of, say, 0.1 per cent more slowly than would have been the case if we'd stayed in. If, against my expectation, the leavers were right, perhaps we would grow 0.1 per cent more quickly. Over the years, these figures would make a big difference to our future. I wrote: 'On the one hand, I don't suppose the earth will open under our feet; but the long-term impact, particularly on the UK's ability to run itself … and to keep itself secure in a dangerous world, seems potentially pretty serious.'

The referendum transformed my job in Vienna. Previous ambassadors had devoted their time to multilateral work. Now, as Brexit devoured the British body politic, my job would be to persuade Austrians of the merits of what the UK was doing, and to make sure Brits living in Austria had the information they needed to navigate looming changes to their status.

On 29 March 2017, I visited the Foreign Ministry to hand my Austrian counterpart – the same Alexander Schallenberg – a copy of the Article 50 letter notifying the Austrians of the UK's intention to leave the EU. On the night of 31 January 2020, I personally lowered the EU flag outside the embassy.

In between, I tried to counter the general assumption among Austrians that the UK had been seized by a collective death wish. This meant countless media appearances, speeches and articles. The task of explaining British policy was complicated by the fact that from 23 June 2016 to 12 December 2019, we did not know what our policy was: our 'lines to take' literally included the phrase 'Brexit means Brexit'. Only when the Conservative

---

[8]   Except in Switzerland. A Swiss colleague said: "Who holds a referendum without knowing the answer?"

Party under Boris Johnson won the December 2019 election on a platform of a 'hard' Brexit did the path – whether right or wrong – become clear.

Trying to explain to British citizens in Austria how Brexit would affect them was gruelling. Most detested what was happening, which had disastrous practical consequences for them. Their anti-Brexit passion, just like the pro-Brexit ardour of many people back in the UK, highlighted three things that perhaps made the dismal, destructive Brexit the UK ended up with on 31 January 2020 inevitable.

The first two were mirror images of one another. For decades, UK political leaders failed to make a clear case for EU membership. Both the main political parties, at least as far back as Margaret Thatcher, were riven by competing pro- and anti-EU factions. Result: as the EU evolved, no serious British leader presented a compelling vision of why membership benefited the UK and its people.

Nor, either before or after 23 June 2016, did anyone formulate a compelling vision of what Brexit was, or what a UK 'freed' from the EU would look like, other than vague assertions about sovereignty and being 'shackled to a corpse'. Without such a vision, arguments about Brexit rights and wrongs remained stuck in an infinite loop of recriminations and accusations.

Neither anti- nor pro-Brexit political forces were able to take their people – in this case, a clear majority of Brits – with them.

The third body of leaders who failed to take the people of either the UK or the rest of Europe with them were idealistic proponents of 'ever closer union' in the European Commission and some EU member states. That failure not only helped usher the Brits towards Brexit, but threatens the future of the European project as a whole.

In March 2009 in Sevastopol, Crimea, I discussed tensions between the UK and EU over a vodka with my friend Jürgen Heimsoeth, the German ambassador to Kyiv.

"Sometimes," Jürgen said, "I think the EU would be better off without the Brits."

"Hold it," I said. "Without the UK, the Single Market would never have happened. The EU would still be spending more than half its budget propping up agriculture. And it would have only 12 members."

The idea that the UK disrupted the smooth development of the EU is, not surprisingly, widespread. In Austrian author Robert Menasse's otherwise terrific *The Capital*, a rollicking Brussels satire, all the Brits are whiny, Machiavellian or both. Other nationalities don't come out too well, either.

The key problem stunting the development of the EU was not Brits but mission drift. The primary purpose of the European Steel and Coal Community, then the European Community, then the European Union, was to make future war between the member states – particularly France and Germany – impossible. It did such a brilliant job that people took peace for granted. Meanwhile, decades of stability, economic cooperation and competition[9] sent living standards soaring.

What do organisations do to prevent stagnation and irrelevance? They reinvent themselves. With the 1992 Maastricht Treaty and the 2007 Treaty of Lisbon, member states and the Commission sought to maintain momentum, like a multinational corporation seeking growth by diversifying from its core business. The new treaties sought to force the pace on integration and to crystallise the 'fundamental values' of what was now the European Union. The motherhood-and-apple-pie list includes respect for human dignity and human rights, freedom, democracy, equality (there is also talk of social equality) and the rule of law.

The professed motives of those pushing this agenda were laudable. They argued that a more integrated Europe, based on values, would be a more cohesive entity, better able to develop policies, promote those policies on the international stage, and support the welfare of its citizens. For them, moving towards a 'United States of Europe' seemed a no-brainer.

The problem was that however compelling such a vision might appear to its architects, not everyone living in Europe found that vision inspirational, or even desirable. Here it was Europe's

---

[9]   Historic exchange rates between the German D-mark and the French franc or the Italian lira from 1960 to 1998 are reminiscent of Gary Lineker's famous quote: 'Football is a simple game. Twenty-two men chase a ball for 90 minutes and at the end, the Germans always win.'

leaders who, despite best efforts, did not take their citizens with them. On the contrary: the push for integration risked leaving some people, and whole countries, behind. Greeks, Brits, Poles, Hungarians and others often felt lectured and patronised by its advocates – who, in turn, looked preachy and out of touch.

I voted against Brexit. It weakens both the UK and the EU. Membership, for all its challenges, boosted UK growth, security and international influence.[10] The UK's absence makes the EU more insular, less nimble on foreign affairs and defence, and less competitive.

Yet even as someone many Brits might regard as pro-European, I scratch my head at the concept of 'European values'. The idea that EU member states have a monopoly on worthy principles after the events of the last couple of centuries seems atavistic, and insulting to much of the rest of the world. As for 'ever closer union', I stand with pride or respect for national anthems. But when Beethoven's magnificent Ninth Symphony is recycled as the Anthem of Europe, it leaves me cold.

Brexit was not inevitable. But nor was the 2016 referendum outcome the freakish result of a slick or mendacious 'leave' campaign. The dearth of British passion for the 'European' or 'integration' agenda, combined with the EU's uncertainty about its own path, lay at the heart of Brexit. The refusal of the EU to make substantive concessions to Prime Minister David Cameron's ill-starred efforts to renegotiate membership in 2015–16, including on the basis that these were, to quote Angela Merkel, incompatible with "fundamental European rights", was the last nail in the coffin.

Whether the drive for ever closer union and a drumbeat of European values will stoke fissiparous pressures within today's EU, or whether tensions can be abated by education, persuasion or leadership, time will tell. But unless EU leaders can take all their people with them, they may find it steadily harder to keep the show on the road.

---

[10] I'll be delighted if the coming decades – I doubt we'll rejoin any time soon – prove me wrong.

Risk appetite and foreign policy

Varying appetites for risk help explain Continental bafflement at Britain's readiness to take a leap in the dark by leaving the EU without having a clue how this actually might be done.

One summer, I was riding an S-Bahn through Vienna when the train ground to a halt. For three minutes, nothing happened. At last, the train moved forward. The driver apologised for the delay.

Nearby, an Austrian pensioner clutching her handbag turned to her neighbour. She shook her head. "Chaos," she muttered. "Chaos."

The incident reminded me of an explanation by a European Commission official in 1983 of different national attitudes to the European Community. The original six member states,[11] he said, had experienced horror, suffering and destruction from 1939 to 1945. Institutions such as the armed forces, the police and the justice system had been tainted by war, National Socialism and occupation. People longed to leave behind the nation state and build something greater and more stable, uncontaminated by the past.

By contrast, the Commission official said, many UK citizens looked back on the Second World War with nostalgia. British institutions had survived and thrived. Some Britons felt the UK had won the war more or less single-handed. They viewed uncertainty and instability as edgy, rather than existential threats. No wonder, he said, that Germans, French and others had different attitudes to EU integration and the stability it was designed to engender.[12]

THE UK'S CAVALIER attitude towards geopolitical change also meant Brexit handicapped the UK's ability to conduct foreign policy. I witnessed this first hand when I was asked to return from Istanbul to the Foreign Office to help run the FCO's crisis response to the Russian invasion of Crimea in 2014.

---

[11] Belgium, France, Germany, Italy, Luxembourg and the Netherlands.

[12] This can be extreme. A top Austrian diplomat once told me he had been astonished as a young man to find that UK and US law prohibited insider trading. "Who," he asked, "would take the risk of buying shares without some insider knowledge?"

My four weeks helping run the crisis unit showed some strengths in British foreign policy. The quality of junior FCO officials, and the deep Russian expertise of the Research Analyst cadre,[13] were undiminished. Motivation was off the scale.

Less positively, the proliferation of email traffic with wide copy lists overwhelmed senior decision makers. The National Security Council, created in 2010 to oversee foreign affairs and defence, confused ownership of policy, created duplication and eroded time for strategic thinking.

Most seriously, British politics was already bogged down in Brexit. Prime Minister David Cameron's 2013 promise of a referendum on EU membership, far from calming things down, had raised the temperature. In May 2014, the UK Independence Party won 27 per cent of the vote in European Parliament elections, the most of any UK party.

With British government ministers half-hearted about building load-bearing relationships with European counterparts, it was left to others to forge an EU response to Russian aggression. The Normandy Format set up to address the crisis comprised France, Germany, Russia and Ukraine and excluded the UK. It soon spiralled into irrelevance; eight years later Russia launched its new, larger invasion.

IT IS CUSTOMARY for diplomats of a certain age to lament the deterioration of their country's foreign policy establishment compared with the halcyon days of their youth. In 2014, my final substantive working period in London, the crisis management machinery working on Crimea struggled valiantly. But the obsession of British politics with Brexit both before and after 2016 not only delivered an ugly clump of geopolitical change that satisfied no one and left the country split as never before. It also crippled the UK's ability to develop policy on, and respond to, events around the rest of the world.

---

[13] One of the most underrated teams in the Foreign Office, charged with developing deep expertise on specific countries or regions rather than day-to-day policy. When I took two Research Analyst Russia experts to a meeting with Foreign Secretary William Hague in March 2014 they told me it was the first time this had ever happened.

4

How (not) to introduce democracy

People living in democracies are often baffled at the longevity of authoritarian states. 'Why don't they have free elections?' they say. 'Everyone knows it works better in the long run. What are they afraid of?'

What authoritarian leaders fear is the loss of control inherent in political reform, and the implications for them personally. Sometimes their people fear reform, too – albeit for very different reasons.

How the Iron Curtain rusted

The rusting of the Iron Curtain after 1985 sent a message to authoritarian leaders worldwide on the perils of introducing democracy.

When I started my posting to Vienna in 1984, communism in the Soviet Bloc seemed set to last forever. Foreign Office security rules prohibited recreational visits to the countries concerned. The risks from hostile intelligence services, they said, were too high.

The advent of Mikhail Gorbachev as general secretary of the Communist Party of the Soviet Union in March 1985 marked a thaw in the Cold War. That October, my friends Carol, Margaret and I secured clearance to visit our mate Pauline at the British embassy in Prague. The conditions were that we must stay in embassy accommodation, not a hotel; must not travel alone; and must get diplomatic visas for the trip (the UK did not yet have diplomatic passports). We later visited Budapest and Warsaw.

Our drive from Vienna to Prague started badly. The Czechoslovak border post sat in an airlock between two military-grade steel roadblocks, a mile apart. Our baggage groaned with bacon, breakfast cereal, baked beans and other goodies for Pauline. The border official, taking my passport, stared into my eye and stroked his chin, indicating that my beard did not feature on the photo. He posted our precious ID documents into a kind of letterbox in the wall.

Might my beard block our entry? Might the officials ignore our CD plates and diplomatic visas and search the car? What was taking so long? Borders embody state power. The 30 minutes we waited, watching officials comb every nook and cranny of neighbouring vehicles, took forever.

Three years later, the removal of barriers between Austria and Hungary would herald the fall of the Berlin Wall. Hungary's minister of foreign affairs, Gyula Horn, and his Austrian counterpart, Alois Mock, would hold a symbolic fence-cutting ceremony at the Sopron border crossing. Yet as late as November 1984, Czechoslovak border guards shot dead would-be defector Frantisek Faktor *after* he crossed the border.[1]

In December 1986, we passed the border again. 'Watchtowers, mist, wrapped-up soldiers, barbed wire, arc lights, like something out of John le Carré,' I wrote. But this time, passing through villages, we saw children dressed up as Father Christmas, angels or devils looming out of the murk. Street markets had colonised Prague, selling satsumas, bananas, oranges and lemons. In Budapest, in April 1986 I noted 'pavement cafes, neon signs, bars … people everywhere selling vegetables, lace and knick-knacks'. The fact Hungarians crossed the road when the man was on red seemed to show a disrespect for authority alien to Vienna, let alone our perceptions of the communist East.

Regimes in Prague, Warsaw and Budapest were grappling with a groundswell of pressure for change from the dead hand of communism. Moscow, too, was about to discover the pitfalls of trying to reform an entire country.

---

[1]   The fortifications were set back from the border itself, allowing Czechoslovak officials to patrol their own territory on the 'Austrian' side of the fence.

GORBACHEV'S 1986 INTRODUCTION of *perestroika* (reform) and *glasnost* (transparency) prompted the collapse of the Soviet Union. In Vienna, too, it triggered a series of mini-revolutions.

Those 1984 security rules also discouraged British diplomats in Vienna from talking to their Warsaw Pact opposite numbers. I once saw a young Soviet[2] diplomat I knew by sight emerge from his flat as I walked to work along the Zaunergasse. I instinctively smiled. He blanched and ducked back inside, perhaps fearing a cultivation attempt.

It came as a surprise in 1986 when the embassy received instructions from London to nominate a diplomat to meet someone from the Soviet embassy at a neutral venue to discuss political affairs.

Those in our team with an interest in all things Moscow were fascinated. Might the Russians send an intelligence officer? What might he or she tell us? Who should go from our side? Where might we meet?

We agreed on a greasy spoon café opposite the British embassy in the Reisnerstraße. I was selected as the representative of HMG.[3]

Weighed down by decades of distrust, both sides approached the exchange with caution. The dingy venue didn't help. We chatted about events in Austria, the Soviet Union and the UK. No secrets changed hands. No meeting of minds took place. Whatever the encounter was meant to achieve, this bland exchange of platitudes wasn't it. Rather, it illustrated the scale of Gorbachev's challenge in trying to change things.

Moscow continued to create openings. The launch of the Conference on Security and Cooperation in Europe (CSCE) in November 1986 brought to Vienna British Foreign Secretary

---

[2] Purists will point out that 'Soviet', meaning 'council', is not a proper adjective for the 'Soviet Union'. We often used 'Russian' as an equally inaccurate adjective, excluding Ukrainians, Kazakhs and so on – like calling citizens of the UK 'English'. The demise of the Soviet Union at least had the benefit of making adjectives more accurate.

[3] At the time, Her Majesty's Government.

Geoffrey Howe and his US and Soviet counterparts, George Schultz[4] and Eduard Shevardnadze.

'The Russians', I wrote, 'displayed extraordinary media skills,' admitting BBC and ITN camera crews to the Soviet Embassy to cover a meeting between Howe and Shevardnadze. None of us had been inside before. 'The Russian side showed us where the crews could stand, suggested lighting positions, offered everyone tea ... Strange to be inside the Russian Embassy, pretending that their diplomats were our colleagues just like everyone else.'[5]

These overtures coincided with Gorbachev's unpopular 1985–88 anti-alcohol crusade in the Soviet Union.[6] After the conference opening, I attended a dinner for delegates. 'We shared a table', I wrote, 'with the Russian CSCE Ambassador and his delegation, who proved with astonishing vigour the theory that the Russians, barred from drinking at home ... will do everything to make up for it when the right opportunity presents itself.'

In February 1987 the Russian bilateral ambassador in Vienna, Shikin, gave an unprecedented press conference, responding gamely to questions such as 'I note the famous novel Dr Zhivago, by Pasternak, is soon to be published in Russia. Can you say when the works of Trotsky will be available?' His comment, "I think it is exaggerated to suggest that the Soviet Union seeks to influence the internal affairs of her Eastern European Neighbours," drew laughter.

But the astonishing thing was that the press conference happened at all.

---

[4]   Before attending a meeting with Schultz I was alarmed to be scrutinised by a ferocious-looking hound large enough to place his paws on my shoulders as he sniffed. "Don't move or he'll bite you," his handlers told us. "He's combat-trained."

[5]   I did not attend the talks. But when it emerged an hour later that a senior figure on the British side had left a classified pack of briefing papers inside the Soviet embassy, I was sent to retrieve them. I waited in the hallway for ages. Was the folder still warm from the photocopier when a grinning diplomat handed it to me?

[6]   When I arrived in Moscow in 1992, defunct mineral water vending machines still littered public parks, alongside crumbling statues of Soviet leaders.

WHILE DIPLOMATS ABROAD battled to project a more positive image of the Soviet Union, reforms at home were fuelling resentment that led to the putsches of 1991 and 1993.

In St Petersburg, during my 1992 language training, I saw an odd reflection of the 1991 coup.

I visited the Piskaryovskoye Memorial Cemetery. It's a tragic place. Of the 600,000 Russians who died in the 900-day siege of Leningrad between 1941 and 1944, 470,000 lie buried there. But two children playing by the statue of the 'Motherland' caught my eye.

Little Girl: I'm Gorbachev. (Adopts solemn stance, walks towards statue as if to lay a wreath.)

Little Boy: I'm a policeman. (Steps smartly forward, seizes 'Gorbachev' by the arm, and marches off with 'him'.)

Gorbachev remained a controversial figure in Russia until his death in 2022.

Shock therapy: chaos in Russia

Post-Soviet Russia offers a powerful lesson to leaders attempting geopolitical change without first gaining the support of those most affected.

In 1989, the Polish government adopted reforms designed to transform the economy from state ownership to capitalism. The programme of removing price controls, monetary reform and floating the currency was masterminded by US economist Jeffrey Sachs. It was a roaring success. From 1990 to 1999, Poland's GDP grew from $66 billion to $170 billion.[7] People talked about a Polish economic miracle.

In 1991, President Yeltsin summoned Sachs to repeat the recipe, dubbed 'Shock Therapy', in Russia.

Things did not go well. Russia was a bigger economy with entrenched political and economic interests, including in the Central Bank itself, that resisted reform. By the end of 1992, inflation surged to over 2,000 per cent. Russian Minister of Finance and later acting Prime Minister Yegor Gaidar

---

[7]   World Bank figures for Poland and Russia in constant nominal 2015 dollars.

commented: "The IMF keeps telling Russia to tighten its belt. Yet Russia has no belt. Or, indeed, trousers, as such."

Sachs, who resigned from his advisory role in 1993, argued that his reforms were never properly implemented in Russia and that Western economic institutions such as the IMF did not provide enough support to back them up. Between 1990 and 1999, Russia's GDP slumped from $517 billion to $196 billion – barely more than Poland's.

Seen from my position as first secretary (economic) at the embassy in Moscow from 1992–95, Western economic help to Russia was substantial. The UK extended the work of the catchily named Know-How Fund from Eastern Europe into Russia. Germany provided billions of dollars' worth of aid, in part to meet the costs of resettling Soviet military forces returning from East Germany. Companies flooded in, from IKEA to Mars and Chevrolet.

But Yeltsin did not manage to persuade either the Russian political class or the Russian people to support the change of direction he planned. Half-baked reform led to instability, the 1993 putsch, and, ultimately, widespread support for a leader – Vladimir Putin – who promised to deliver stability.

THE FACT THAT many ordinary Russians fear that the alternative to authoritarianism is chaos in part reflects their grim experience of the 1990s.[8]

In 1992, Russia was the world's largest oil producer. Yet fuel stations remained empty, and shuttered, throughout my 1992–95 posting.

'My chronically unreliable Lada Niva is familiar with jerrycans,' I wrote, 'but has yet to know the nozzle of a petrol pump.' One night in December, the fuel gauge of the Niva fell below 'empty'. The temperature was minus 20. The streets grew bleaker with every flash of the warning light. We were far from home with our three-month-old child in the back seat. After a string of closed petrol stations, eventually a steamed-up kiosk yielded one Sergei.

---

[8]   I recommend the 2022 BBC series 'Russia 1985–1999: TraumaZone' (also known as 'TraumaZone: What It Felt Like to Live Through the Collapse of Communism and Democracy') for a vivid account of how grim it was.

Sergei said he had no fuel. But when we offered him a $10 bill, he remembered he had some stashed away, and reappeared with a full jerrycan – for a 1,000 per cent mark-up.

As he filled our vehicle through a funnel on the forecourt of the deserted filling station, fumes clogged the air. A citizen approached.

"Got some fuel, then?" he asked.

Sergei did not look up. "No," he said. The would-be customer departed without a murmur.

In later months I would phone Yuri, a Russian contact, who arrived with the boot of his ancient Zhiguli (a small saloon car based on the Fiat 124) stuffed with fuel canisters. One winter's day he pulled a snow shovel from the boot, its blade about two feet square, and tossed it to me with a flourish.

"What do you think of that?" he said. "Very light," I replied. "You can't buy one like this in the shops," he said. "The blade is titanium. A mate of mine at the aircraft factory made it for me."

From 1993, bowsers operated by groups of Chechens appeared on roadsides around Moscow, offering a relatively reliable source of fuel. The tankers had no display to show how much petrol had been pumped; the operator would scrutinise a counter only he could see, and tell you how much you had bought.

On one occasion, the operator filled my Nissan Sunny[9] and told me that he had pumped 45 litres of fuel. I protested, pointing out that the Sunny's tank had a capacity of only 40 litres. After a vigorous argument, he reluctantly accepted payment for that quantity, and I drove off. I later double-checked the handbook and discovered that this particular model had a 50-litre tank. I never visited that bowser again.

CRIME BURGEONED IN Moscow in the early 1990s. One day, climbing into my car, I saw that someone afflicted by the chronic shortage of spare parts had pinched my wiper blades. Driving on icy streets thick with grit and slush, I repeatedly squirted fluid at the windscreen, stopping to wipe the glass with a cloth.

---

[9] The Niva spluttered and died in January 1993. The same year, our replacement Sunny was among the first diplomatic-registered cars to be stolen in Moscow.

My heart sank when a police officer raised his black-and-white baton[10] to flag me down.

"You have performed a traffic violation," he said. His nose wrinkled. "Have you been drinking?"

I said I had not. He asked me to step to one side, and sniffed my breath. He frowned and approached the car, then peered at the windscreen. "What is this?" he asked.

I explained that because windscreen-wiper fluid was scarce and ruinously expensive, we had used vodka, which was cheap and plentiful. The police officer shook his head and sent me on my way.

It took me months to find a pair of replacement wiper blades. We got through a lot of vodka.

QUITE APART FROM the assault on their living standards from hyperinflation, collapsing healthcare and rising unemployment, Russians found the chaotic state of the country in the early 1990s humiliating. Smirking Western analysts caused outrage by saying the chaos proved that, as they had always expected, Russia was simply 'Upper Volta with nukes'.[11]

In summer 1993 I visited Khabarovsk, in eastern Siberia. We stayed overnight at a Soviet-era hostelry of the class we dubbed in those days the 'Hotel Concrete'.

It soon became clear that the place specialised in a specific business. The bar was crowded with Japanese men, who had made the shortish flight to Russia in search of female companionship. Local women, desperate for hard currency, flocked in to satisfy their needs.

Visiting my room, I shared a lift with a tall, heavily built Russian woman wearing a plastic apron over a grubby white T-shirt and jeans and clutching a huge container of what looked like talcum powder. She hummed to herself as the lift ascended and got out at my floor. I saw her hammer on the door before mine.

---

[10] Dubbed a '*пожалуйста stick*' or 'please stick' by expats.

[11] US President Barack Obama continued this theme in 2014, branding Russia 'a regional power that is threatening some of its immediate neighbours, not out of strength but out of weakness'. True or not, one may discuss the benefits of saying this.

A Japanese man emerged and looked up at the figure towering over him. Eyes wide, jaw quivering, he shrank away to one side. The woman walked past him into his bedroom. I never knew what service he ordered. But the transaction seemed grim and desperate – on both sides.

In May 1994, I visited another dodgy hotel, in Kazan, capital of the Russian republic of Tatarstan. Tatarstan had declared independence in 1990, only to have its constitution struck down by the Russian Constitutional Court. In response, the tiny entity threatened to 'blockade' Russia, which surrounded it on all sides.

'The fearsome Hotel Kazan', I wrote, 'had not improved since my last visit. The staff proudly pointed out the television (not working), the telephone (not working) and the huge Zil fridge (working, but roaring into life with a noise like an Atlas rocket every 10 minutes and therefore having to be turned off). Improvements – this year there was no broken glass in the bed[12] and the stench from the drains had been muffled by a rubber bath mat – were outweighed by new problems – a plague of world-class cockroaches had broken out and at night the mosquitos just kept on coming.'

In 1993 I REPORTED on the attempt to issue 'vouchers' to Russians, allowing them to invest in privatised enterprises. At the Moscow main post office, where citizens could exchange vouchers for shares, I watched a pensioner totter towards the counter.

'Her shabby appearance', I wrote, 'suggested her to be one of those who have not been treated well by economic reform. She looked on anxiously as her voucher was taken away and exchanged for an impressive-looking share certificate which she folded up neatly and put in her handbag. "Now, we'll all be rich," she said.'

The woman's cynicism was justified. The botched privatisation concentrated wealth and property in the hands of a few oligarchs.

---

[12] When I climbed into bed on my first visit, I thought a bit of horse-hair mattress stuffing was pricking my feet. Or could it be fleas? I investigated and found black dots on the mattress – too stationary for insects. It was spots of my own blood, from where tiny fragments of broken glass in the bed – origin unknown – had pierced my flesh.

While a small slice of the population was better off as a result, many – particularly state employees and pensioners – suffered deep economic hardship. For the mass in the middle who were neither much better nor much worse off, the comfortable certainty of Soviet life was replaced by a yawning void of chaos.

Nowhere was the turmoil starker than when travelling. Domestic flights in early 1990s Russia were anarchic. Boarding an Ilyushin 86, you were required to carry your own 'check-in' luggage up steps inside the aircraft, the Soviet Union's answer to the Boeing 747, and stow it in a hold area halfway up. Shabbily dressed flight attendants – one, memorably, munching an apple – directed passengers to occupy seats in a certain pattern, to prevent the plane from tipping over.

'Flying by Tatarstan Airlines (newly hived-off bit of Aeroflot)', I wrote, 'is no picnic, indeed no inflight service at all except for a plastic tea-cup of cola. The seats look like rejects from a Salvation Army hostel, all stains and foam rubber poking out and bits missing.'

As Soviet-era institutions corroded, staff training and maintenance collapsed. Accidents included the chilling March 1994 downing of Aeroflot Flight 593 from Moscow to Hong Kong. The pilot decided to give his son and daughter a go at the controls of the Airbus A310. The plane crashed, killing all 75 passengers and crew on board.

Many Aeroflot pilots flew with panache, coming in to land more rapidly than I was used to, yet setting the aircraft down on the runway gently. On-board food gave birth to the phrase 'Aeroflot rubber chicken'.

Thus it was that when I boarded a nine-hour flight from Vladivostok to Moscow I watched a family of ethnic Sakha, or Yakuts, in front of me, unload from their baggage half a dozen aluminium pots of stew and rice, which they stowed on the floor around their feet. Delicious smells seeped out as the aircraft prepared for take-off. Then I became aware of a more ominous aroma.

Smoke billowed from the back of one of the seats the Sakha occupied. A hole grew, ringed with flames, the plastic covering melting as the fire took hold. The bearded, robed patriarch occupying the seat leapt up and beat at the flames with his gnarled hands until only a smoking mess of fabric and charred wires remained.

"Really." The man shook his head. "It's not acceptable." Passengers crowding in around us to witness the conflagration murmured their assent. The bearded man strode off towards the cockpit and returned with the pilot, who peered at the back of the seat. He stuffed the blackened wiring back into the smouldering hole with his finger.

"Looks OK to me," the pilot said. "Let's fly."

Our fellow passenger's decision to go directly to the captain was typical of relaxed Russian attitudes towards flight safety. The atmosphere was closer to a bus ride than a long-haul flight. After we had taken off, several large dogs, accompanied by screaming children, rampaged down the aisles, happily transiting the cockpit to complete a circuit. When standards go into free fall in a country, everything falls (out of the sky).

Who broke up the Soviet Union?

Russia's 1990s reforms were successful in one respect. They killed off the Soviet Union for good. When President Putin complains that every problem is the fault of someone else, it is worth recalling it was Russia that broke up the union. That included not only joint legal steps set out in the next chapter, but unilateral Russian economic action.

In June 1948, the introduction of the Deutschmark in the US, British and French occupation zones of Germany precipitated the introduction of the Ostmark by the Soviet Union, creating East Germany as a separate economic entity. On 26 July 1993, President Yeltsin's Russia followed suit, replacing Soviet rouble notes printed from 1961 to 1992, overnight, with new Russian rouble notes.

The July 1993 currency reform was another hammer blow to long-suffering Russian citizens. On the Monday after the reform, which the government organised on a mid-summer weekend, I wandered central Moscow to find a city in shock. Queues snaked everywhere, supermarket shelves yawned empty. In a bid to counter organised crime, citizens could exchange only a small amount of Soviet-era cash ('leninki'). Many people were on holiday and missed the deadline to convert their savings.

The action also, at a stroke, required other ex-Soviet republics to introduce their own currencies and economic policies – giving them a mighty shove towards independent statehood.

THE FISSIPAROUS FORCES unleashed by Gorbachev's reforms were swift and unpredictable. During the August 1991 coup, one politician to speak in support of President Yeltsin was Eduard Shevardnadze, born in the Soviet Republic of Georgia and Soviet foreign minister from 1985–91. He returned to Tbilisi as leader of the new country in 1992.

At this time the British ambassador in Moscow, accompanied by experts from the embassy, regularly toured other ex-Soviet republics where the UK was not yet represented. Travel was complicated and dangerous. So the Foreign Office authorised the ambassador to charter an antique Yak 40 'executive jet' to visit his patch.

The Yak had a range of only 1,800 kilometres – barely enough to reach the end of the runway, we would joke. To reach other capitals, we had to refuel. When in 1994 we landed at Mineralnye Vody in the North Caucasus to tank up en route to Tbilisi, the airport authorities asked us to park up at a remote spot on the airport perimeter, lest the presence of a private charter attract the unwelcome attention of local kidnappers. We stood by rolling wheat fields while the bowser topped us up.

On arrival in Tbilisi, we checked in at the Metechi Palace Hotel. A sign alongside a metal detector instructed us not to bring firearms inside. In South Ossetia we saw detritus from the 1991–92 conflict, after Russian-backed Ossetian forces declared independence from Georgia.[13] 'After a 2-hour drive through the pretty Georgian countryside', I wrote, 'we reached a shambolic check-point manned by a lot of chaps with Kalashnikovs (the Georgian army) and a burned-out troop carrier.'

We looked forward to a fascinating conversation with Shevardnadze, given his former job as Soviet foreign minister. All the British delegation spoke Russian. We were stunned

---

[13] Other conflicts after 1991 included wars between Armenia and Azerbaijan; in the Transnistria region of Moldova; in Tajikistan; and in the Abkhazia region of Georgia.

when Shevardnadze introduced himself in Georgian, speaking through an interpreter, and conducting the entire meeting in that language.

I had never before heard a Soviet politician speak a language other than Russian. The use of consecutive interpretation not only crippled our ability to have a free-flowing exchange – something I was to witness later in our negotiation with China on the handover of Hong Kong – but also reduced by more than half the time available for discussion.

Our veteran interlocutor, however, considered the inconvenience of the set-up a small price to pay for transmitting a clear message: *Georgia is no longer part of the Russian empire. We are an independent country.*

ANOTHER SYMBOL OF Russia's tension with its Soviet past lies in Red Square.

In 2005 I visited Moscow for the first time since 1995. Swathes of suburban housing had sprung up; private restaurants had proliferated;[14] and Sad Sam,[15] the decrepit foreigners' compound where we lived in the 1990s, had been restored into anonymity and relet to Russian companies.

One of the most striking new structures was the Cathedral of Christ the Saviour, destroyed in 1931 and replaced by an open-air swimming pool until 1995. Back in 1993, we had been thrilled to see Russians queueing at churches to celebrate Easter after the failure of communism to crush religion. By 2005 Putin had embraced the church: the soaring, pristine structure radiated power.[16]

We visited Lenin's mausoleum on Red Square, where the embalmed body of the communist leader has lain since his death in 1924. Josef Stalin shared the mausoleum from 1953 to 1961.

---

[14] When I first arrived in Moscow in 1992, some restaurants still closed for lunch.

[15] Sadovaya-Samotechnaya Ulitsa, built by German prisoners of war in 1949.

[16] In February 2012, feminist punk band Pussy Riot protested there against the support of the Orthodox Church for President Putin's election campaign, drawing two-year jail terms.

His body was removed after Soviet leader Nikita Khrushchev denounced Stalin's crimes and cult of personality.

Lenin, himself the subject of a personality cult,[17] remains. 'Lenin seems unchanged,' I wrote in 2005; 'a pink pixie apparently glowing from within, at the bottom of a gloomy shaft of black marble, guarded by fierce men in uniform who erupt with rage if you speak, or dally, or put your hands in your pockets. We were pleased that the children could see Mr L while he's still available.'

Given the atrocities that occurred under Lenin's leadership and the sheer weirdness of keeping a dead body on public display, it seems high time that the founding leader of Soviet Russia followed his successor to a decent burial. But tellingly, President Putin supports keeping the body in the mausoleum, reportedly because removal would suggest – perish the thought – that generations of citizens had observed 'false values' under Soviet rule.

PUTIN'S REFUSAL TO disavow Lenin is a reminder of why the Russian leader launched his catastrophic wars against Ukraine in 2014 and 2022.[18] Putin's goal since 2000 has been to keep Russia's democratic neighbour dependent, unsuccessful and poor. As Ukraine sought to move beyond Moscow's orbit, Putin became increasingly concerned that a successful Ukraine would offer Russians an alternative, democratic model to authoritarianism.

Democracy – a system where no one knows who will win the next election – terrifies the Russian leader. If he loses office, his decades in power and personal wealth will come under scrutiny. The persecution of Alexei Navalny, leading to his death in 2024, shows Putin's fear of corruption allegations against him. Many ordinary Russians are content to put up with authoritarianism so long as living standards keep rising, because their experience of 1990s reform was so dismal. But for Putin himself, the motivation for staying in control of an autocratic Russia is 100 per cent personal: lose power, and he risks losing everything.

---

[17] After Lenin's death the Soviet government founded an Institute for Brain Research to study Lenin's brain, cut into 31,000 slices. In 1993, the then-director of what had become the Moscow Brain Institute ranked the brain as 'nothing special'.

[18] See Chapter 5, 'How to understand Putin's war on Ukraine'.

Why Chinese leaders fear democracy

China, at first sight, is in a different place from Russia in every sense. Despite a near-total absence of democracy, Beijing stands in the first rank of world powers. In 1991, the Russian economy was about one-third bigger than China's. Now, according to the World Bank, China's economy is *ten times* bigger than Russia's in nominal terms. Surely, China's leaders should feel strong and confident?

No. Despite China's manifest strengths, its leaders are as fallible and make mistakes as often as anyone else. Above all, they are terrified of instability – and of losing power.

Following my first work visit to Hong Kong in 1995, I travelled to Beijing overland – at that time, an overnight journey requiring a train from Kowloon to Guangzhou, then a switch to a Beijing service. Arriving in Guangzhou, I saw vast masses of people stretching into the distance. What was happening? Was it a political protest, or some kind of sporting event? My destination, the Soviet-style station for the train to Beijing, lay beyond the crowd.

Gingerly, I approached. The mood seemed calm. People stood in groups, chatting, gazing at the railway building, or jammed together in queues, single-file, in contact from head to toe. Showing my ticket to enter the station, I looked back across the sea of humanity. What I had witnessed was an everyday crowd of locals going about their business in the square in front of the station.

China in 1995 was in the midst of tumultuous growth ushered in by the 1980s economic reform policies of Deng Xiaoping. Flying into Hong Kong, one passed the border city of Shenzhen, a mass of new skyscrapers whose population grew from 1 million to 7 million between 1987 and 2000. In Beijing, vast areas of picturesque but run-down housing known as *hutongs* were cleared and thousands of modern apartment blocks erected. World Bank figures show China's poverty rate plummeting from 88 per cent in 1981 to 0.7 per cent in 2015, lifting around 850 million people out of extreme poverty. But the Chinese communist party ensured it retained an iron grip on power – as it does to this day.

In 1997 I visited the Shanghai Museum, reopened in a splendid privately funded building in 1996. 'You begin to see why the

Chinese think they're better than the rest of us, the centre of the world, etc.', I wrote, 'when you see the exquisite sets of melodious bronze bells their people were casting 3,000 years ago, fine stone carvings, calligraphy, the well-known pottery ("china") etc.'

China has its problems, including demographic.[19] But scale, history and economic power explain why China's leaders feel history is on their side. Why risk political reform?

THAT SENSE OF destiny helps explain why China was at first sceptical of the need to discuss the return of Hong Kong to Chinese sovereignty in 1997 with the UK. They argued that the 19th-century agreements that ceded Hong Kong Island and part of Kowloon to the UK in perpetuity, and the New Territories for 99 years from 1898, were 'unequal treaties' and therefore invalid. Sovereignty remained with China, Beijing said, and they had no need to discuss the future of Hong Kong with the UK.

The problem was that this position created uncertainty for the people of Hong Kong as the end of the lease on the New Territories loomed. Who would agree loans or property deals extending beyond 1997, without knowing what laws might apply then?

Mrs Thatcher, too, was not keen to negotiate. The 1997 deadline, she argued, applied only to the New Territories. Why could the UK not hold onto Hong Kong Island and Kowloon? Only when massed ranks of Sinologists showed her that the border between Kowloon and the New Territories ran through the centre of a dense urban area (roughly where Boundary Street lies) was she persuaded to start talking.

The decision to negotiate required U-turns on both sides.

Talks ran for 18 years, from 1979 to 1997.[20] They covered everything from telecom licences through the establishment of

---

[19] A 2020 study in *The Lancet* forecast that China's population would age and shrink from 1.4 billion now to 732 million in 2100. A World Economic Forum paper of July 2022 put the 2100 figure even lower, at 587 million, and a Shanghai Academy of Social Science projection of January 2024 lower still, at 525 million. Long-term population forecasting is an imprecise art, but these figures are dramatic.

[20] This period contrasts with the UK's withdrawal from the EU, where the triggering of Article 50 on 29 March 2017 set what was supposed to be a two-year deadline. The UK left the EU on 31 January 2020. Negotiations continue.

the Court of Final Appeal to nationality and citizenship issues, the maintenance of Commonwealth War Graves and who would sit where at the handover ceremony. Both sides made concessions. Whether the final outcome could have been better for either side – in particular, whether the UK could have done more to guarantee democratic rights in Hong Kong – remains fiercely debated. But the idea that China was an implacable opponent who could not be moved on matters of principle is wrong, too.

FLYING INTO KAI TAK Airport in January 1996 on the postage-stamp-sized runway between the apartment blocks, I was picked up by a fat Mercedes and driven to my hotel by a diminutive woman in a black dinner jacket and bow tie. She spoke no English and wove through the traffic like a maniac.

My programme was packed – in the way of official trips where all concerned are keen to avoid any suggestion of enjoyment – and included meetings with Governor Chris Patten and Chief Secretary Anson Chan. The city already felt Chinese. 'Welcome China' merchandise, from T-shirts to watches, crammed the shops. A 'History of Hong Kong' attraction at the Peak set out a distinctly pro-Beijing view of events. The business elite of the city hung out in the China Club, 'a place', I wrote, 'done up as a pastiche of 1920s Shanghai, all dark wood and live song-birds in cages, plus upstairs a kitsch "Long March Bar" full of Mao memorabilia'.

Everything in Hong Kong moved quickly. People charged up and down the moving stairways that linked the different levels of the city; everyone punched the 'close door' button as they entered packed elevators. While zones of the city such as Kowloon, Kennedy Town and Wanchai still conformed to Far East stereotypes of bustling streets, stalls and neon, Central was a sterile desert of skyscrapers and scaffolding. "No one's building under 80 storeys these days," a banker told me.

At Government House, the governor's residence from 1855 to 1997, also used for official meetings, the atmosphere on the eve of the handover was febrile. By 1995, the vast majority of senior civil servants in the Hong Kong government were Hong Kong Chinese. Nearly all would stay on after the handover. Until then, they negotiated alongside Chris Patten, and the UK-based diplomats of the Joint Liaison Group,[21] on the future of the colony after 30 June 1997.

Beijing criticised Patten, a senior Conservative Party politician who had been appointed as governor of Hong Kong after he lost his parliamentary seat in the 1992 general election, for promoting democratic reform. Tensions over policy arose between London and Government House, between London and Beijing, between politicians in London, and between Hong Kong politicians with pro-Beijing views and those more sympathetic to the UK.

Tensions probably simmered within the Beijing political establishment, too, but were less visible to us. In theory, the 'Joint Declaration' meant Hong Kong retained a high degree of autonomy. In practice, Beijing was – and remains – terrified of anything that could allow democracy or free speech from Hong Kong to take root in mainland China.

China's instability neuralgia

The UK, like the US, is fortunate that in recent centuries it has not suffered invasion or anarchy. Major schools of political thought in both countries tend to approach high-risk events, such as Brexit or the invasion of Iraq, with a 'suck it and see' nonchalance baffling to those inhabiting less blessed geographies.[22] This does not always end well.

But instability over the past century has devastated China.[23] From the collectivisation of agriculture in the 1950s through the forced industrialisation of the Great Leap Forward to the violence and chaos of the Cultural Revolution launched in 1966, the country suffered convulsions, famines and massacres. Battles raged between Mao and other Communist Party leaders as the former sought to assert himself against rivals.

---

[21] A group of Chinese and British officials that worked from 1985 to 1999 to implement the transfer of sovereignty.

[22] Brits and Americans tend to think their superior democratic institutions are responsible for this happy state of affairs, but geographical isolation may be more important.

[23] Nor did political chaos in Moscow and the dwindling to insignificance of communism in 1990s Russia encourage the Chinese Communist Party to experiment.

As the 1960s drew to a close, many Western progressive types saw the Cultural Revolution, which they perceived as a revolutionary struggle against the bourgeoisie in China, to be rather admirable. When I went to boarding school in Swaziland in 1969 it was considered cool to own a copy of Mao's *Little Red Book*, although no one really knew what it meant. The contrast between this myopic adulation of a distant leader and actual cataclysms for the people of China is a lesson in being cautious on leaping to judgement about events in distant countries.

In November 1997 the Chinese authorities took us from Beijing to Shanghai[24] to show us the city's development. We visited the Bund, a rare relic of pre-Communist times to have survived the reconstruction of the city. Promenading Shanghainese packed the broad walkway along the Huangpu River.

As we gazed across at Pudong, my colleague Alan Paul, who had served in Beijing in the 1970s, observed that one of the first signs that China was becoming a more normal country after the excesses of the Cultural Revolution had been when young couples began to appear on the Bund, holding hands and even kissing in public. Before that, young people had been kept busy gathering to chant revolutionary slogans, to bang drums to frighten sparrows, or to destroy anything old.

THE PHOBIA OF Beijing's authoritarian leaders of losing control has devastated Hong Kong. For a time after the June 1997 handover, much continued much as before. When I visited that November, the city felt largely unchanged. At immigration, you were still given leaflets inviting you to vote for 'the most courteous immigration official' – not common at all borders. But tension was in the air. 'Hong Kong ...' I wrote, 'still has the "borrowed place living on borrowed time" feel to it ... I'm hoping that if China can leave Hong Kong to its own devices for, say, a year or two, and witness the fact that this doesn't create any particular problems, it will then feel free to continue not to intervene.'

It was not to be. Following protests in Hong Kong in 2019–20 against plans to allow extradition to China, Beijing introduced

---

[24] I had flown up from Hong Kong on an Air China 747 whose dog-eared safety leaflet boasted 'no accidents since 1955'.

a new Hong Kong security law, considered by the UK a serious violation of the Joint Declaration. The period since has seen a crackdown on free speech and democracy in Hong Kong, including the closure of leading newspapers, the incarceration of pro-democracy politicians and activists and elections at which opposition candidates are not allowed to stand.

Logic might suggest that China, a country of 1.4 billion people, has no more to fear from a free and prosperous Hong Kong – population 7 million – than Russia has to tremble at a successful, democratic Ukraine. Surely they could show their strength best by allowing, in the words of Chairman Mao, a hundred flowers to bloom?[25]

But authoritarian leaders know that allowing genuine democracy in their own countries – no matter how popular their own statistics suggest them to be – will carry with it a risk that they, personally, could be voted out of office and face an uncertain future. In response, they will pull any lever they can to prevent that happening – even, in the case of President Putin, killing horrifying numbers of Ukrainians and Russians in a totally unnecessary war.

PERHAPS IT IS no surprise that authoritarian leaders are prepared to do almost anything to keep hold of what they have, rather than risk losing power, ill-gotten wealth, and – perhaps – their freedom, or even lives.

The unease of citizens of authoritarian states with ditching the status quo is less obvious. But we should never forget that people's experience of democratic reform is not universally delightful. Sometimes, the devil you know – in the form of stability and limited freedoms – may seem preferable, to some, to leaping into a black hole of uncertainty.

---

[25] Some historians argue that the Hundred Flowers Campaign of 1957, where Chairman Mao encouraged intellectuals to voice opinions in an apparent outbreak of free speech, was actually designed to identify and destroy dissidents. It was cancelled after a few months.

5

How to understand Putin's war on Ukraine

President Putin's unprovoked invasions of Ukraine in 2014 and 2022 turned diplomacy on its head. In response, countries supporting Ukraine must show strategic patience. Delivering an outcome that Ukraine can accept will be a marathon, not a sprint. The biggest challenge will be to maintain unity for as long as it takes to face down Russian aggression.

To understand the war, it is worth exploring why Putin took the action that he did, the history, and how the Russian leader got his decision so wrong. We should consider how Putin's war fatally undermines the cause of nuclear disarmament and raises the risk of conflict elsewhere. Russian misinformation campaigns also repay study.

Why did Putin invade Ukraine?

Russia's invasion of Ukraine was a clear breach of international law. Why did it happen?

Interpreting the Kremlin is complicated because misleading people about what you are doing, or *maskirovka*, is part of Russian military tactics. Putin has recycled a plethora of arguments on the lines of the bully in the playground who, having struck another child, whines that 'they made me do it'.

Putin has called Ukraine a hostile country. In fact, it was a friendly neighbour until Russia's 2014 invasion of Crimea and eastern Ukraine. I visited Donetsk and Crimea often between 2008 and 2012. Russian-speaking Ukrainians in the east and south lived in peace and stability. Russia's 2014 invasion plunged the region into conflict, killing 14,000 people up to 2022. At no point before 2014 did Ukraine pose a military threat to Russia.

Putin has also claimed that Ukrainians are 'Nazis'. This repeats the propaganda playbook from 2014 – when Russia claimed a fascist threat from Ukraine to justify its invasion – and 1961, when builders of the Berlin Wall, designed to stop East Germans fleeing to West Germany, called it an 'anti-fascist protection wall'. It is straight-out nonsense.

Russian propagandists speak about a threat from NATO expansion. But at no point has NATO threatened Russia. Even if Russia perceived a threat, nothing had changed since NATO rejected Ukraine's application to join in 2008 – to avoid provoking Moscow.[1] Nor did NATO ever promise, during negotiations leading to the Two Plus Four Agreement of 1990 on the future of Germany or subsequently, that NATO would not expand east – although it did agree that foreign troops and nuclear weapons would not be stationed on the territory of the former East Germany.

Vladimir Putin invaded Ukraine to keep himself in power. The real threat from Kyiv, as discussed in the last chapter, is that a strong and successful Ukraine could introduce the bacillus of democracy – deadly to authoritarian leaders – into the Russian body politic. That prospect terrifies Putin.

The Russian leader may believe he has a secondary, related aim – to secure himself a place in history as the leader who restored Russian 'greatness'. In fact, all Russia's interventions in Ukraine since 2013 have weakened Russia, slowing economic growth and encouraging suspicion of Russian territorial intentions across Europe and Asia.

This matters to all of us. If Russia is allowed to break international law to invade its neighbour and steal their land, the world will face a Pandora's box of potential new conflicts

---

[1] When Boris Johnson visited Vienna as foreign secretary in 2016, I argued over a late-night beer that we should arm Ukraine to the teeth to reduce the risk of further Russian aggression following their 2014 invasion. The only argument Moscow understood, I said, was military might. But others argued that arming Ukraine would provoke Moscow and *increase* the risk of Russian aggression. Until Russia invaded again in 2022, Ukraine mostly had to make do with non-lethal supplies such as body armour and night-vision goggles.

such as Venezuela's claim, renewed in 2023, to oil-rich tracts of neighbouring Guyana.

WHAT ABOUT THE HISTORY? Nationalists of all kinds love to say 'X territory is the ancient home of our people'. You have to be careful of this argument. What if the Romans, the Mongols, the Ottomans or the Lithuanian Commonwealth were to reclaim their lost lands?

For Ukraine and Russia, the date that matters is 1991.

On 1 December 1991, Ukraine held a referendum on independence from the Soviet Union. Eighty-four per cent of the electorate took part, of whom 92.3 per cent voted for independence. Both Luhansk and Donetsk, the two regions partly occupied by Russia since 2014, voted 83.9 per cent in favour of Ukrainian independence. In Crimea, the figure was 54.2 per cent.

One week later, on 8 December 1991, the leaders of Russia, Ukraine and Belarus signed the Belovezha Accords, declaring that the Soviet Union had ceased to exist. On 21 December, 11 of the 12 remaining Soviet republics – all except Georgia, and the Baltic states, whose independence the Soviet Union had recognised on 6 September 1991 – signed the Alma-Ata Protocol, reiterating the end of the Soviet Union and the creation of a Commonwealth of Independent States. On 25 December, Soviet President Gorbachev resigned. The flag of the Soviet Union was lowered at the Kremlin and the flag of Russia was hoisted. The introduction of the Russian rouble in July 1993 was the final nail in the coffin of the Soviet Union.

The Belovezha Accords left plenty of loose ends. They included the presence on Ukrainian territory of the world's third-largest stockpile of nuclear warheads – leftover Soviet weapons – and the presence in Sevastopol, Crimea, of the Soviet Black Sea Fleet.

To sort out the nukes, in December 1994, Russia, the US and the UK signed the Budapest Memorandum. In exchange for Ukraine, Belarus and Kazakhstan giving up nuclear weapons on their territory, the signatories promised they would respect those countries' independence and sovereignty within existing borders; refrain from the threat or the use of force against them; and refrain from using economic pressure on them to influence their policies. Russia, the US and the UK did not, however, commit themselves to offering military support to defend against any threat to the sovereignty of the three countries.

On 28 May 1997, Ukraine and Russia signed the Partition Treaty on the Status and Conditions of the Black Sea Fleet, dividing the fleet and its armaments between them. Ukraine also agreed to lease naval facilities in Sevastopol, Crimea, to Russia for 20 years until 2017 (extended in 2010 by Ukraine's President Yanukovych to 2042) and to allow Russia to maintain up to 25,000 troops and related weaponry in the city.

On 31 May 1997, Ukraine and Russia signed the bilateral Treaty on Friendship, Cooperation and Partnership, also known as the 'Big Treaty'. The treaty promised the inviolability of existing borders and respect for territorial integrity, and committed each side not to invade the other's country. That's right: Russia voluntarily signed treaties guaranteeing never to threaten or invade Ukraine, and recognising Ukraine's 1991 borders – including Crimea. Putin abrogated both treaties on 31 March 2014 after his first invasion of Ukraine.

WHAT ABOUT THE argument that Russia somehow had to invade Ukraine because of the EU? After Russia annexed Crimea and invaded eastern Ukraine in 2014, Moscow said that they had not been consulted about Ukraine's EU integration efforts; and that Brussels was being provocative. Some Western critics, shamefully, echoed these arguments.

In fact, the EU held regular summits with Russia from 1991 onwards, including detailed briefings on Ukraine's efforts to draw closer. In 1994, Ukraine signed a Partnership and Cooperation Agreement with the EU, designed to boost economic integration. For years, Moscow never objected.

Over the following decade, some EU member states such as Poland and the UK supported granting Ukraine a 'membership perspective', confirming that Ukraine would one day join the EU. Others, notably Germany and France, did not.[2]

---

[2]   It was not until June 2022, after Russia's full-scale invasion in February that year, that the EU at last granted Ukraine candidate status. In December 2023 the EU went further, and agreed to start accession talks – a powerful political signal of support.

Yet the EU and Ukraine continued to pursue practical steps to deepen integration – including under pro-Russian President Yanukovych, elected in 2010. Discussion focused on an Association Agreement between the EU and Ukraine, including a Deep and Comprehensive Free Trade Area (DCFTA). This would have given Ukraine access to the EU's Four Freedoms – goods, services, capital and people, including visa-free travel. By November 2013, the EU was ready to sign the Association Agreement. So was Yanukovych. Russia up to this point had always been relaxed about the whole process.

I visited Moscow, as British ambassador to Kyiv, in 2009. I was intrigued that Russia was so laid back about Ukraine's cosying up to the EU, which conflicted with Russia's efforts to build its own Kremlin-dominated 'customs union' with other former Soviet states. I called on the head of Russia's Ukraine department in the Ministry of Foreign Affairs and asked him if Russia minded Ukraine getting closer to the EU. "Not at all," he said. "Of course, we would rather they joined our customs union, but it's up to them."

Then, in late 2013, in an abrupt policy U-turn, Moscow told Yanukovych not to sign the Association Agreement. What happened?

What changed everything was events in Russia. In 2011–13, large-scale, pro-democracy demonstrations erupted in Moscow and other cities following alleged electoral fraud: the so-called Bolotnaya protests. The unrest convinced Putin he faced a threat from democracy washing over from a successful, democratic Ukraine. Under Putin, Russia has, since 1999, become an autocratic state, without genuine opposition parties or free media. The Bolotnaya protests showed Putin that democracy, if left unchecked on the territory of the former Soviet Union, could sweep him away.

Moscow's block on President Yanukovych signing the DCFTA in 2013 precipitated the Maidan Square protests in Kyiv and the ejection of President Yanukovych from power. Putin's policy backfired,[3] creating a more, rather than less, pro-Western Ukraine.

---

[3] I like the German expression for something backfiring: *in die Hose gehen*, literally 'to go off in your trousers'.

As the Maidan Square protests raged in Kyiv, the Russian leadership saw an opportunity to seize Crimea. They also attempted to foment uprisings in various Russian-speaking areas of Ukraine, including Odesa in the far west. These failed completely in some cities. Even with support from regular Russian troops, by the end of 2014, Russia controlled only half of the two most easterly regions of Ukraine – with Crimea, about 7 per cent of the country.

Crimea: not Russian

After Russia's invasion and annexation of Crimea in 2014, some politicians in Western countries would say: 'Well, that's it. They'll never give it back.' Or 'It was only given to Ukraine in 1954, it was always Russian in the first place.'

Both arguments are wrong. Ukraine's supporters should view the 'annexation' of Crimea with strategic patience. For example, the UK and other states never recognised Soviet sovereignty over Estonia, Latvia and Lithuania after Moscow's invasion of the Baltic States in June 1940. It took 51 years – until 1991 – for them to re-establish their independence following Soviet, German and renewed Soviet occupation.

When deciding what territory belongs to which country, it is better to rely on international law than vague musings about ancient lands. A glance at the history of Crimea shows it has been occupied by Scythians, Greeks, Romans, Goths, Huns, Bulgars, Genoese, Mongols and Ottomans – some for far longer than Russia's century and a bit.

When I visited Crimea in 2008, a retired Russian sailor from the Black Sea Fleet drove me around for the day in his taxi. A controversy raged at the time over whether it was reasonable to have traffic signs in Crimea in the Ukrainian language, or whether they should be in Russian. I asked my driver – a voluble fellow – what he thought. "It's a lot of fuss about nothing," he said, and shrugged. "Crimea is fine as it is."

Outside Sevastopol, where the Russian Black Sea Fleet was based, I rarely met anyone in Crimea who expressed a strong view about its status. The exception was the Crimean Tatar minority of 250,000, around 15 per cent of the population. Exiled to Uzbekistan in 1944 by Stalin, who accused them of being Nazi collaborators, they began to return only after Ukrainian independence. They consistently expressed strong pro-Ukrainian sentiments and a visceral hatred of Moscow.

In 2014, after seizing the peninsula, Russia staged a 'referendum' on merging Crimea with Russia. The supposed result? An incredible 96.7 per cent in favour. The figure is meaningless: Moscow could have plucked out of the air any figure it wished. Were there hard-core separatists in Crimea before 2014? Yes. How strong were they? We know precisely, because in 2010 Crimea held internationally recognised parliamentary elections. Sergei Aksyonov, the man installed by Russia as 'prime minister' of Crimea after the 2014 invasion, led a party called 'Russian Unity'. What share of the vote did 'Russian Unity' win in 2010? Four per cent.

Why Putin doesn't understand Ukraine

In 2014, and again in 2022, President Putin seemed to believe his own propaganda that Ukrainians were, basically, Russians who had been led astray. He seemed to think Ukrainians would welcome Russian troops. How did he get it so wrong?

We can find the answer in a long essay titled 'On the historical unity of Russians and Ukrainians', which Putin published on 12 July 2021.[4]

Long essays by political leaders are rarely a good idea. They smack of hubris. If your president is a brilliant historian, why isn't he (it's rarely a she) teaching history somewhere? Such screeds tend to be authored by authoritarian rulers who have convinced themselves that their brilliance is the only thing standing between the country they lead and the apocalypse.

Putin's treatise is no exception. He argues that Russians and Ukrainians share not only a common heritage (debatable) but also a common destiny (making him a soothsayer). He talks about

---

[4] Putin recycled arguments from the paper in a rambling interview with conservative US journalist Tucker Carlson in February 2024, in which the Russian president also said Poland, invaded by Nazi Germany in 1939, had 'collaborated with Hitler'.

'ethnic Russians', as if Russians are unique, as opposed to – like every other nationality on Earth – a mishmash of DNA fragments stretching back through time. He says that Ukraine includes 'Russian lands' – as if these could possibly be defined and as if all countries, most notably Russia itself, don't incorporate territory that used to belong to someone else.

This is dangerous stuff because, as we saw in 2022, it seeks to legitimise the destruction of some or all of Ukraine and the Ukrainian people. It is based on mystic mumbo-jumbo: the confused, out-of-date rant of a 71-year-old who has never lived in Ukraine

People across the former Soviet Union (FSU), as in any post-imperialist set-up, have a mixture of identities. When I arrived in Russia in 1992, the country had existed for less than a year. The idea that other 'Newly Independent States' were real countries was difficult for us, too. But 30 years have passed. That is longer than the period between the First and Second World Wars, or the lifetime of the Berlin Wall.

In that time, much has changed. Russia faces a demographic crisis, with a shrinking, ageing population. The 2020 study in *The Lancet* forecast that Russia's population would fall from around 146 million in 2017 to 106 million in 2100 – even including inward migration from Central Asia, where populations would surge.

The ethnic makeup of the rest of the FSU has changed, too. In Kazakhstan, Russians outnumbered Kazakhs as recently as 1979. Now Kazakhs outnumber Russians four to one.

Nearly all countries of the FSU are loosening their ties to Russia – and not just in Europe. China and Turkey have boosted links with countries in the South Caucasus and Central Asia such as Uzbekistan, Kazakhstan and Azerbaijan. When I visited Nazarbayev University in the Kazakh capital Astana in 2012, the language of instruction was English. In 2014 the National Museum of Kazakhstan, with its giant mechanical eagle in the entrance, contained no reference to the Soviet Union at all. Since Russia's 2022 invasion of Ukraine, Kazakh President Tokayev, formerly an ally of Putin, has refused to recognise the fake Russian 'referendums' held in occupied zones of Ukraine and has said Kazakhstan upholds the inviolability of international borders.

None of this is the result of a plot by anyone. Rather, it is peoples from the former Russian empire choosing their own paths.

Ukraine is a special case. Its economy is the second largest in the FSU after Russia. It has close historic, cultural and linguistic ties. That history includes bitter conflicts, from the brutal invasion of eastern Poland – now western Ukraine – by the Soviet Union in 1939 to the Holodomor, a famine brought about by Soviet policies that killed millions of Ukrainians in 1932–33. Solzhenitsyn's gulag memoir *One Day in the Life of Ivan Denisovich* features Ukrainians among the political prisoners.

After independence in 1991, Ukrainian nationalism surged. This is not the place to debate the history of the Slavs from the 9th century, although Ukrainians like to point out that Kyiv was a sophisticated city for centuries before Moscow existed. But anyone who has lived in modern Ukraine can see that Ukrainians are as different from Russians as, say, the Irish from the English. Speaking Russian no more makes Ukrainians Russian than speaking German makes Swiss citizens Germans.

In 2009 I attended the opening of the Donbass Arena in Donetsk – a magnificent football stadium[5] by the same team that designed stadia for Bayern Munich and Manchester City. In addition to a set by Beyoncé, the highlight was a speech by President Yushchenko, who always spoke Ukrainian in public.

When Yushchenko began speaking, the Russophone crowd, few of whom had voted for him, booed and whistled. But as he began to praise Donetsk, the Shakhtar football team and Rinat Akhmetov, the owner of the club, the crowd began to cheer and clap, applauding the Ukrainian-speaking president's wisdom and judgement.

Unfortunately, President Putin witnessed none of this. If he had – or if he had spent more time experiencing other aspects of post-1991 Ukraine – he might have been less likely to launch his catastrophic wars of 2014 and 2022.

---

[5]   Damaged by fighting after Russia's 2014 invasion.

Russia torpedoes nuclear disarmament

Putin's invasions of Ukraine have also set back nuclear disarmament. To understand how, visit the Strategic Missile Forces Museum, lying halfway between Odesa and Kyiv in rich, flat, agricultural land. Ever wondered what nuclear Armageddon looks like? The museum shows you the details.

In 1991, Ukraine housed hundreds of intercontinental ballistic missiles, each with six to ten warheads, plus dozens of heavy bombers. In 1994, in exchange for Russia's promise in the Budapest Memorandum to respect Ukraine's independence and sovereignty within existing borders, Kyiv transferred the weapons to Russia and joined the Treaty on the Non-Proliferation of Nuclear Weapons – a legal agreement designed to stop the spread of nukes.

Ukraine's pre-1991 weapons were under Soviet command. One may debate whether they would have made any difference to Putin's calculations in deciding whether to invade. But the presence of nuclear weapons on Ukrainian soil would at least have damped down Moscow's tendency to threaten the unilateral use of its own nuclear arsenal. Russia's invasions and trashing of the Budapest Memorandum put up a country-sized neon billboard to any other state considering abandoning its nuclear arsenal: DON'T GIVE UP YOUR NUKES.[6]

Thanks for that.

When I visited the museum in 2010, you could view full-sized model missiles above ground and the massive trucks that transported them. A silo gaped, complete with a 120-ton cover that could be blown open to launch a missile within six seconds. You could walk down an underground tunnel to the entrance of the 'unified command post' – a prefabricated 12-storey metal tube inside a silo designed to resist a direct nuclear hit.

A staff of three inside the command post could launch nine or ten intercontinental ballistic missiles from silos nearby, capable of delivering dozens of warheads. In the event of an attack, the crew could in theory survive up to 45 days, isolated from the outside world, equipped to kill millions of people. Visitors could sit in

---

6   Russia further undermined the international nuclear arms control regime by
     deratifying the Comprehensive Nuclear-Test-Ban Treaty in November 2023.

the death seat and press the – deactivated – launch button. "The movies always show us pushing a big red button," the guide said, "but actually it's small and grey."

'Fascinating and, in a way, cheering,' I wrote in 2010, 'since the likelihood of the world being destroyed has actually fallen in the last few years. Famous last words!'

Famous last words, indeed.

Russian official statements

Russia's war against Ukraine has yielded a bewildering array of often self-contradictory statements by Putin and Kremlin mouthpieces. To understand them, it is worth examining Russian (mis)information policy.

On 4 March 2018 Sergei Skripal, a former Russian military intelligence officer settled in the UK, and his daughter Yulia, visiting from Moscow, were poisoned in Salisbury with a Novichok nerve agent. The UK said Russia was responsible. Many other countries agreed, expelling over 150 Russian diplomats.

In response, Russia denied all involvement. Denials continued even after a UK police investigation identified two suspects, based in Moscow. In an interview on Russian TV, the two claimed to be tourists interested in Salisbury Cathedral's 123-metre spire. Russia also denied involvement in the poisoning of Russian defector Alexander Litvinenko in London in 2006 with polonium-210.

Moscow adheres to the KGB mantra 'never confess'. This was set out by Kim Philby in a talk to trainees of the East German state security service, the Stasi, in 1981.

"If they confront you", Philby said, "with a document with your own handwriting, then it's a forgery – just deny everything ... They interrogated me to break my nerve and force me to confess. And all I had to do really was keep my nerve. So my advice to you is to tell all your agents that they are never to confess."

Next comes the Russian doctrine of *maskirovka*, or military deception. This says that it is OK to mislead your enemy about what you are doing. In 2014, during the invasion of Crimea, Moscow flatly denied that Russian troops were involved – until later it admitted they were. In 2022, President Putin repeatedly denied Russia would invade Ukraine – until it did.

You may think 'What about Western leaders lying? Surely they are just as bad? What about the invasion of Iraq, atrocities committed under colonialism, Brexit, or other examples of people saying what they did or didn't do?'

Indeed, 'whataboutism', seeking to change the subject by raising others' wrongdoing, is a standard response of Russian leaders to accusations against Moscow of every kind.

There are countless examples of Western leaders lying. The difference is one of consistency and scale. In most countries, if a leader lies, he or she will come under pressure to resign. Voters may punish them at the next election. In Russia, the regime has crushed the opposition and pummelled media outlets into submission. In 2008 in St Petersburg, I remember being shocked to buy a copy of *Izvestia*, a newspaper which during my time in Moscow from 1992–95 had been a useful source of news, and finding it contained only the official line.

Three tragic cases where military forces shot down civilian airliners illustrate the extreme nature of Russian disinformation. In 1988, the USS *Vincennes*, a US warship, shot down Iran Air flight 655, killing 290 people. The US did not deny shooting down the plane, but said it was an accident, and eventually paid compensation to Iran. In 2020, Iran shot down Ukrainian International Airlines flight 752, killing all 176 occupants. Within days, the Iranian government admitted that they had shot down the aircraft by mistake and apologised, although arguments about compensation continue.

In 2014, a Russian Buk surface-to-air missile shot down MH17, a Malaysia Airlines plane from Schiphol carrying 283 mostly Dutch passengers and 15 crew, over Russian-occupied eastern Ukraine. A Dutch official investigation found Russia responsible. Yet despite overwhelming evidence, the Kremlin continues to deny *any role whatsoever* in the destruction of MH17.

MH17 is an example of another technique the Kremlin deploys to mask the truth. This is repeatedly to float alternative theories. In 2014, Russia first said a Ukrainian fighter jet had shot down MH17 (not true); then that a Ukrainian Buk was responsible (not true); then that the path of MH17 was deliberately shifted into a war zone (not true) and other contradictory theories. The aim is to generate a fog of confusion among the public in the spirit of 'it's impossible to know the truth', and to give supporters and conspiracy theorists something to cling to.

Next time you listen to a Russian official statement, bear in mind: Kim Philby, *maskirovka* and MH17.

Russia–Ukraine: what next?

How could the conflict be ended? At the time of writing, prospects for a negotiated outcome look bleak. Early in the war, Ukraine suggested a ceasefire and talks based on the pre-February 2022 boundaries. The suffering caused by Russia's invasion since then makes any such outcome unlikely. Ukraine now says Russia must withdraw from the whole of Ukraine, including areas occupied in 2014, before peace talks. They argue that a ceasefire on any other basis would reward aggression and allow Russian military forces to regroup.

On the Russian side, Putin cannot agree to anything that leaves his troops occupying no more of Ukraine than they did in February 2022. How could he justify to the Russian people the chaos and destruction he has wrought – including hundreds of thousands of Russian soldiers dead and wounded – for no gain? That would surely be the end of his rule – the very outcome he launched his war against Ukraine to prevent. For Putin, the war is existential.

Many observers expect a grinding war of attrition. Russia will try to seize more land and resist Ukrainian advances. Ukraine will try to push forward. At the time of writing, the war is far from 'won' for either side.

The situation inside Russia is fluid. Every decision Putin has made since 2013 has been wrong. He has turned Ukraine, a friendly neighbour, into a bitter foe. His actions have caused Finland and Sweden to join NATO, and turned previously sympathetic countries such as Germany against him. Putin has spent years building a system where he is difficult to overthrow. But the longer the war goes on, the greater the likelihood that Russian families suffering personal tragedies from the loss of loved ones will demand a change, as they did during the 1979–89 Soviet occupation of Afghanistan. The June 2023 mutiny by the forces of mercenary leader and Putin ally Yevgeny Prigozhin, who stated that the reasons given for the invasion of Ukraine were lies, showed how quickly the situation could change.[7]

Putin hopes that a long war will sap the collective will of countries supporting Ukraine. To begin with, the opposite happened. Each time evidence of Russian atrocities emerged, such as mass graves or attacks on civilians, the resolve of Ukraine's allies grew. But maintaining political cohesion among those allies to support Ukraine financially and militarily in the long term is a challenge, as debates in the US and other countries have shown. They have their own economic and political problems to deal with – particularly as fresh crises erupt, in the Middle East or elsewhere.

The top priority in responding to Russia's invasion of Ukraine must be to maintain unity among the countries opposing it. Only that will make it possible to keep providing Ukraine with the weapons and material it needs to defend itself against the biggest war launched on European soil since 1945. It is a grim prospect. But the alternatives are grimmer still.

---

[7] Prigozhin died in an air-crash, widely attributed to an on-board explosion, in August 2023.

6

How to grapple with
a legacy of colonialism

Many observers of diplomatic or political life are inclined to think
that if only they were put in charge, they could swiftly sort things
out. But as presidents and potentates have found throughout
history, running countries is tricky. Foreign policy is especially
fiddly: people beyond your borders are strangely sceptical that
you have the answers to their problems.

In few places is the contrast between 'easy-looking path to
solution' and 'ghastly morass of quicksand' so stark as in the
British Overseas Territories. Yet, on a good day, they are diverse,
magnificent and fascinating.

Problems left over by history

Just as I had barely heard of the Falkland Islands before Argentina
invaded them in 1982, so most Brits have only the haziest
understanding that the UK still possesses numerous overseas
territories, or OTs, around the world. Many people would struggle
to place South Georgia, Anguilla or Pitcairn on a map, let alone
Tristan da Cunha, the South Sandwich Islands or Providenciales.

The Chinese liked to say that Hong Kong was a 'problem left
over by history'. The remaining OTs have diverse constitutional,
economic and political arrangements, rooted in history and
geography. Some, such as Bermuda and the Cayman Islands –
which between them account for around half the OTs' combined
population of 270,000 – have strong economies but don't want to
be independent. Others are too small to be viable: step forward
Pitcairn, with its population of around fifty. Several are disputed;

for example, Gibraltar, the Falklands, or the British Indian Ocean Territory (BIOT). (I was not responsible for Gibraltar or the Sovereign Base Areas of Cyprus).

But if the OTs are indeed 'problems left over by history' that is not the fault of the people who live there.

The inhabitants of most OTs want maximum freedom to run their own affairs. They resent London's ability to impose laws with which they disagree – for example, a 2001 Order in Council to decriminalise homosexuality in some Caribbean territories. But they do not want independence, lest this endanger UK ties that help them build financial services industries, repair hurricane damage, or protect their security.[1]

As director of Overseas Territories from 2006 to 2008, I was commissioner, that is, non-resident governor, of BIOT and the British Antarctic Territory. 'Her Majesty has been pleased to direct', the document appointing me as commissioner, BIOT read, 'pursuant to Section 4(1) of the British Indian Ocean Territory Order 1976 as amended by section 2 of the British Indian Ocean Territory (Amendment) Order 1981, that ROBERT LEIGH TURNER shall be, with effect from 31 July 2006, Commissioner for the British Indian Ocean Territory, to hold office during Her Majesty's Pleasure.' I was sworn in to the new position with my hand on a Bible.

THE QUASI-COLONIAL STATUS of the territories meant they sat awkwardly with the rest of the Foreign and Commonwealth Office. Senior figures rarely had much idea what was happening there unless a problem blew up. The remote and vulnerable nature of the OTs meant such issues detonated regularly. From child abuse on Pitcairn to corruption allegations in the Turks and Caicos Islands; from airworthiness certificates for the planes of the British Antarctic Survey to repairing the rotten runway on Ascension Island, something was always happening.

'My week', I wrote to my parents in May 2007, 'was the usual round, including the decision of the Appeal Court against

---

[1] Despite the fact that the OTs do not want independence, the UN Special Committee on Decolonization continues to list many of them as non-self-governing territories and debates their status every year.

HM Government on the British Indian Ocean Territory.[2] ... On other fronts, we're preparing for the final month of the Falklands' 25-year commemorations of the Argentine invasion; in the death-throes of our negotiations with the British Virgin Islands on a new constitution; and are urgently reviewing our whole policy on the OTs by the end of June, by special request of the minister. So, plenty to do.'

CONFLICT BETWEEN LONDON and the territories is pre-programmed. Not one territory brings in a penny to the British taxpayer; some represent a massive financial commitment. London would be delighted in most cases if the local populations decided to become independent. Yet that is entirely a matter for them: unless the territories themselves take the initiative to seek that status, any attempts by the UK to encourage them to do so are likely to be nugatory if not counterproductive. For disputed territories, independence is not an option.

Some people say that overseas territories are like hyphens: if you take them seriously, you will go mad. Yet for their inhabitants, together with their worldwide diaspora, OT governance is an existential issue. The British taxpayer, in turn, yearns for stable administration, minimal expenditure and zero problems from these remaining fragments of empire.

All this puts pressure on the governors of the territories, who are appointed by the UK, to advise, cajole and persuade local politicians to act wisely – and legally – at all times.

Policy and depopulation

Perhaps the most headache-inducing of the mind-expanding challenges generated by the OTs are those concerning money. Everything, from zoning decisions to allow lucrative real estate development, to offshore domiciling of companies keen to avoid taxation while enjoying the British legal system, risks the territories', and the UK's, reputations. The semi-detached nature of governance, whereby territories press to run their own affairs

---

[2]   On whether an Order in Council preventing people living in BIOT could be subject to judicial review.

so far as possible and London seeks to intervene only when necessary, makes future horrors inevitable.

Trying to square these circles makes working with the OTs both challenging and – often – rewarding. As I wrote in my 2008 handover note, 'I recommend OT work to anyone who wants a high level of responsibility, fulfilling work and unexpected challenges … Given the cataclysmic nature of many OT issues, whether in terms of contingent liabilities or plain ghastliness if things go wrong, you will want to make sure that you are up to speed on all the main subjects.'

A particular regret of my 21 months at the helm, as we navigated our way – sometimes literally – through stormy seas, was that I did not visit more of the OTs. I was fortunate that my boss encouraged me to visit as many as I did.[3] Yet when the British Antarctic Survey urged me, as commissioner of the British Antarctic Territory, to travel to South Georgia and the Antarctic Peninsula, I failed to find time in my diary to do so.[4] Nor did I ever make it to Pitcairn, in the South Pacific. I still long to see both.

MOST NEW BRITISH foreign secretaries are baffled at the diverse constitutional arrangements that bind the Overseas Territories to the United Kingdom. In territory A, the local budget pays the governor's salary; in territory B, this falls to London. In territory C, the uniform worn by the governor was abolished as anachronistic decades ago; in territory D, a push from London to abolish the uniform is met with suspicion and hostility. 'Our policy on the OTs needs a review,' British politicians say.

The 1997 Labour government led by Tony Blair was no exception. In 1999, London published a White Paper, *Partnership for Progress and Prosperity*. Foreign Secretary Robin Cook called it 'a milestone in Britain's relationship with the Overseas

---

[3] Quite apart from their intrinsic fascination, many territories have distinctive and collectable passport stamps.

[4] I even had in the drawer of my desk in the department my personal British Antarctic Territory pennant, featuring a lion and a penguin, which I would like to have seen flying from a snowmobile.

Territories'.[5] It proposed to update the constitutions of the OTs and give them greater powers to run themselves.

I partook in numerous discussions on the reform of overseas territory constitutions. All were scratchy: 'The talks themselves were fairly predictable,' I wrote to my parents in 2006 from one territory, 'lengthy all-day meetings in the disaster management centre with the [territory] side attacking us for our colonial mentality, and our delegation leader (a lawyer) explaining how we were seeking to give them more powers. Highly interesting in its way but gruelling after the first 8 hours.' Having visited another territory, I wrote: 'Quite a difficult political scene here, with lots of people unhappy or aggrieved, and I've had many difficult conversations with them.'

At another set of constitutional talks, I noted: 'Unfortunately, the [territory] side in the talks comprises the entire … legislative assembly, made up of four or five different political parties, with the Chief Minister being the only member of his own party in a fragile coalition, so everyone had views to express … by the end of three days we had inched forward a little …'

People in the OTs often asked about the UK's long-term policy. Surely, they said, there must be a master plan?[6] Thus it was that under the heading 'British diplomat in Anguilla says no "secret plan" for overseas territories', the Caribbean Media Corporation reported on 16 January 2008 that 'a senior British diplomat says political independence is a matter entirely for the Overseas Territories, even as he said he would welcome some of them breaking ties with the United Kingdom …

'Leigh Turner, Director of the Foreign and Commonwealth Office's Overseas Territories Directorate,' the report went on, 'told reporters here Wednesday that the territories hold their future in their own hands. He recalled that during a recent visit to another OT, advocates of independence told him that the British

---

[5]   The White Paper also noted that the government had 'ended Britain's isolation in Europe'. In 2012 the Conservative–Liberal Democrat coalition published a further alliteratively titled White Paper: *The Overseas Territories: Security, Success and Sustainability*.

[6]   If Germany was running the OTs, they would no doubt have a *Gesamtkonzept* (see Chapter 10, 'How to know people').

government was "holding them back from independence and that we had a secret plan to try and frustrate those territories which wish to become independent". Turner denied that there is any "secret plan" by the UK government. "It would save me a bit of work if one or two territories decided that they want to become independent," Turner said.'

Did I mention that none of these problems have simple solutions? I suspect no set of constitutional arrangements will create long-term harmony between London and the OTs except – where possible, and democratically decided – independence.

As DIRECTOR OF Overseas Territories, one of the most common suggestions I heard, when describing the challenges of the OTs, was that depopulating remote territories would be more economical and simpler than the status quo. 'Given the amount the UK's spending on them,' people would say to me, 'it would be cheaper to buy each of them a house in London. Every year.'

The UK has attempted several times to depopulate OTs, always with mixed-to-disastrous results. In 1856, the entire population of Pitcairn, then 193, was resettled on Norfolk Island, now an external territory of Australia. Their descendants live there still. But some families returned to Pitcairn in 1858 and 1863 and have been there ever since.

Similarly, in 1907, the British government offered to resettle the population of Tristan da Cunha following years of hardship.[7] The islanders declined the offer. In 1961, following a volcanic eruption, the entire population – by then 264 – was evacuated to the UK. Most returned in 1963.

More notoriously, from 1966 onwards, the British government evacuated the entire population of the British Indian Ocean Territory, known as the Chagossians, to Mauritius and the Seychelles in advance of leasing the territory to the US to build a military base. The decision led to decades of legal action from

---

[7] The Tristan archipelago, one of the remotest inhabited places in the world, includes the uninhabited Inaccessible Island. Incredibly, a party from Denstone College in Uttoxeter visited Inaccessible Island for a *five-month school trip* in 1982. I recommend their deadpan autumn 1983 account 'Denstone Expedition to Inaccessible Island'.

those evacuated to be allowed to return.[8] In November 2022 the UK announced that it would open negotiations with Mauritius about sovereignty over BIOT, 'including the status of the former inhabitants of the Chagos Archipelago'.

In 2002, the British Overseas Territories Act gave full British citizenship to all British Overseas Territory citizens, including the right to live in the UK (although not vice-versa). This appears to have led to a slight shift of population from some OTs to the UK.

The future of the Falklands

Thanks to the Argentine invasion of 1982, the Falkland Islands[9] is one of the highest-profile of the UK's overseas territories. Many people around the world, particularly those who have suffered a history of colonialism, imagine that the inhabitants of the islands are an oppressed indigenous people.

This is not the case. The Falkland Islanders are a tough, independent-minded bunch, overwhelmingly descended from British settlers, who, when asked whether they supported the continuation of the islands' status as an overseas territory of the UK in a 2013 referendum, voted 99.8 per cent in favour on a 92 per cent turnout (only three voters supported a change).

As director of Overseas Territories, I had plenty of opportunities to witness first-hand the plain speaking of the Falkland Islanders.[10] In 2007 I entered a small hotel in East Falkland with the governor, Alan Huckle, to find the reception desk empty. I was surprised to see on the wall a painting of an Argentine Hercules aircraft flying over Stanley, the capital of the islands.

---

[8] In 2016 the British government apologised for 'The manner in which the Chagossian community was removed from the Territory in the 1960s and 1970s, and the way they were treated'.

[9] Argentina refers to the islands as the *Malvinas*, from the French name, *Les Îles Malouines*, given to them in 1764 by French explorer Louis-Antoine de Bougainville, whose ships had set off from St Malo in Brittany. In talks with the Argentines, both sides referred to them as 'The Islands' to keep things simple.

[10] Falkland Island councillors sometimes visit South American countries or the United Nations to explain why they are content with their current status. This is good diplomacy.

When the proprietor arrived, we introduced ourselves. I remarked on the painting. Why, I asked, did it hang there?

She fixed me with a flinty gaze. "That's to remind us what happens", she said, "when you trust the Foreign Office."

Her comment had its origins in discussions between the UK and Argentine governments in the 1960s and 1970s about a possible transfer of sovereignty over the islands. Some analysts – and many Falklanders – believe the fact that the British government seemed prepared to countenance such a transfer, despite bitter opposition from the islanders, encouraged Argentina to invade in 1982 in the expectation that the UK would not retaliate.[11]

Under Néstor Kirchner, president from 2003 to 2007, and his successor (and wife) Cristina Fernández de Kirchner (2007–15), Argentina adopted a policy of maximum pressure on the Falklands in the hope that this would bring them to the negotiating table. This included cutting off flights between Argentina and the islands. Unsurprisingly for anyone who has met any Falkland Islanders, this policy was counterproductive, stoking mistrust of Buenos Aires and determination to resist such pressure.

In my discussions with Argentina, or the media, I advocated a different approach. I argued that Buenos Aires should be as nice as possible to the Falkland islanders, to build trust and normalise the relationship, including economic ties and people–people confidence-building measures. Unless the islanders themselves wanted a change in the relationship with Argentina, nothing would ever happen.

The invasion of 1982 and subsequent periods of Argentine pressure, I said, meant trust building would be a lengthy process. Twenty-five or 50 years of niceness would be needed. But in the context of the centuries-long dispute over the islands' status, it was the most promising way forward. It also had the bonus that building economic ties between the Falklands and Argentina was a win–win for both.

---

[11] If so, a misreading of the situation on a par with President Putin's apparent belief in his own propaganda that the people of Ukraine would welcome Russian troops as liberators when they invaded Ukraine in 2014 and again in 2022.

This suggestion drew long faces from Argentine interlocutors. But it remains my view. Indeed, the only thing harder than building the trust of the Falkland Islanders in Argentina would probably be rebuilding their trust in the Foreign Office.[12]

The stability of St Helena

The OTs teach us to take nothing for granted. When I visited St Helena, midway between Africa and South America, by ship in 2006, I was struck both by the beauty of the island, and by the fact some people seemed to enjoy its isolation. Lush pastures topped sheer volcanic cliffs. English pubs sold local prickly pear spirit. Tropical flowers surrounded Napoleon's tomb. The Peaks area was home to 22 species of spider.

Before the opening of the Suez Canal in 1869, St Helena bestrode the sea-lanes: the Duke of Wellington, Captain Bligh, James Cook, Charles Darwin and the astronomer Edmond Halley all came here. After 1869, it slumbered, with the collapse of the flax industry in the 1960s a further blow. Many island residents, or 'Saints', emigrated to the Falkland Islands or the UK.

The opening of St Helena Airport to commercial flights in 2017 offered new connectivity, and the chance of a fresh start. But my earlier visit highlighted the self-sufficiency of the islanders. On a walk, I passed 'Banyan Cottage', hidden in the remotest south-eastern corner of the isolated island. The cottage was advertised as having 'running water, a wood stove, and NO ELECTRICITY'. Saints living on the island told me they went to Banyan Cottage 'to get away from it all'. In an age of ever-more-crowded tourist destinations, one of the most isolated spots on Earth has much to offer.

---

[12] By contrast, the islanders like the Ministry of Defence, whose presence in the Falklands is muscular. In 2007 a hard-bitten army sergeant drove me around the Mount Pleasant Royal Air Force station. The UK's army, navy ('the senior service') and air force are famously antagonistic to one another. But after a couple of cool RAF pilots had shown me the Tornado F3 interceptors at the site, the sergeant grimaced. "I don't like to say it, sir," he said, "but they're fucking impressive, ain't they?"

ST HELENA CAN also teach us about political stability.

Jonathan, a Seychelles giant tortoise, came to the island in 1882. Based on the fact that he was fully mature when he arrived, his date of hatching has been estimated at 1832. In 2022 he turned 190 – perhaps the world's oldest living land animal.

I met Jonathan in 2007. To be in the presence of such an ancient creature was humbling. But his longevity tells us a lot about the stability of St Helena.

Jonathan's age owes much to his robust constitution and appetites.[13] Yet where else on Earth would a 200 kg[14] tortoise be able to roam freely in a paddock accessible to members of the public for centuries without anyone molesting him? Where else would someone come with clockwork regularity, over centuries, to feed him? It's a bit like opening a battered, long-lost family board game to find that all the pieces, cards and dice are still complete.

'Jonathan is alive and well!' Joe Hollins, the island vet, wrote in 2015. 'I fed him yesterday ... and his appetite was vigorous. He's blind from cataracts, has lost his sense of smell ... but he has retained excellent hearing.' The extraordinary life-span of this terrific tortoise demonstrates a community, and polity, of remarkable stability. Long may it, and he, thrive.

Bermuda: a lesson in political will

Bermuda, too, has some illuminating features.

In 2007 I travelled from the Cayman Islands to Hamilton. Like many things involving the OTs, the trip was complicated: a flight from George Town to Miami, a connection to New York's JFK airport, and a third flight to Bermuda. The fact JFK was frosted by an ice-storm, making it impossible to disembark from aircraft and later requiring me to sleep on the floor of the

---

[13] Jonathan suffered a mid-life crisis in 1969, frequently escaping his enclosure. He calmed down after a mate and a friend, Emma and David, arrived from the Seychelles that year. Governor Andrew Gurr said in 2008 that "Jonathan only groans when he's mating." Owing to uncertainty about the gender of another tortoise he has been seen trying to mount, Jonathan's sexual orientation has been the subject of speculation.

[14] Estimate. No adequate scales exist on St Helena to weigh him.

'JetBlue' terminal ('a state-of-the-art airport experience') was an exotic bonus.

I arrived at Government House as the guests at my welcome dinner were eating their puddings. John Vereker, the governor, introduced an impressive array of high-powered guests. A fine host, he later showed me around the island.

Bermuda is sometimes said to have the most 'advanced' constitution of any overseas territory. The Bermuda parliament, whose foundation in 1620 makes it one of the oldest in the world, has extensive powers to run its own affairs. Indeed, when the constitution was introduced in 1968, Bermuda was expected to become independent imminently.

Bermuda's non-independence illustrates why so many overseas territories still exist. In 2022, according to the World Bank, the island's population had a nominal GDP per capita of roughly $119,000 – well over twice the level of the UK. The Progressive Labour Party, which has been in power for much of the time since 1998, has in the past advocated independence. But since 74 per cent of voters in a 1995 referendum rejected it, the project has remained becalmed. Bermudians appear to consider the status quo a safer bet than the uncertain prospect of independence.

One curiosity of Bermuda is that because of the territory's small area and limited road network, the size of cars is strictly controlled. Bermuda is the ninth most densely populated country or dependency in the world, with 1,200 inhabitants per square kilometre. Before importing a vehicle, you must notify the Transport Control Department of its dimensions. Maximum length is 175 inches (4.4 m); width, 71 inches (1.8 m) and engine capacity 2.5 litres – leading to lots of modest Kia, Renault or Toyota hatchbacks. Only one vehicle per household is allowed, and individuals (rather than businesses) may not own pick-up trucks as private vehicles.

In most countries of the world, such rules would be unthinkable. Yet in these days of climate crisis, with car manufacturers constantly introducing more and more gigantic models,[15] I would

---

[15] The lead designer of a luxury car company told me in 2014 that electric motors could make cars far smaller, without reducing the size of passenger compartments. But many drivers felt a larger car gave them more status.

encourage other governments to follow Bermuda's lead. Who, after all, really needs a car that's longer than 175 inches?[16]

Climate change and the ice-core room

Mention of the climate crisis highlights the importance of another OT in bringing to the world's attention the facts of climate change.

The British Antarctic Territory, like most other OTs, is afflicted by insoluble problems. Its entire area is disputed by Chile and Argentina. But the 1961 Antarctic Treaty freezes (yes) all territorial claims to the continent.

The British Antarctic Survey (BAS) has operated permanent bases in the territory since the 1940s. Their study of Antarctic ice cores reveals a record of the Earth's climate covering 800,000 years – including recent warming.

I visited the BAS near Cambridge in 2007 and viewed the 'ice-core room'. '"This is 50,000 years old," the guy says,' I wrote, 'giving me a piece about 50 cm long. "If you cut a piece thinly and put it at room temperature it starts melting, and you can hear the gas it contains being released, a bit like the snap crackle and pop of Rice Krispies."'

Polar regions experts and scientists are a specialised and admirable breed. Lifetimes studying the Antarctic can have strange rewards. 'We also had the retirement party for Mike Richardson, head of the Polar Regions Unit,' I wrote, 'with many scientists and specialists. It turned out that someone had arranged to name a cove after Mike on a remote Antarctic island, and presented him with a map of the place.'

The work of the scientists of the BAS is vital to all of us. What happens to the thinning West Antarctic Ice Sheet and to the climate in Antarctica more widely will be an indicator of the future path of climate change and the degree to which the Earth remains habitable to human beings. Let's hope for good news.

---

[16] In February 2024 the city of Paris unwittingly followed in Bermuda's footsteps by voting to triple parking costs for so-called sports utility vehicles, or SUVs, and 4-wheel drives weighing 1.6 tonnes or more. But turnout was only 5.7 per cent of registered voters.

How do you get a job like that?

Every OT has enough character and history for a full-time country. Caribbean territories, for all their financial and governance challenges, excel in easy charm.

When I visited the British Virgin Islands in 2006 for constitutional talks, Orlando Smith, chief minister (prime minister equivalent), spared no opportunity to exhibit his awesome dance moves at the end of a hard day of negotiations. I kicked myself when I did not seize an opportunity to meet soca star Arrow, in Montserrat (he died in 2010). In 2007 I was impressed by District Commissioner Ernie Scott's firm grip on the administration of Cayman Brac, south of Cuba. 'Ernie invited me to lunch at a local hotel', I wrote, 'where he introduced me to his immigration, police and customs officers – none of them under twenty stone. No wonder crime is so low there.'

Granville was the governor's driver in Anguilla. At the end of an official programme including the prison, press interviews and meetings with elected politicians, he took me on a quick tour in the official Range Rover, distinguished by having a silver crown on a black background instead of a number plate. Tall, organised and a wry observer of life on the island, he responded to any comment by me with the answer "Definitely," stretching the four syllables out to the full. Between him and a visit to the island museum, I learned about Anguilla's 1967 revolution, when Anguillans objected to being part of St Kitts and Nevis (about 100 km away) and briefly declared their independence.

It rained every day in Anguilla and the clouds were leaden. Driving in a cloudburst, Granville told me the island was famous as the place Jennifer Aniston had split up with Brad Pitt. He said Chuck Norris, the action film star, had also broken up with his wife there – she had left him for an Anguillan singer. "Look," Granville said, "here she is now." I turned and saw a blonde woman in a mighty 4x4 drive past. Was he pulling my leg? It was hard to be sure.

When the sun broke through, Granville suggested a visit to a beach before I headed to the airport. He turned down a narrow dirt track to a remote bay where a café stood by glistening blue water. I changed behind the door of the Range Rover and enjoyed a brief splash. On my return an imperturbable Granville, resplendent in his driver's uniform, passed me a towel and stood nearby while I changed back into my travel gear. An American tourist, sitting alone in the café, watched this performance. He shook his head. "How do you get a job like that?" he said.

I told him you had to take a couple of exams.

THE OVERSEAS TERRITORIES are unique. Dealing with them is a crash course in the complexities of politics, diplomacy, and creating durable solutions to long-term problems. They also contain some of the most stupendous places, and people, in the world.

7

How to handle politicians

Former Conservative minister Alan Clark said of politics in his diaries that 'if you are a serious player, it's no good being "straight". You just won't last.'

In fact, the best politicians are those who work hard, network ceaselessly and avoid hubris. 'Being straight' may be a positive blessing when it comes to resisting some of the temptations that confront them.

Politicians and hubris

On 1 November 1989, I was sitting in the resident clerks' flat in the Foreign Office when the door handle rattled. I felt a pang of relief that I had turned the key. I blinked at my Swedish girlfriend, who was with me on the couch, then went to open up. A familiar-looking man in spectacles walked in.

In the 1980s, the Foreign Office still operated an ancient and clunky system of night-time cover known as the resident clerks.[1] The concept was simple: young, single officers were allocated to the clerkery, a suite of bedrooms with shared amenities overlooking St James's Park, to fill a night-duty rota. You weren't on the night shift: you slept in the clerkery and went to work in the morning. But if something happened in the silent hours, anywhere in the world, you would get up and deal with it.

---

[1]   Better comms, the 24-hour news cycle and growing expectations for what a government should do for its citizens later led to a 24/7 global response centre.

In addition to receiving a small allowance, you could in theory live in the clerkery. But by the time I became an occasional resident clerk in 1988, no one actually lived there – or so I thought.

The crises a resident clerk could face were legion. A security cupboard contained scary instructions on how to respond to a daunting range of incidents: a radioactive leak from a nuclear power station, a satellite crashing on UK territory, or an attack on an embassy overseas. On my first night, I received from Baghdad a 'flash' telegram, then the most urgent form of communication, telling me to contact immediately the wives of two men for whose release Foreign Office minister David Mellor had lobbied on a visit to Iraq. One man had been released; the other hadn't.

Most cases were consular: one night in February 1989 I heard from 'a woman stranded at a station in New York, a man penniless in Nassau, a man dying in Managua, and our gallant embassy staff in Kabul'. Anxious parents phoned around pub closing time, asking for news of their offspring travelling in Africa or Latin America, from whom they had not heard for months. Often, common sense was all we could offer.

Another night, the captain of a Royal Navy vessel in the Far East contacted me. His ship had rescued some Vietnamese boat people and wanted to put them ashore in the region. But the country concerned wanted a written assurance from London that the captain was authorised to land the migrants. Could the Foreign Office provide such an assurance?

Without hesitation, I sent the captain the required instruction. It never occurred to me to consult anyone; indeed, I never did so on any of my stints in the clerkery. In the days before mobile phones, more junior people made bigger decisions.

The clerkery could be lonely. That night in November, I had invited my friend, visiting London and properly signed into the FCO, to come and keep me company for the evening. Her presence in the clerkery was a bit of a grey area, so although the place was deserted I had locked the door shortly before our unexpected visitor arrived.

My first thought when the man walked in was that he looked like John Major. But why would Major, who had taken over as chancellor from Nigel Lawson when the latter resigned the month before, be in the clerkery when the Treasury was next door? He asked if there was any news, in such a matter-of-fact way that I assumed he must be a colleague popping in on his way out of the building.

"Not much going on," I said, and mentioned some South African troop incursions into Angola.[2] He smiled at my friend and asked how she was enjoying the evening. Then he said that he was expecting some papers from John Gieve. I stood up a little straighter. Gieve was the chancellor's private secretary. But Major was already ambling off, telling us over his shoulder which of the bedrooms he was staying in.

Later enquiries resolved the mystery. The reshuffle that transferred John Major from the FCO to the Treasury had obliged him to vacate the foreign secretary's official country residence, Chevening, in favour of the new incumbent, Douglas Hurd. Meanwhile, Geoffrey Howe, who had left the FCO in July for the largely ceremonial office of deputy prime minister, had, in compensation for what was seen as a demotion, moved into Dorneywood – previously the chancellor's official residence. Stuck for somewhere to live, Major – with characteristic modesty – stayed in a bedroom in the clerkery.

John Major was one of the most down-to-earth and likeable politicians I ever came across. He was also a Stakhanovite worker. When he was foreign secretary I often submitted to him briefing for meetings with European counterparts; and, later, received them back for filing. In the interim, he had covered the papers in dense, handwritten annotations – evidence of hours spent preparing for each meeting.

I later met John Major in both Kyiv and Vienna. He said he had no recollection of our encounter in the clerkery.

I SAW THE perils of hubris in politics first-hand on the night of 19 May 1980 in the House of Lords, during the passage of legislation to privatise the National Freight Corporation (NFC).

Sitting in the officials' box, my job was to support the parliamentary under-secretary, Lord Bellwin, in debate with his

---

[2]   One quirk of being resident clerk was that you received all FCO telegram traffic throughout the night.

Labour opposite number, Lord Mishcon. I was not allowed on the floor of the House; to communicate with the minister I scrawled handwritten notes on scraps of paper carried to and from the front bench by clerks or, sometimes, their Lordships themselves.

The duel was ill-matched. Lord Mishcon, a famed orator, had a forensic approach to debate and a ready wit. Always polite, he was fond of saying things like: 'I am sure the committee will have listened with respect to what the minister has just said but I do not know that the respect will necessarily be accompanied in this case by sympathy or understanding.' Lord Bellwin was a less accomplished speaker.

That night in the Lords, the opposition introduced an amendment proposing that any private company succeeding the NFC should, like the NFC itself, have a statutory obligation to promote transport research ('research into relevant matters'). Lord Bellwin said such nebulous obligations were precisely the kind of handicap that held nationalised industries back. Viscount Simon, an opposition peer, asked what would happen to NFC staff engaged in such research after privatisation. Would they be 'thrown to one side'?

Lord Bellwin replied that he did not know how many such staff existed, Lord Mishcon, filled with righteous indignation, denounced 'the complete callousness with which the transfer of a great corporation such as this to a private enterprise is made'.

As the debate heated up, I scurried out to a coin-operated telephone from which to call my contact at the NFC. He said the corporation employed precisely zero staff in R&D. Back in the officials' box, I scribbled a note to the minister. But the debate had moved on, and no opportunity arose for Lord Bellwin to deploy the devastating argument I had secured for him – and with which, arguably, I should have furnished him before the debate.

An hour later, Lord Mishcon, for once, made a mistake. Debating another matter, the Labour peer could not resist a dig at the government's ignorance not 'even to know how many people there were in the research department' of the NFC. Lord Bellwin rose to his feet. 'I should not have mentioned this particular matter again today,' he said, 'but in view of the fact that the noble Lord very kindly has given me the opportunity so to do, I think that both he and the noble Viscount, Lord Simon, will be interested to learn that I now do know the number of NFC people employed on R and D. The fact is that there are no people employed full-time on R and D by the NFC. I think that that information will comfort the noble Viscount.'

This tiny victory in the wee hours of the House of Lords committee stage of the 1979 Transport Bill provided a lesson in hubris. Once you have won the argument, shut up.

FOR POLITICIANS, AVOIDING hubris also includes knowing when to quit, and shunning the advice of courtiers that your unique qualities make you irreplaceable.

Days after my arrival in Germany on 3 July 1998, the Christian Democratic Union (CDU) , part of Germany's ruling coalition, unveiled a weird election poster. It showed a wizened elephant bathing in an Alpine lake with the slogan, in English, 'Keep Kohl!'

The surreal image sought to trade on the chancellor's longevity and experience – he had been in office for 16 years. In elections on 27 September, German voters instead installed the Social Democrat candidate, Gerhard Schröder.[3]

Kohl's departure from politics came after that of UK Prime Minister Margaret Thatcher (1979–90) and French President Mitterrand (1981–95). The 22nd amendment of the constitution specifically bars US presidents from serving more than two four-year terms. Do elected politicians have a natural shelf-life?

Yes. Leaders who stay in office too long cannot make good decisions. Over time, awkward ministers are replaced by flunkies and flatterers. Advisers become more willing to filter out inconvenient facts that suggest the leader's inclinations, or past decisions, are wrong. Hubris blossoms. Leaders start to believe that past decisions have always been correct – so whatever they plan to do next must be right, too.

Long-in-the-tooth elected leaders should step down after a decade, their reputations intact, rather than wait to be forced out. Exceptions such as German Chancellor Angela Merkel –seen

---

[3] A 1998 anti-Schröder poster, showing three random women with the slogan 'Three women say: Schröder is the wrong man', based on the fact that he had been divorced three times, did not sway voters. In 2018 Schröder wed for the fifth time.

as a factor for stability in Germany and Europe in her tenure from 2005 to 2021 but subject to more criticism since the 2022 Russian invasion of Ukraine – simply prove the rule.

Some leaders of authoritarian states, or 'managed democracies' where media freedoms are constrained, opposition parties harassed and elections predictable, stay in power for decades – sometimes changing the law to make this possible. They cannot afford to lose power lest this opens up scrutiny of their actions in office – and an uncertain future.[4] I leave it to the reader to decide whether such leaders – mostly men – consistently make decisions that are good for their countries and their people.

Feet of clay

Diplomats come into contact with politicians regularly. These encounters – perhaps on both sides – can recall the biblical expression 'feet of clay', where King Nebuchadnezzar of Babylon dreams of a statue with a head of gold, only to find on closer examination that the rest of the body is made of cheaper materials.

Politicians, like diplomats and ambassadors, are fallible human beings. The difference is that politicians are obliged to make it appear that everything they have ever said was correct – an impossible task. The trick is to admit your mistakes.

Geoffrey Howe, a wise old cove and a former chancellor of the exchequer and foreign secretary, visited Moscow when I was posted there.[5] He told me that his most anxious moment in politics had been the night before the abolition of UK exchange controls in October 1979. "We honestly weren't sure what would happen," he said. Would it lead to a catastrophic collapse in the currency, or yield huge financial benefits?

In fact, the City of London experienced the 'Big Bang' and boomed throughout the 1980s. But Howe candidly admitted that he could not be sure of this.

---

[4]   As the proverb has it, 'He who rides the tiger is afraid to dismount.'

[5]   Howe's masterful 1990 resignation speech attacking Prime Minister Margaret Thatcher had eclipsed Labour politician Denis Healey's earlier, cruel jibe that being attacked by Howe was 'like being savaged by a dead sheep'.

In 2003, US President George Bush and British Prime Minister Tony Blair sought to justify the invasion of Saddam Hussein's Iraq by the need to disarm the country of 'weapons of mass destruction' (WMD). I argued with my father about the invasion: he opposed it passionately, on the grounds that there was no UN Security Council authorisation.

I argued that the UK and US intelligence communities must have convincing evidence. Saddam's cat-and-mouse games with UN weapons inspectors did not seem like the actions of a man with nothing to hide. My confidence was eroded when the British government published its 'Iraq Dossier'[6] in February 2003, which felt thin; and when US Secretary of State Colin Powell spoke at the UN the same month about Saddam's alleged mobile toxin labs, which sounded fanciful.

When no WMD were subsequently found, Blair was denounced as a liar. I was not convinced that he had deliberately dissembled; rather, he and others – perhaps including Powell – had chosen to believe intelligence that they should, with hindsight, have interrogated more thoroughly given the stakes involved. I continue to respect Blair, whom I met several times, including for his work in helping to bring about the 1998 Good Friday Agreement on Northern Ireland.

When politicians are wrong it is not necessarily the case that they are mendacious or idiots, although some may be both. But in the unforgiving age of social media, voters will be less and less inclined to give them the benefit of the doubt.

NO ONE CAN change the rules of politics. In the year 2000 I attended the bizarrely titled 'Young Node', a leadership course at the Sunningdale Civil Service College[7] for supposedly upwardly mobile managers from the civil service and the private sector. A highlight was a talk by Douglas Hurd, former home secretary and, from 1989–95, foreign secretary. An ex-diplomat, Hurd had enjoyed respect in the Foreign Office, which he would enter wearing a voluminous green Loden coat.

---

[6] Soon dubbed the 'dodgy dossier'.

[7] Later called the National School of Government. It closed in 2012.

At Sunningdale, Hurd reminisced amiably about his time as a politician. Then someone asked whether Prime Minister Tony Blair, whose rebranded New Labour party had come to power in 1997 and seemed politically invincible (he would win another landslide general election victory in 2001) had changed the rules of politics. Hurd stirred. "Every party winning a big majority", he said, "thinks they can change the rules of politics. But the rules of politics never change. Something will always happen to bring them down."

Hurd did not quite say 'Events, dear boy, events,'[8] but his meaning was clear.

Three years later, when Blair supported the unpopular 2003 invasion of Iraq, he suffered a blow to his reputation from which he never recovered.

I have often thought of Douglas Hurd when it seems a government is riding high and armour-plated. I quoted him to Austrian friends when we discussed the charismatic Chancellor Sebastian Kurz, who won landslide victories in elections with his rebranded New People's Party in 2017 (aged 31) and 2019. Kurz resigned in October 2021, after a scandal.

Gas and corruption

What is the most poisonous substance on Earth?

Step forward, natural gas. Not for its chemical properties, but for its noxious impact on politics and politicians.

The first Russian gas delivered to Western Europe arrived at Baumgarten, near Vienna, in 1969. In 2019, President Putin visited Austria to celebrate 50 years of exports.

As Russia extended its network of export pipelines after 1991, Russia hawks argued that European dependence on Russian gas could allow Moscow to build influence and put pressure on importing nations. Others argued, plausibly, that flows of gas and money could help integrate Russia into the global economy and political structures, to everyone's benefit.

---

8   Attributed to British Prime Minister Harold Macmillan, when asked what was the greatest challenge for a statesman.

In January 2009 Russia cut gas supplies to Ukraine, over gas debts, prices and transit fees. Because gas for European markets transited Ukraine, the shutdown severed supplies to Slovakia, Bulgaria, Greece, Austria and others. Russia and Ukraine blamed each other for the crisis. 'A lot of activity on gas, with Europe freezing as the result of Russia cutting off supplies,' I wrote from Kyiv. 'Exactly who has done most wrong is obscure, but Russia holds most of the cards and has been throwing its weight around.'

The dispute was a foretaste of controversy over the Nord Stream 1 and 2 pipelines, designed to bypass Ukraine, deprive it of transit fees, and deliver Russian gas directly to Germany and beyond. The US, and Central and East European countries, fought the project. Despite this, Nord Stream 1 opened in 2011, two years after the Ukraine gas crisis. Nord Stream 2 was completed in 2021 – only for Germany to suspend it two days before Russia's 24 February 2022 invasion of Ukraine.[9]

The argument that integrating Russia into the global economy should make it a more normal country hasn't worked. The problem is not that Russia can blackmail people. On the contrary: when Moscow cuts supplies, as in 2022, it is effectively shouting from the rooftops that it is not a reliable supplier.

The real poison in gas is its corrupting effect on politics. Gas is less fungible than oil: it's hard to turn on and off and tends to be transported through expensive pipelines under long-term contracts. The cash involved is so eye-popping that Western business types involved, and politicians close to them, develop an irresistible urge to go easy on Russia on everything from Crimea sanctions to condemning Russian assassinations at home and abroad. Donations by oligarchs thrill everyone from ancient universities to political parties, including in the UK. In fact, it's not really the gas that's poisonous. It's the money. Many politicians are mesmerised by the whiff of billions – for their countries, their institutions – or sometimes themselves.

If gas corrupts, gas pipelines corrupt absolutely.

---

[9]   Both pipelines were destroyed by undersea explosions in September 2022. Responsibility remains unclear. It is not obvious which side would gain from their destruction.

TECHNOLOGY IS MAKING political corruption harder to hide. One evening in 2019, I met a top Austrian contact for a beer. We did a bit of business, and then the conversation moved to other areas. I mentioned my sci-fi comedy thriller *Eternal Life*, part of which is set in Vienna, and which referred to corruption in the Alpine republic.

My interlocutor frowned. "Really?" he asked. "Do you think Austria is more corrupt than anywhere else?"

I said that during my stay in Austria from 1984–87 I had witnessed many dodgy events. An insurance fraud had come to light over the 1977 sinking of a ship, the *Lucona*, in the Indian Ocean, costing the lives of six sailors. In 1985, the Austrian wine scandal had erupted.[10] Procurement was often suspect, as in the case of the Vienna AKH (general hospital). People talked about 'Vitamin B' (for '*Beziehung*', or 'relationship') being essential for success in life.

But perhaps he was right, I concluded. It was hard to compare corruption between countries. Maybe it was more about a *Freunderlwirtschaft* – a closely networked society, where everyone knew everyone else and was ready to do and return favours. Corruption indices didn't show Austria in too bad a light.[11] We ordered another beer.

Shortly after, in May 2019, a new scandal exploded. A covert video appeared to show two politicians from the Austrian Freedom Party (FPÖ) at a villa in Ibiza discussing corrupt practices, including securing positive media coverage by granting government contracts. Although the video had been made two years earlier, the shock-waves forced the collapse of the ruling coalition, which included the FPÖ.

The fact the video featured a young woman posing as the niece of a Russian oligarch, copious alcohol, the proposed purchase of Austria's biggest newspaper, the *Kronen Zeitung* and alleged connections to Vladimir Putin lent colour to the story.

---

[10] The addition of antifreeze to make wine sweeter turned out to be a blessing. Tough new laws transformed the quality of Austrian wine.

[11] The 2023 Transparency International Corruption Perceptions Index rated Austria 20th of 180 countries: tied with the UK, worse than Germany and better than the US.

The 'Ibiza scandal' led to the release of damaging text messages from the phones of leading politicians, and the revival of an old political saying in Austria: *ein Schrifterl ist ein Gifterl* (anything you write down can come back and bite you). Worldwide, the spread of intrusive technology, including cheap and easy audio and video recording, may actually benefit those politicians who are 'straight'.

How to network

Not all politicians are natural networkers. A lesson in how they can nonetheless build a vast web of contacts comes from an unexpected place: the Élysée Treaty, signed by the President of France, Charles de Gaulle, and West German Chancellor Konrad Adenauer, in 1963.

The Élysée Treaty is designed to overcome centuries of conflict and distrust between France and Germany. Its text is short, simple and mechanical. Among other things, it mandates the ministers of foreign affairs and defence of the two countries to meet 'at least once every three months'. So, too, education ministers and those responsible for youth and sports. Chiefs of staff should meet at least every two months. Such contacts are baked into the Franco-German system at every level, including officials and diplomats.

Many Anglo-Saxons find mandated meetings of this kind preposterous. Ask a British minister to meet her or his foreign counterpart and they will invariably ask 'What is the goal?'

This is not daft. British ministers are usually members of Parliament. They have ferociously busy schedules. What is the point of meeting someone, they ask, if the objectives are not clear? Surely they should prioritise meetings likely to bring about crunchy, concrete results, or 'deliverables'?

It is not daft, but it is mistaken. Politics, like business, diplomacy or most forms of human interaction, is about relationships. The time to build up those relationships is *before* a problem emerges. If, when crisis comes, you find yourself seeking help from someone to whom you are speaking for the first time, chances of success are lower than if you have spent hours in that person's company learning about their opinions, politics, children and favourite authors or artists.

The working of the European Union takes this into account. Ministers of, say, agriculture or social affairs meet regularly, year in, year out, whatever else is going on. They get to know one another, supposedly increasing their chances of working effectively together. The fact that some sub-units of members – such as the so-called Visegrád Group of Czechia, Slovakia, Hungary and Poland – caucus separately to hammer out positions in turn increases their chances of pushing through their objectives. The Élysée Treaty simply takes relationship building to the next level.

ONE PERSON I saw deliver masterclasses in networking was Queen Elizabeth.

The first time I met Her Majesty was during her only state visit to Moscow, in October 1994. Heavy-handed Russian security disrupted the programme. A walkabout on a deserted Red Square fell flat. Guests invited to the embassy for a reception to meet her encountered, in the way of Russian VIP protocol, an impenetrable security cordon.

We had established two holding areas for guests: a small, exclusive one – the tidied-up embassy post room – for the 50 most senior VVIPs, and a larger one for everyone else. Her Majesty, too, was delayed. As we waited endlessly for her to arrive, a colleague came to ask my help with an irate guest in the senior waiting room.

Unfortunately, only two VVIP guests had arrived early enough to penetrate security: Anatoly Chubais, the deputy prime minister in charge of economic reform, and his wife. Chubais, precisely the type of contact to whom a royal visit gives junior officials privileged access, was furious. "Is this the right place?" he asked, peering around the empty pigeon-holes in the bare, deserted room. His wife, glamorously clad for the reception in a bare-shouldered evening dress, shivered with cold. Meanwhile, as in 'The one with the two parties' in *Friends*, the chill draft carried sounds of merrymaking from the more heavily populated room reserved for junior guests. By the time Her Majesty arrived, neither I nor Chubais ever wanted to see one another again.

Her Majesty, meanwhile, fulfilled her gruelling schedule with professionalism, purpose and persistence, greeting and gruntling starry-eyed Russians from dawn to dusk – not in search of

'outcomes' or 'deliverables', but to build up a bedrock of goodwill
and respect for the UK and its institutions.

The Queen's programme also included a visit to the Bolshoi
Ballet, as a guest of President Yeltsin, to see *Giselle*. As they sat
together, watching the show, the following exchange was said to
have taken place.

Yeltsin: I like *Giselle*. It is very short.

The Queen: *The Nutcracker* is shorter.

IN MAKING THE case for hard work and networking, I often point
to Marilyn Monroe. She initially had little success in Hollywood.
But she took dancing, singing and acting lessons and fought her
way to the top.

Politicians and diplomats, too, can increase their chances of
success by studying their craft. But politics comes more easily
to some than to others. When I worked in the Department of
the Environment in 1981–82, Michael Heseltine was secretary
of state for the environment. John Stanley had the more junior
position of minister for housing.

As Anthony Trollope describes through the character of
Augustus Melmotte in *The Way We Live Now*, standing up to make
a speech in the bear pit of the House of Commons is a daunting
ordeal. Heseltine and Stanley prepared for it in different ways.

Stanley would swot intensely, requesting reams of briefing
and summoning teams of officials to quiz him in mock debates.
But once he rose to his feet in the chamber, the impact of this
conscientious preparation was not always conspicuous.

Heseltine would prepare for his parliamentary appearances
with a good lunch. We sometimes spotted him in the lifts of the
22-storey Marsham Street HQ of the DOE en route to the House
in a state of conspicuous good humour. Yet once he took up his
post at the despatch box, he commanded the House.

Heseltine also worked hard and networked. But natural talent
never hurts.

Deadly cheese: when officials turn

Politicians can increase their chances of success by making
the most of their officials. The choice is not between issuing

ceaseless demands for policy reviews, briefings and think-pieces[12] or passively accepting officials' ideas. Rather, ministers should harvest ideas, decide on policy, and focus on ensuring officials implement those decisions.

Two of the best Foreign Secretaries I encountered were David Miliband and William Hague. Miliband visited Kyiv in 2008 during the Russia–Georgia war to show support for Ukraine's territorial integrity. He made a good speech, dealt with a chaotic programme and difficult Ukrainian personalities, and came up with policy ideas that made sense. Hague, foreign secretary during Russia's 2014 invasion of Crimea and eastern Ukraine, was outstanding at making decisions amid uncertainty.

Jeremy Hunt, briefly foreign secretary in mid-Brexit and later chancellor, took a radical approach. Arriving in Vienna in July 2018, he took his accompanying team to a nearby beer garden. The evening was sultry; everyone relaxed as the sun set. He then invited each of us to say what we considered the qualities of a good minister. He rounded off the evening by picking up the tab, earning bonus points from thirsty officials.

The consequences of ministers failing to inspire loyalty can be cringe-making. In February 2018 Sir Christopher Mallaby, a former British ambassador to Bonn and Paris, visited Vienna to publicise his memoir, *Living the Cold War*. Foreign Minister Karin Kneissl, appointed by the right-wing Austrian Freedom Party (FPÖ), came to lunch with her team. Following Russia's annexation of Crimea in 2014, the FPÖ opposed EU sanctions against Moscow. I took the opportunity to ask Kneissl what she thought.

She said, without hesitation, that she was against sanctions. They were ineffective, they harmed Austrian pig meat exporters, and they strengthened the Russian economy. Now, she said, the Russians even manufactured their own mozzarella! Who did that benefit?

As host, I did not respond, but one of my chancery team spoke up. Was it not the case, he said, that Austrian pork exports to

---

[12] Robert Cooper, deputy head of mission in Bonn, once observed of an ambassador that he had the excellent quality of "not creating unnecessary work".

China had grown by ten times the amount of the lost exports to Russia? To my surprise, a senior Austrian foreign ministry official chipped in. It might be true that Russia was manufacturing its own mozzarella. But, she said, reports indicated that it tasted awful; and no one was buying it.

A still more senior Austrian, a pillar of the foreign policy establishment and renowned Russia expert, then spoke. "It is not so much that the Moscow mozzarella is unpleasant," he said. "It is more the case that Russians have died after eating it."

Kneissl left office in 2019.

8

How to learn
from diplomatic tradecraft

Concepts of diplomatic tradecraft such as etiquette, immunity, cocktail parties, discretion and secrecy sound old-fashioned. Do we, in our sleek new digital age, even need to meet people physically, let alone have rules about how to interact?

The answer is yes. Diplomatic traditions have built up over centuries precisely because they facilitate the core business of diplomacy and, arguably, life: getting to know people, learning from them and influencing them.

Immunity – and intelligence

Leaving the Foreign Office for lunch on 17 April 1984 I ran into a colleague outside at Clive Steps.[1] "Something big has happened at the Libyan embassy," he said. "It'll be on the news."

During a protest that morning outside the Libyan People's Bureau[2] by opponents of the Gaddafi regime, someone inside the building had opened fire with an automatic weapon on the crowd. The hail of bullets injured 11 protesters and killed Police Constable Yvonne Fletcher.

A stand-off followed. The Libyan government refused police access to the 'People's Bureau'. Someone planted a series of

---

[1]   I shall watch with interest how long the statue of Robert Clive, a colonial figure sometimes termed 'Clive of India', remains in the heart of Whitehall.

[2]   The title of the Libyan embassy in London under Muammar Gaddafi.

bombs in London, one exploding at Heathrow Airport. Members of the Libyan Revolutionary Guard Corps besieged the British embassy in Tripoli. On 22 April, Britain broke off diplomatic relations with Libya.

Then, on 27 April, the British government allowed the Libyan staff of the 'People's Bureau' to leave. The Vienna Convention on Diplomatic Relations gave the staff immunity from prosecution; they left for Libya that evening. They took with them sealed diplomatic luggage which, under the convention, was immune from search or seizure. Members of the British embassy in Tripoli returned to London the same day.

The events of April 1984 highlight both the challenges and – in a limited way – the benefits of diplomatic immunity.

The principle that an accredited diplomat cannot be prosecuted for a crime unless his or her home country agrees to lift immunity is mostly an anachronism. If, in a country where the rule of law operates, a diplomat is caught speeding, shoplifting or committing a murder, he or she should – obviously – face justice. Cases where countries decline to waive immunity under these circumstances rightly cause outrage. British diplomats posted overseas are warned to respect the rules and regulations of the receiving state – including parking tickets.

Sadly, the rule of law is not above reproach in every country. Where undue government influence afflicts the justice system, diplomatic immunity remains vital. In 1984, had members of the 'People's Bureau' not been allowed to return to Libya, diplomats at the British embassy in Tripoli would have faced an uncertain fate – regardless of the fact that, unlike in London, no one had sprayed bullets from the building.

The list of abuses of diplomatic immunity is a long one – and often features the murder of Yvonne Fletcher. The controversial case of Harry Dunn, a 19-year-old motorcyclist killed in 2019 in a traffic accident by the wife of a US government employee based in England, damaged UK–US relations. But without immunity, diplomats would be unable to operate in some countries.

A 14 JULY EVENT at the French embassy in Vienna in 1986 showed the difficulty of maintaining diplomatic conventions about secrecy. Champagne flowed freely.[3] Joining a French group, I asked if they were diplomats. "My husband is a diplomat," one woman replied, swigging her drink and pointing her chin at a swarthy man opposite. "Or at least, he pretends to be." His face like thunder, he took her arm and marched out of the room.

The relationship between espionage and diplomacy is delicate. The Official Secrets Act and common sense prevent me from saying too much about it here. But Vienna has a reputation: when in September 2016 Foreign Secretary Boris Johnson stepped in front of an unclassified all-staff meeting in the conference room of the embassy and gazed around the room, his opening words were: "Ah, Vienna, capital of spies."

In the 1980s, as embassy press officer, I attended meetings organised by the Austrian Federal Press Service (BPD) for foreign correspondents. The bowling evenings and booze-ups with free food drew a devoted following of peckish press attachés from countries of what was then the Warsaw Pact.

The presence of diplomats from Eastern Europe happy to chat with Western diplomats proved, with near certainty, that they were spies.

One evening in 1986 the BPD arranged a cruise on the Danube. I sat next to the pipe-smoking Herr Krebs, the DDR[4] press attaché. He waxed lyrical about his country's high living standards, its democratic elections, its freedom of speech. "We allow reception of all West German TV channels," he said. "We're not afraid to let our people see life on the other side." I asked about the Berlin Wall. He said it was a temporary necessity. At this point the Polish press attaché strolled by, beer in hand. He clapped Krebs on the shoulder and pointed at me. "You'll never recruit him," he said. "I've been trying for years."

A student in a lecture on diplomacy once asked me what working with spies was like. "I can't confirm that I've ever worked with any," I said. "But if you were, hypothetically, to interact with them, my advice would be to treat them the same as you would

---

[3] I was shocked at a 14 July 1999 event at Schloss Ernich, then residence of the French ambassador in Bonn, to find only sparkling wine served. I hope this was a one-off aberration.

[4] Deutsche Demokratische Republik – the former East Germany.

representatives of any other constituent part of the civil service that may, or may not, operate in your working environment."

"Eh?" he said.

"Supposing you were in the economic section of the British embassy in Berlin during the epidemic of mad cow disease," I said, "working with an agricultural attaché to ease the way for exports of British beef. This attaché is not a Foreign Office employee. She has a different network, and different bosses back in London. But she shares the same objectives, signed off by elected ministers, to promote the security and prosperity of the UK. How do you ensure your working relationship with this colleague is positive?"

"I'm a vegetarian," the student said.

"You'd do it by talking to each other," I said. "By building up a relationship; and discussing her tasking, so far as you need to know, to understand how it fits in with your goals. If you're senior – a head of mission, say – you might want gently to encourage her to participate in embassy life more widely, for example by taking a role in the crisis response team, or sitting on the housing committee. Any good agricultural attaché would do all these things anyhow, because she'd be a passionate networker and a highly trained professional. In brief, you would want to include your agricultural attaché as part of the team, not as a mysterious 'other' that you ignored and hoped would go away."

"Does that work with spies?" the insistent student asked.

"In my experience, the local leadership of most organisations that work closely with the Foreign Office is well aware of the importance of a good relationship with their diplomatic colleagues and will be keen to make it work."

"Why are you talking in riddles?"

"It's hard not to, sometimes. But read between the lines."

KEEPING SECRETS IS a skill. In 2009 I received a lunch invitation from the head of a Ukrainian intelligence agency. I had not met him, and accepted with alacrity.

I arrived with several interested colleagues at a trendy diner in Kyiv to find a private room decorated in a nautical theme including lifebelts, portholes, a ship's wheel and mermaids. Our host was a bluff military type who arrived with a delegation, shook our hands with enthusiasm, and invited us to sit. He then launched into an explanation of his work.

While he spoke, waiters brought drinks; then an initial course of soup. He continued his address. Plates were cleared, and *zakuski*[5] arrived. We munched and listened. Once or twice, when he paused, I attempted to interject a word; but he politely indicated that he had not yet finished. A disappointing hot dish followed. Then a sweet. By the time coffee and tea were served, our host had spoken for 80 minutes. At last, he drew breath, and invited questions.

Too little time remained for a meaningful discussion.

Filibustering, the art of speaking at length to prevent others from intervening or decisions being taken, is a technique much deployed in parliaments. It is also a ghastly feature of UN debates. Whether our interlocutor was doing it on purpose or was simply loquacious, we never found out.

Fear of cocktail parties

Few fields of diplomatic endeavour attract more attention than so-called cocktail parties.[6] To irritate a British ambassador, simply mention the words 'Ferrero Rocher'.[7]

If cultivating contacts is core diplomatic work, larger functions provide rich hunting grounds. The problem is that while some people love having a drink and a chat, for others cocktail parties are as enjoyable as a visit to the dentist. Attendees comprise a mix of diplomats, contacts and 'embassy groupies' – people who enjoy diplomatic hobnobbing, but are not useful contacts.[8] The more marginal the guest, the more likely he or she is to share with you a life story or pet project, not necessarily concisely,

---

[5] Traditional cold appetisers served in Slavic countries, well-suited to accompany vodka shots. Usually followed by a disappointing hot dish.

[6] More accurately, 'diplomatic receptions'. Cocktails rarely feature, with a few glorious exceptions.

[7] A brand of chocolates in a 1993 TV advert set at an 'ambassador's reception'.

[8] This does not mean they are not lovely, fun and fascinating people, although not all have all or indeed any of these qualities.

while ensuring your full attention by bringing their face within centimetres of your own.

Many diplomats resort to alcohol to help them navigate such events. Some find it numbs the pain; for others, it intensifies the despair. 'Dry', or alcohol-free, receptions have the advantage that few people stay late or, indeed, come in the first place. Countries with renowned cuisine tend to attract good turn-outs, although not always of the right people.

Speeches are a special ordeal. Not all speakers understand the golden rule of speech making, to 'stand up, speak up and shut up'. Instead, ambassadors or VIPs grind through stodgy sermons about the glories of their home countries while guests check the time, their empty glasses, or escape routes.

Several renowned diplomats have suggested tactics for making the most of cocktail parties.[9] Some are ways to escape a guest ('I mustn't monopolise you. Can I introduce you to X?') Others include projecting confidence, asking open questions, and always saying 'How nice to see you,' rather than 'How nice to meet you'. I like the advice to 'get in the right mindset: you will be in a room with lots of important, useful or remarkable people. Use and enjoy the opportunity to connect with some of them.' And, to bear in mind in countries with a colonial history: 'The axe forgets. The tree doesn't.'

While years of practice helped me overcome my early horror of making speeches, nothing inured me to cocktail parties. I described in a letter from Kyiv in 2009 'The dread situation when someone turns to you ... and says "let me tell you an interesting story to illustrate that point", which usually starts off with a reference to some distant relative or friend whose identity you never quite manage to establish, followed by an account of their experiences in the 19th century; the great famine of 1932–33; the repression of 1937–39; the repression of 1939–41; World War 2; the repression of 1945–56; the slow decline of the Soviet Union from 1956–91; the economic crisis of 1991–98; the Orange revolution of 2004; the experience of a number of the

---

[9] Notably but not only Dame Nicola Brewer, former high commissioner to South Africa.

first-named person's friends or relatives during the same period; or, more usually, all of the above.'

Despite these pitfalls, diplomatic receptions remain essential tools of information gathering and influence. 'The value of the cocktail circuit', I wrote from Kyiv in 2008, 'was demonstrated at a reception at the Cuban embassy, when I had a call from London asking me to lobby the Belgian ambassador about a meeting about to begin in Brussels. I promptly did so, and he hurried from the room. We later heard that the Belgian position in Brussels on a key Ukraine-related issue had changed. Extraordinary.'

At an embassy reception in Vienna in 1986, I spoke to a woman who introduced me to her grumpy-looking, silent husband. He was Austrian sculptor Alfred Hrdlicka. He had recently caused a furore by sculpting a wooden horse, mocking Austrian President Kurt Waldheim, whose murky Second World War record had led former Chancellor Fred Sinowatz[10] to say of him: 'Waldheim was not in the SA,[11] only his horse.' Hrdlicka later invited me to an event at his studio at which I met Mayor of Vienna Helmut Zilk and Interior Minister Karl Blecha.

HAVING THE RIGHT structures to promote contact building helps, too. When I arrived in Vienna in 2016 and saw the magnificent ambassador's residence, I thought: 'I must hold a salon here.'

I had a notion of salons from Balzac and Tolstoy, and from powerful women of the 19th century holding court in Vienna. My goal was to build a regular series of evenings to discuss political, social and economic issues with the most fascinating figures I could entice. I hoped not only to build my knowledge of Austria, but to meet new people and extend UK influence.

The first stage was a name. My team came up with 'The Charles Stewart Conversations', arguing that my dodgy predecessor had qualities that might lure potential guests. Charles Vane-Stewart, Third Marquess of Londonderry, was British ambassador in Vienna from 1814 to 1823 and great-grandfather to Winston Churchill. He was famed, among other things, for punching a

---

[10] Famous for his epigram *Es ist alles sehr kompliziert* (Everything is very complicated).

[11] The Nazi 'brownshirts'.

horse, consuming 10,000 bottles of wine between September 1814 and January 1815, and for bringing with him a hunting pack of 40 dogs because 'Austrian hounds do not understand anything'.

It was an inspired choice.

We then had the good fortune to recruit a new events organiser, Lisa Ludwiczak, a German hotelier with imagination and enthusiasm. First, we would pick a theme and a speaker – subjects included gay rights in Austria, the running of a presidential cabinet, the relationship between art and money, the Waldheim Affair and Brexit. Lisa would assemble a sparkling list of invitees. I chaired the discussions – which took place late in the evening, in German, using the Chatham House Rule.[12]

The formula was a hit. Diverse top people were delighted to be invited to the British ambassador's residence for a discussion over drinks. I introduced each session by saying that the object of the exercise was for me to learn more about Austria in a way enjoyable and mind-stretching for all concerned. Once the conversation flagged, I would wind things up over a nightcap.

I received two accolades for my contact making in Vienna. The first was in 2018 when Danielle Spera, the director of the Jewish Museum, organised an exhibition, 'The Place to Be. Salons – Spaces of Emancipation', about Jewish hostesses running salons in Vienna between 1780 and 1938. A former TV journalist, she interviewed me about the Charles Stewart Conversations and put the results on a video loop in her exhibition.

The second was at my farewell events in 2021, where the turnout of senior and interesting guests, from President Van der Bellen down, was better than I could have dreamed of when I began my posting.

AMBASSADOR CHARLES STEWART's record in consuming 10,000 bottles of wine in a few months was somewhat extreme. But alcohol has long played a role in diplomacy. A top diplomat once told me that 'to really make friends with a German, you

---

[12] 'When a meeting, or part thereof, is held under the Chatham House Rule, participants are free to use the information received, but neither the identity nor the affiliation of the speaker(s), nor that of any other participant, may be revealed.' (Chatham House)

must drink a beer and eat a sausage with him or her'. This works well in Austria, too. In Russia in 1992–95, a visit to a collective farm at 10 a.m. began with shots of vodka; it was standard to consume substantial quantities, usually sold in hundred-gram units, at lunch. W. Somerset Maugham, who worked in the Secret Intelligence Service, spoke of 'the state of intoxication that enables so many ... to look upon all men as their brothers'.[13]

The liberal use of booze to oil the wheels of diplomatic intercourse has left many victims in its wake. Unwary diplomats may find themselves offered alcohol at lunch, an early evening reception, an official dinner and a late-night snifter with a contact, only to return home to find a spouse keen to raise a cosy glass together. The fact alcohol is often cheaper overseas than at home can fuel the fire.

How you cope with alcohol depends on who you are. Some diplomats enjoy social tippling until the last guest has staggered off; others find mass drinking exhausting. Many do not drink at all, for religious, health or other reasons. But diplomacy is a contact sport. In many societies, alcohol makes social interaction easier.

Specific drinks may also be part of a country's diplomatic brand. If you are heading to the Belgians, you may anticipate a chilled Leffe. The Irish may offer Guinness, the Japanese sake, and so on. In Vienna, as well as serving the best G&Ts in Austria at the residence, I spent five years promoting Nyetimber, an English sparkling wine. "The only difference between Nyetimber and Champagne", I would tell guests, "is that it's more expensive – and better."[14]

Against this background, you have to drink intelligently. Be conscious of how much alcohol you are consuming, and stay in control. One top diplomat used to counsel people never to drink standing up. I wouldn't go that far. But I kept track of the number of units of alcohol I drank each week for 40 years.

LEST THESE ANECDOTES risk suggesting that diplomatic life is one long party, I should perhaps interject a counterexample.

---

[13] W. Somerset Maugham, 'The Summing Up,' 1938.

[14] It is, in fact, not necessarily more expensive.

Diplomats in early 1990s Moscow had it far easier than most Russians. But things were not always straightforward. Fresh food, in particular, was hard to get hold of.

On one occasion we celebrated a success in the embassy by serving cartons of long-life orange juice at the morning meeting.[15] As the ambo[16] droned on, people at my end of the table noticed that the liquid a young colleague was pouring into her plastic disposable cup contained long strings of shiny, mucus-like, bright-blue mould.

No one wanted to interrupt the ambassador with a service message. So we watched as the colleague raised the cup to her lips, oblivious to what lurked within, and began to drink before a series of nudges and hand gestures reached her around the table. For the rest of the meeting, we went thirsty as people probed their own cups to reveal a range of slimy and unappetising residues.

Etiquette and contact making

At the opposite end of the scale, a lavish lunch when Prince Andrew, Duke of York, visited Kyiv as special representative for international trade and investment highlighted the benefits and bear-traps of royal visits in contact making.

The pulling power of royalty is unparalleled. When the Duke of York visited Kyiv, the Prince of Wales Vienna or Queen Elizabeth Berlin or Moscow, everyone you invited turned up – at the highest level.

Because the Royal Family are globally known, even the most senior leaders are inclined to let down their guard a bit in a private discussion – particularly over a meal. Embassies can share in the benefits.

When Prince Andrew visited Kyiv in 2010, he had a long lunch with Ukrainian President Viktor Yanukovych, a plain-speaking power politician from the east of the country. Yanukovych expounded his view of the world for hours. As the two men formed a rapport, Andrew raised a number of substantive

---

[15] Sometimes called 'morning prayers', for the ambassador to check in with key staff.
[16] Diplomat-speak for 'ambassador'.

and difficult points on which we had briefed him – to which Yanukovych responded helpfully.

The pitfalls? Yanukovych, elected in 2010, developed into an authoritarian leader, including jailing his political opponent, former prime minister Yulia Tymoshenko.[17] On the UK side, subsequent events relating to Prince Andrew are well documented.

A curiosity: in 'The Prince's Trousers', episode 2 of the 2013 Mitchell and Webb comedy series *Ambassadors*, 'Prince Mark', a parodic royal played by Tom Hollander who is obsessed with ironing boards, visits the imaginary country of Tazbekistan. The series featured more missed opportunities than belly laughs. But the scene where Prince Mark, via a boozy lunch with the President of Tazbekistan, resolves a political crisis, struck me as uncannily realistic. I congratulate all those who advised on it.

A GRISLY ENCOUNTER with a fruit salad illustrates the enduring benefits of diplomatic etiquette.

During my time as director of Overseas Territories from 2006 to 2008, Argentina maintained constant pressure on the Falkland Islands and cut off most diplomatic contacts between London and Buenos Aires. One exception was fisheries. I became an expert in the mating habits of the Loligo squid.

Who knew that many of the *calamari* we eat come from around the Falkland Islands?

Squid migrate between Argentine waters and Falkland waters without documentation or immigration control, reproducing with scant regard to borders. Both Argentina and the UK had an interest in preventing overfishing across the maritime boundary, to ensure sustainability. The Argentine side therefore agreed, exceptionally, to hold talks on the issue in the format of the South Atlantic Fisheries Commission.

This was my first experience of chairing formal diplomatic negotiations. Each delegation had six people at the table but, as with our talks with China on Hong Kong, only the heads of

---

[17] Advice to world leaders: jailing your political opponents is never a good look, no matter how much you hate them, unless your justice system is internationally acknowledged to meet the highest standards of independence.

delegation actually spoke. My opposite number was Ambassador Airaldi, the head of the Argentine Foreign Ministry's 'Malvinas' department, who brought a delegation from Buenos Aires for talks in London. After each round of exchanges, we would break to discuss how we should respond.

Progress was slow. Airaldi, a consummate professional, had a poker face and a fine sense of humour. On one occasion, after I had described a proposal from the British side as a win–win, he sighed. "Mr Turner," he said, "you describe your proposals as win–win. But it seems to me that what you are proposing is, 'we win, you lose'."

Some months later, following discussions in Buenos Aires, things took an unexpected turn. 'After the talks,' I wrote, 'we took a minibus to the Argentine Foreign Ministry's "fine rooms", at a grand palace, and were treated to a mighty lunch – an excellent steak, followed by a fruit salad. The latter was rather marred in my case by containing a chunk of glass … Being diplomatic I did not draw attention to this curious incident.'

I never knew if the shard of glass in the pud placed before the leader of the British delegation was an accident, the work of a disgruntled kitchen worker, or a deliberate political act. At the time, I spat it onto my spoon and let it fall on my side plate with an audible tinkle. The Argentine diplomat sitting on my right glanced down, but none of us referred to the matter again.

Our fishing talks made little progress. But they showed how diplomatic niceties may make meaningful exchanges possible even when governments are at daggers drawn. We ended up with a working, if frosty, relationship between the two sides. The fact I knew and respected Ambassador Airaldi made it easy for me, in the split second between discovering the broken glass in my mouth and deciding what to do about it, to decide that this could surely not have been a deliberate political act.

ANOTHER DIPLOMATIC TRADITION designed to make possible progress under the most unpromising circumstances is what we may call 'other types of events'.

I coined the phrase in a letter to my parents during our negotiations with China on Hong Kong. 'The main formal meetings of the Joint Liaison Group', I wrote, 'are accompanied by other types of events. This is really where most of the progress is made.'

The plenary sessions of formal negotiations, whether on squid quotas off the Falklands or the future of Hong Kong, are often stultifyingly dull. These are the 'talks' we see on TV. Rows of people sit on each side of a table. Each side reads out texts they have prepared earlier. Translation may slow things down, whether simultaneous or, all too often, consecutive.[18]

Breakthroughs during plenary sessions are rare.

Fortunately, set-piece discussions are accompanied by informal meetings – break-out sessions on issues too sensitive or difficult to be tackled in plenary. Principal negotiators may decide that no formal note will be taken. The sides may exchange non-papers or *bouts de papier* – informal documents setting out positions or proposals. This is where most progress is made.

To provide further opportunities for minds to meet, many diplomatic negotiations are accompanied by entertainment. This can range from the excruciating – interminable set-piece dinners of indifferent quality where you sit between people with no interest in talking to you and you can't wait for the coffee – to the life-affirming, such as a boozy dinner at a London club for an inbound diplomatic delegation.

The 1995–98 meetings of the Sino-British Joint Liaison Group on Hong Kong were accompanied by many hard-to-classify entertainments, including formal dinners at the Beijing state guest house, the Diaoyutai, featuring enigmatic dishes such as 'Abalone and four delicacies'; or karaoke evenings in Soho with the Chinese embassy in London.[19] But a curiosity of the JLG was The Outing.

The Outing was designed to bring the teams together in a more relaxed atmosphere than the conference table. Fierce arguments

---

[18] With simultaneous translation you hear what the other person is saying, usually on headphones, while they are speaking. With consecutive, the interpreter takes notes while one side speaks, then translates. A long intervention by one side might be divided into 20 little chunks of translation. Simultaneous is quicker, but costlier.

[19] I recommend 'The Green, Green Grass of Home', which requires almost no singing at all.

about aspects of the handover were punctuated by trips to Castle Howard or the Ming tombs. Forming personal connections with these truest of communist believers was not straightforward. One delegate spent the train journey to York explaining to me why Tibet had always been part of China and how grateful Tibetans were to the government in Beijing for their enlightened policies. But it all helped us build relationships with the other side during complex, challenging negotiations.

Do we need the UN?

The natural home of the most intractable diplomatic issues is the United Nations. If you think negotiating with another country is tough, try doing it with 193 states simultaneously.

The UN is an extraordinary, brilliant and ghastly organisation. Created in the aftermath of the Second World War and the failure of the League of Nations, its founders gave a special role – permanent membership of the Security Council, with a veto – to five countries: the US, UK, China (initially the Republic of China, later the People's Republic), the Soviet Union (later Russia) and France. It was a compromise: if important countries were liable to be overruled by the new body, they would not participate.[20] Yet without them, the UN could not function.

At early meetings, 51 nations were represented. With decolonisation, membership grew. So did the UN's agenda. Having focused initially on peacekeeping, the UN system now encompasses institutions from the UN Economic and Social Council to the International Maritime Organization, the Food and Agriculture Organization, the UN Industrial Development Organization and many more. The rotation of chairmanships to ensure 'fairness' can lead, for example, to North Korea chairing the Conference on Disarmament in 2022.

Decades of expanding membership have frayed consensus with the governance structures of the UN. Why, Brazil, India, Indonesia and Nigeria ask, should places with such puny populations as Russia, the UK and France have permanent seats

---

[20]   As, for example, the US, Russia, China, India and some others refuse to join the International Criminal Court, founded in 2002.

on the Security Council? What about other countries that run a sophisticated foreign policy machinery, such as Germany, Mexico or Egypt?

The result is a permanent state of insurgency by the have-nots at the UN – including the so-called G-77 group[21] of so-called developing countries[22] – against those they see as enjoying excessive privilege within the UN. Bitter trench warfare rages on personnel, budgetary allocations and policies of every kind.

To make things worse, capitals often set diplomats representing them on UN bodies unnegotiable objectives. The status and experience of the diplomats concerned determines whether they can persuade folks back home to send more reasonable instructions; ignore or sidestep them; or must stick to them, paralysing progress.

Experienced UN operators[23] know that, to keep the ship moving forward, compromise and consensus must be found. Both are forged by networks of painstakingly constructed relationships between diplomats, building trust and respect in difficult circumstances. My best moments at the UN were where disparate ambassadors gathered in a side room to thrash out an agreement to take back to the main meeting. There, personal relationships, past favours and future promises created the alchemy of progress.

It is popular to argue that the UN is beyond reform. It certainly is reform-resistant. But if it didn't exist, we would have to invent something to do many of its tasks. I take my hat off to all those who work there.[24]

---

[21] It recently had 134 members.

[22] Statistician Hans Rosling argued in his 2018 book *Factfulness* that rising global incomes made it no longer meaningful to group countries into 'developed' and 'developing'. G-77 members include China, one of the richest countries in the world.

[23] Having only done one substantive UN job, I do not count myself among their number.

[24] Excluding those who do scandalously little actual work.

The Motswana in Maun

The BBC World Service is a great British diplomatic tradition under constant threat of reinvention.

In March 1983, I tried to hitchhike along a dusty road from Maun, in the north west of Botswana, to Kasane, near the border with Zambia, Zimbabwe and Namibia.[25] For three hours, not a single car passed.

At last, someone took me to Crocodile Camp, in Maun, where he said the hitching was better. Again, no one stopped. I ended up staying at the Camp, sleeping in the open, and catching a light plane the following morning into the Okavango Delta with a South African teacher from Pietermaritzburg, a parent and the group of schoolgirls they were minding.

While I waited for the plane in the shade of a hangar at Maun, a Motswana[26] airport worker asked where I was from. When I said the UK, he nodded. "The Labour Party will never win the general election if they don't sort out the Militant tendency," he said. "The Social Democratic Party have really taken the wind out of their sails." It turned out he was a regular listener to the BBC World Service.

The World Service is the strongest purveyor of British influence worldwide. From the early days of shortwave from Ascension Island, the announcement 'This is London' and the evocative 'Lilliburlero' theme tune, through to DAB and internet transmission, the World Service delivers unbiased news to global audiences. In addition to eight regional feeds in English, dozens of foreign language services, from the Afaan Oromo spoken in East Africa, notably Ethiopia, to Yoruba (West Africa, notably Nigeria) via Ukrainian, Russian, Mandarin and Vietnamese, reach key audiences.

I have lost count of the number of times that presidents, prime ministers, foreign ministers and other opinion formers have told me they listen regularly to the BBC as a reliable source of news.

---

[25] Among the fine people I met on the road from Gaborone to Maun and back was the hospitable family of the Francistown chief of police.

[26] An inhabitant of Botswana is a Motswana, just as an inhabitant of Lesotho is a Mosotho.

Such an impartial voice becomes all the more important when war is raging – wherever that may be.

Unfortunately for the BBC, it also broadcasts in the UK. In an era of polarised politics, the BBC's neutrality – vital to its soft power overseas – regularly earns it criticism from British as well as foreign politicians of every hue, from rival media organisations and from deluded opponents of traditional media who do not realise the abyss of chaos and misinformation that is the alternative. The result is bumpy, unpredictable funding as successive governments proclaim, dispute or dismiss the significance of the BBC as a source of global influence. It deserves long-term stability.

When diplomats dissemble

Any discussion of tradecraft must include the reluctance of diplomats publicly to badmouth the country in which they are posted. Indeed, many diplomats overseas suffer from 'postitis' – a tendency, as years go by, increasingly to see things from the point of view of one's host government. 'The frequent beheadings in my country,' the ambassador will write, 'must not be allowed to overshadow widespread improvements in human rights.' When asked by a local to rate his or her host country, any rational diplomat will praise it.

In every country, people are eager to hear which posting you have enjoyed most – provided the answer is correct. Few people in Istanbul want to hear that your favourite posting was Kyiv. Few in Vienna want to learn that your favourite posting was Moscow – and so on. When asked to name my favourite, I would reply with a quote attributed to Oscar Wilde:[27] 'Comparisons are odious.'

All places have qualities. I used my Twitter[28] hashtags #reasonstolikeIstanbul[29] and #keenonWien hundreds of times. But I have seen outstanding social media posts from ambassadors

---

[27] Also attributed to John Lydgate. Wilde has a rich repertory of quotes. One of my favourites is 'We are all in the gutter, but some of us are looking at the stars.'

[28] Rebranded as 'X' in 2023.

[29] I eschewed #reasonstoloveIstanbul to maintain British reserve.

in capitals as varied as Havana, Tashkent, Ulaanbaatar and Paris. Most diplomats will have postings to more than one city with which they develop a deep and meaningful relationship.

The main feature distinguishing the cities to which I was posted was not any natural attribute but the degree of desperation of the inhabitants to be told that theirs was the finest city on Earth.[30] If you are a proud citizen of country X, about to ask a foreign ambassador or diplomat which has been his or her favourite posting, please bear this in mind.

Under surveillance

Surveillance poses challenges to diplomats in many countries. Before our FCO language class went to Moscow in April 1992, a woman from the Security Service gave us a briefing. "My number one rule", she said, "would be not to allow yourself to be in a room at any one time with only Russians. Try always to have another Brit with you."

I raised my hand. "We're going to Moscow for Russian language immersion training," I said. "The whole point is to spend time with Russians."

The woman sighed. "Just be careful," she said.

Prior to 1991, the security risks were deemed too high to allow FCO language classes to attempt immersion in the Russian capital. But following Gorbachev's reforms, we were packed off to a student dormitory in central Moscow for seven weeks on our own.

Looking back, the optimism we had about Russia developing into a friendly, like-minded country seems laughable. The Russian Federation took over the rights and obligations of the former Soviet Union – including key security institutions. Such institutions remained suspicious of Western diplomats and kept tabs on them.

Interactions with Russian security services took two main forms: surveillance and compromise attempts. We assumed 100 per cent coverage of anything we said in Moscow, whether in the embassy or our homes, and adjusted what we said accordingly. 'According to the IMF head here,' I wrote, 'when the EBRD refurbished their office in the huge tower block which used

---

[30] It would be undiplomatic to say here which city won the prize.

to house all the COMECON[31] delegations, they found 16 microphones in the ceiling, left over from a previous occupant.'

When we were out and about, it was impossible to know whether we were being followed, with a few rare exceptions. You just had to ignore it.

On one occasion, I arranged on the telephone to meet a Russian friend to play tennis. We agreed to meet on the platform of a certain underground station after work. But either he or I got the station wrong and I ended up waiting for an hour on the railway platform.

This must have seemed suspicious behaviour to my tails. It also made it hard for them to remain in cover. I eventually spotted a woman and two men, who then accompanied me back to my metro station at Tsvetnoy Bulvar via several changes of line. Here, the three of them stood between me and the station exit so that I had to walk around them – perhaps to remind me who was boss in Moscow.

Compromise attempts were more common and obvious. Travelling widely in Russia as first secretary (economic), I seemed to be targeted regularly – perhaps a couple of times a year. A colleague with expertise in this area once suggested that my scruffy appearance and unpredictable behaviour might lead the Russian authorities to think I was working for a UK intelligence agency, and therefore worth special attention.

Some encounters were a bit too X-rated – or sordid – for this volume. But as an example, I once visited Volgograd on business, and stayed at the hotel Intourist. My room was, even by the standards of Russian hotel rooms of the early 1990s, particularly uncomfortable;[32] so I asked to move. The management expressed outrage, but eventually transferred me to a different part of the hotel.

---

[31] IMF: International Monetary Fund. EBRD: European Bank for Reconstruction and Development. COMECON: Council for Mutual Economic Assistance, a Soviet-era body to foster Eastern Bloc economic integration.

[32] 'The restaurant of the Intourist', I wrote, 'closes for a "sanitary day" for the whole of Wednesday; the hot water in the bathroom comes out treacle-black; and the rugs have not been changed since the hotel was rebuilt in 1950.'

That evening I stayed in my room to record the (unclassified) notes of my visit on a Dictaphone. As I sat there, someone hammered on my door. I opened it to find one of the most beautiful women I had ever seen in my life. She had argued with her boyfriend, she said. Could she come in for a few moments to drink a glass of water? I apologised and said I was too busy. She pleaded with me to let her in, but eventually departed.

An hour later, I heard more hammering. The woman had returned, in an emotional and distressed state. Now she and her boyfriend had had a fight, she said. He had threatened her. She was frightened for her life. Please could she take refuge in my room, until the danger had passed?

I looked at her. What if she genuinely was a damsel in distress? What if my refusal to admit her to my room was condemning her to actual violence? I thought of the John Grisham book, *The Firm*, where the hero saves a woman being assaulted on a Caribbean beach, only to learn later it is a set-up. I peered down the corridor for any sign of the violent boyfriend. I offered to accompany her to the reception. She accused me of not caring about her safety and flounced off.

By the time I visited St Petersburg in 2008 to brush up my Russian before starting as British ambassador in Kyiv, much had changed – but much had stayed the same. I stayed with a woman, her grown-up son and two cats in a block of flats at Prospekt Bolshevikov. A friend of hers who took me for walks around the city was openly critical of Russia's leadership. "What do you think of Prime Minister Putin?" I asked her. "He is very short," she said. "What do you think of President Medvedev?" I said. "He is even shorter," came the reply.

During my wanderings around St Petersburg in 2008, I often suspected I was under observation – particularly in deserted areas such as parks. But it was my language teacher who surprised me most, with her example to illustrate the Russian language's fabulously complicated verbs of motion.

"Suppose", she said, "that you leave your flat to come to the language school. The first FSB[33] surveillance operative is hiding in an ice-cream stall. As you approach, he says to his handler 'Turner

---

[33] Federal Security Service – the main successor organisation to the KGB.

is coming.' He then says, 'Turner has reached me,' 'Turner has passed me,' and 'Turner is walking beyond me.'" She repeated the cycle of phrases at a number of points on my route – picturing an FSB man observing me from the newspaper kiosk at the metro; another accompanying me on the train; and a fourth watching me arrive at the language school. She drew stick figures of the FSB operatives, and my route, on a scrap of paper, with me approaching and passing them at each stage. I still have it.

The place where I encountered the most obvious surveillance was in Minsk, the capital of Belarus, during a visit in 2009. When Ambassador Rosemary Thomas took me for a walk around the city centre there seemed to be teams of people behind and in front of us at all times, regularly swapping positions so that they could brush by us as we chatted. When the two of us entered the central area of the memorial to the Afghanistan war on an island in a lake, two men squeezed into the cramped space with us. 'We then had dinner with an opposition bloke ...' I wrote. 'During this a man literally sat at the next table taking notes.'

I DO NOT CONSIDER myself a traditional diplomat. Few diplomats do. But diplomatic traditions and tradecraft, absurd and archaic as they may seem at first, have served me well – and continue to do so, now that I have retired.

9

How to drink wine and know things

If you think lifelong learning sounds dull, you're doing it wrong.

Lifelong learning is a key to happiness. It means seizing experience at every opportunity. It means making a habit of, and taking pleasure in, growing your stock of knowledge. With time, it can mean becoming wise – or, at least, wiser.

How to learn languages

Diplomats pick up a lot of languages. The key to success is to recognise that people learn in different ways.

Arriving in Moscow for my seven-week Russian immersion course in April 1992 I found the student dormitory had more cockroaches than sink-plugs, and sheets, but no towels. I tracked down a staff member to ask where I could get one.

Finding the woman in the corridor, I realised I did not know the Russian word for 'towel'. "What is it you want?" she said. "Shower," I said – a word I knew – and mimed drying myself. She peered at me as at a particularly dim child, shook her head, and walked off. After six months of Russian language training, I could say "We demand peace." But I did not know the most basic household vocabulary.

My nine-month Russian course from October 1991 was my only full-time programme of FCO language training. Our class of diplomats, mostly destined for the embassy in Moscow, was highly motivated and, in most cases, talented.

The exception was me. Learning German at school I had famously scored *nul points* for grammar in three successive exams leading to my O-level in 1973. When I joined the FCO ten

137

years later and scored a pathetic mark in the Modern Language Aptitude Test (MLAT), personnel banished me to that category of persons unsuited to hard languages. Come 1991, only the fact I was going on a joint posting to Moscow with someone who already spoke Russian enabled me to sneak into a class.

To my surprise, Russian revealed that I not only enjoyed learning a difficult new language, but – despite the MLAT score – was good at it. Grammar paralysed me with fear – then as now. But the availability of audio and video tapes made it more possible than ever before to immerse yourself in a language. After our four hours of tuition each morning, I'd watch a movie,[1] do my homework and go for a stroll with a Russian cassette in my Walkman. In the exams in June 1992, I was overjoyed to pass the required C1 level, and passed C2 after a few months in Moscow.

I have friends who love nothing better than to sit down and get intimate with a German or Russian grammar book. I would rather saw off my extremities with a rusty hacksaw. If at first you struggle with languages, try different ways of learning.

Start with the teacher. Are they using a method that scrambles your brain? Ask them to try something else. If they won't, try another teacher. If you love grammar, great. If you hate it, try an immersive method such as Berlitz or Duolingo. Or go to a place where your target language is spoken and avoid your mother tongue for as long as possible.

Next, focus on your motivation. The harder you work at a new language, the better. I set myself targets, such as 30–60 minutes a day. If you're not that bothered whether you make progress, your chances of success go down the toilet.

Self-belief is vital. Everyone learning a language has days when they confront impossible new concepts such as aspect in Russian, or vowel harmony in Turkish, and ponder giving up. But once you have learned one language, you know it is possible; and that barriers to learning the next one, however insuperable they appear, will be overcome.

Finally, be prepared to make a fool of yourself. No one can learn to ski without falling over, or pick up pottery without

---

[1]   Glasnost classics such as *Comrade Stalin Goes to Africa* (1991) or *The Fountain* (1988) made compulsive viewing.

binning their first efforts. No one speaks a new language faultlessly straight off. If you start by mangling the language, you'll improve. If you wait for perfection before opening your mouth – you'll wait forever.

Languages changed my life. Knowing German secured me my short-notice despatch to Vienna in 1984. Russian got me to Kyiv as ambassador in 2008. In both cases, my predecessor left early and they needed a language speaker quickly. German also gave me a leg-up to jobs as counsellor (EU and economic) in Germany and as ambassador in Vienna.

The system is not consistent. Diplomats quip that if you want to be sent to Brazil, the first thing you should do is learn Russian.

But that didn't work for me.

THE UBIQUITY OF English can make languages seem old hat. 'If it weren't for the French, we wouldn't have interpreters,' I wrote from a G7 meeting in Washington in April 1990, 'since everyone present, including the French, can speak English. It is, however, French government policy for its representatives always to speak French at such gatherings.'[2]

Translation software, too, looks set to advance inexorably. It has the benefit, once installed, of costing next to nothing – unlike interpreters. For now, though, it remains some way from being able to understand nuance, irony or context that seem obvious to human beings.

The United Nations has six official languages: Arabic, Chinese, English, French, Russian and Spanish. Turks, Germans, Brazilians, Japanese and speakers of other tongues must be able to work in one of those. The European Union has 24 official languages – 'a unique approach', the EU website says modestly, 'unequalled by multilingual countries or international organisations'.

In break-out meetings at the United Nations and unofficial meetings at the EU, the general rule is that English or French can be used, based on the formerly widespread use of French in diplomacy. But by the third decade of the 21st century, to use

---

[2] This policy seems to have been relaxed in recent years and French diplomats are now free to display their English language skills.

French in larger meetings risks furrowed brows. Others ask: if French, why not German? Or Hindi?

I continue to work on my languages. I regularly torment my partner, Gözde, with my poor Turkish, and am learning Dutch. The key to my motivation is not only that speaking in the other person's language is a small act of courtesy and respect. Rather, penetrating that language opens up a new world of communication, understanding and experience.

In Ukraine, it was invaluable to be able to chat with President Yushchenko in Ukrainian, or President Yanukovych in Russian. But it was life-changing to talk to my security detail in Istanbul, or co-travellers on a bus in Anatolia, in Turkish; to be interviewed by journalists in Novosibirsk or Vladivostok in Russian; or in Vienna to attempt to justify Brexit in live TV talk shows in German. Many of the exchanges that have left the deepest impressions on me have been in languages other than English.

Vive la différence!

EVEN WATCHING THE right stuff on TV can teach you languages – and illuminate countries and cultures.

The cult German police procedural *Tatort* launched in 1970. Every Sunday evening at 8.15 p.m., a 90-minute episode airs in Germany, Austria and Switzerland. The series is made by different German regional TV stations (and Swiss and Austrian ones), each with distinctive and occasionally overlapping teams of detectives.

Whenever I'm in a German-speaking country I tune in to *Tatort* on Sunday evening. Not only is the series fun and great for polishing your German, but it helps explain German-speaking Europe. *Tatort* teems with texture. Sure, it's fiction. It is no more a manual on Germany than, say, *Midsomer Murders* (popular in Germany under the name 'Inspector Barnaby') is an accurate guide to life in rural England. But *Tatort's* settings and its evolving preoccupations hold up an intriguing, warped mirror to contemporary concerns.

I once visited Baden-Württemberg to address some students. They were a rum bunch. 'The audience for my lecture on the UK and the EU,' I wrote, 'the Katholische Jugend Verbindung, turned out to be a kind of Catholic fraternity, all funny hats, sashes and no women members … tho' they emphasised that they were a *nicht schlagende Verbindung*, i.e. a non-duelling fraternity.'

Luckily I had recently seen a *Tatort* episode about a detective from western Germany, sent to investigate a murder in the former East Germany, who found evidence implicating a right-wing duelling fraternity. Otherwise, I'd have thought my audience's bizarre costumes meant they'd all taken leave of their senses.

Back in the 1990s, nearly all *Tatort* detectives were White men, many apparently beyond retirement age. Now they are more diverse, more female and younger. The police teams are often riddled with conflict and ineptitude – a Keystone Cops quality reminiscent of the chaotic *flics* in the visually unparalleled 1981 French movie *Diva*.

Come to think of it, even the fantasy-packed *Diva* included a number of French preoccupations of the moment, including a pet cat called Ayatollah and, of course, police corruption.

FOREIGN WRITERS, TOO, can reveal new worlds.

When learning a language, I always seek out easy fiction to build fluency and vocabulary. On my first visit to Moscow in 1992 I was delighted to find in a bookshop a single Russian-language copy of *The Lord of the Rings*. In the apparent absence of any thrillers, a story I liked and knew well would be just the thing.

I took it to the counter. The grumpy cashier[3] said I could order the book. Delivery would take six weeks. Instead, I bought a copy of *The Day of the Triffids*, which for some reason was available at once.

The scarcity of consumer goods and rigid control of culture and information in the Soviet Union is the subject of much black humour. The authorities vetted all literature, banning and mounting campaigns against works such as *Doctor Zhivago* that did not present the communist one-party system in the 'correct' light.[4]

One by-product was that many Russians owned a complete library of 'the classics' – Russian and foreign literature approved by the authorities. The list included masterpieces, such as Dickens,

---

[3] Tautology. In the early 1990s all Russian sales staff were beyond grumpy.

[4] *The Zhivago Affair*, by Peter Finn and Petra Couvée, details how the authorities banned the book and hounded Pasternak to his death in 1960.

but also works by authors who had fallen out of fashion in the West – such as Nobel Prize-winner John Galsworthy's *The Forsyte Saga*, which happens to show that owning things does not lead to happiness. An intellectual[5] could reasonably claim to own, and to have read, all important literature.

Censorship and authoritarianism mean a finite quantity of literature. Just as some children are said to benefit from clear rules about bedtime, some citizens might feel comforted at the idea of having explored every corner of the literary landscape, rather than wandering in an endless jungle of world literature stretching to the horizon in every direction. Others might be appalled at the thought of being allowed to read only pre-approved books.

How you feel about either option may be a good guide to how well you would cope with living in an authoritarian state.

See it yourself

I started my first full-time job, in the Freight Central Division of the Department of Transport in London in 1979, after seven weeks of hitchhiking around 27 states of the continental United States, plus British Columbia. The rides included hours in the cabs of Peterbilts, Kenwoods and Freightliners. My new work seemed somehow appropriate.

Riding in lorries is a unique joy. The elevated driving position and hydraulically damped seat suspension create a thrilling sensation of weightless, low-level flight along the road – albeit in a 40-ton 'rig'. Long journey times generate camaraderie, as did – in the 1970s – the use of citizens band radios.

In March 1980, shortly after I started work in Freight Central, far-sighted executives at Denby Transport, a trucking firm in the cathedral city of Lincoln, suggested that officials working on road transport policy might benefit from real-life exposure to the life of heavy goods vehicle drivers.

I volunteered immediately.

---

[5]   In Russia, unlike in the UK, no one is shy of calling themselves an intellectual. In the 1990s a Union of Intellectuals even existed. 'How do they join?' foreigners mused. 'Do they have to take an exam?'

The trip from Portsmouth to Clermont-Ferrand (dropping off Michelin tyres from Stoke-on-Trent) then on to Péronne to pick up chemicals bound for Grangemouth, was a crash course in trucking and life. Driver Joe Staines made me welcome, giving me one of two bunks in the cab of his DAF 2800 truck as we overnighted in lay-bys and truck stops across France, none luxurious. His stoicism, calm and patience as we crossed borders, loaded cargo and navigated the continent were a masterclass in getting a tough job done without fuss. It was also the best lesson imaginable in what being a truck driver was really like.

LEARNING FROM NEW experiences means keeping an open mind.

I first visited West Berlin in 1980. We transited the 'air corridor' in a British Airways plane that shuddered and stuttered as it fought to stay airborne at the 10,000 feet (3,048 metres) maximum ceiling agreed by occupation authorities after 1945 – too low for modern aircraft. I was coming to inspect the Berlin barracks, airfields and tank sheds of the British Army of the Rhine.

For a British 22-year-old, West Berlin was a kaleidoscope of in-your-face decadence, decay and Cold War menace. 'The whole place is weird – rotten is too strong,' I wrote, 'but a bit like Tadzio in *Death in Venice*.' Costly prestige projects and corporate HQs rose from grey tenements blighted by the wall. Even the Kongresshalle (now the Haus der Kulturen der Welt), a conference hall gifted to the city by the US in 1957, lay slumped in ruins after collapsing a few months earlier.

On arrival, I was invited to a dinner hosted by the cavalry colonel commanding the Chieftain tanks of the British armoured squadron at his house at 51 Stallupöner Allee. Colonel Johnson debated the optics of holding the Queen's Birthday Parade on the Maifeld, where Hitler had staged rallies, or the difference between patriotism and nationalism. He joked about military contingency planning ("If the Soviets attack we'll drive our tanks into the Grünewald and hide"). His intellectual liveliness – a hallmark of British military officers, I was to discover – was not what I, naively, had expected from a soldier. Between us, the table groaned with historic regimental silver.

On the third evening we donned uniform or dinner jackets and drove in a military vehicle to the opera (*Der Freischütz*) in

East Berlin, exercising the right of the four occupying powers – France, the UK, the US and the USSR – to travel to all sectors of the city. Our route took us through Checkpoint Charlie, where we did not exit the vehicle but held our passports up to the window for inspection.

The opera was a catalogue of embarrassments. For me, wearing a dinner jacket, or tuxedo, was an uncommon experience. Only on the night did I realise that my dress shirt needed cufflinks – something I did not own. I fashioned a shabby-chic substitute from two red India tags.[6] Colonel Johnson sported dress uniform: a scarlet jacket, cavalry breeches and boots with gleaming silver spurs. At the interval, we drank Champagne in the bar. As casually dressed East Germans eyed our group, I felt like a story-book representation of a militaristic, exploitative capitalist flaunting my conspicuous consumption.

The youth of West Berlin were welcoming. On my second evening, I met Ute, recorded in my diary as 'willowy'. She invited me to a club called Sounds, from which I did not return until 3.30 a.m. We rendezvoused the next night, after the opera; this time I did not return until 4.15 a.m. The West Berlin party culture seemed turbo-charged by the fact that male residents were exempt from military service. On my final night, I visited Joe's Bierhaus until 4.45 a.m., made new friends, and missed the 8.40 a.m. British military train to Braunschweig.

Berlin changed me, and my politics.[7] As a student at Cambridge from 1976–79, I had read Orwell and Hemingway without really focusing on the politics. When the Union Society debated the motion 'This House believes that Communism is morally superior to Capitalism' I had filed through the 'aye' door, along with most other attendees.

West Berlin's parties, peep shows and politics felt raw, like a nightclub with the lights turned on. When I went on a tour of

---

[6] Short strips of metal or plastic, connected with a cord, colour-coded according to length, used to bind papers together through a hole punched in the corner.

[7] 'Those who can't change their minds, can't change anything' – George Bernard Shaw.

the wall, my guide was a young man who had spent two years in an East German prison after a failed escape attempt.

'It is two walls', I wrote, 'separated by 150 metres of mines, tank traps, barbed wire and, main obstacle, clear land with watchtower lookouts … gruesome.' The idea that the communist authorities had constructed this pornography of barriers and barbs to keep their own people in, while cynically describing the resulting death-strip wasteland as an 'anti-fascist protection wall', was as good an education in the moral challenges of authoritarianism as – later – reading Solzhenitsyn.

After eschewing the West Berlin nightlife on my final, extra day in town, I got up in time to catch the military train back home. The carriages were sealed on leaving West Berlin.

A leaflet issued to passengers warned in red letters that 'CAMERAS AND BINOCULARS ARE NOT TO BE USED OR EXPOSED DURING THE TRAIN JOURNEY' and set out points of interest: '10.40, 87 miles: Before crossing the **River Elbe** there is a large **Soviet Engineer Barracks** on your left.' Or '11.24, 113 miles: On arrival at **Marienborn**, the **OC Train, TCWO** and **Russian Interpreter** alight, and present all the documents to the **Soviet Army Officer** for checking, while the engine is detached and searched. Shortly afterwards, the train leaves the "**Corridor**". Watch out on both sides for the **guard dogs, barbed wire, minefields** and **watch towers**.'

At one point, an East German train travelled alongside ours for a minute or two. I looked down and saw a long-haired man my own age, clad head-to-toe in denim, gazing back at me. He smiled and raised his hand in a peace sign. I did the same. It was a splendid reminder that authoritarian regimes do not necessarily reflect the views of those they control.

MANY DIPLOMATS LAY WREATHS. For a British diplomat, doing so at concentration camps is both a sombre duty and an education.

When posted in Berlin, I once went alone one November to commemorate British Commandos murdered at the Buchenwald concentration camp, near Weimar. The site is a horrific indictment of humankind's capacity for inhumanity.

On a bleak, cold day, a local woman showed me around, describing the atrocities that had taken place.

Afterwards, over a cup of coffee, she told me she had been a guide at the camp for years. "When I was growing up in the DDR," she said, "they told us that this had been a camp where communists and Soviet troops were murdered. Later, we learned that thousands of Jews and others had died here. Finally, after 1989, we learned that the Soviets themselves interned people here from 1945 to 1950 – many of them died, also. I sometimes wonder what we will discover next."

I left Buchenwald chilled at the horrors experienced by those imprisoned and murdered there. My guide's comments also unsettled me. She had lived through a gut-wrenching shift of historical paradigms. We should all bear in mind that our understanding of past – or current – events may not be as accurate, or objective, as we believe.

To LEARN FROM new experiences, you must have the experiences in the first place. Several times, I failed at this.

On 8 November 1989 in London, I had my regular German lesson. On 9 November, the Berlin Wall came down.

A week earlier, I'd told John Major in the clerkery of the Foreign Office there was "not much going on". With hindsight, I could not have been more wrong.

In the 1980s I didn't own a television and the internet did not exist. The extraordinary images of people swarming on top of the Wall at the Brandenburg Gate and pouring through Checkpoint Charlie did not reach me for three days. I thought: 'I should fly to Berlin and witness this historic event.' Then I thought: 'Work is busy and I've already missed the moment.'

I've regretted that decision ever since.

'Last year was probably the most important in world affairs since 1945,' I wrote in July 1990 to my German friend Rüdiger. 'I was discussing with my father whether Gorbachev would be able to retain power or not. My father said Gorbachev faced a strong challenge from the right-wing, the hard-line communists. Surely, I said, you mean the left wing? Ah, yes, said he: one has always tended to assume that the reactionaries will be on the right.'

In the same letter, I argued the European Community had a role: 'after years developing into a ... rich nations' economic club, we see it coming back towards its roots as an association to bring nations so politically close together that no-one can imagine them fighting each other ... What', I wrote, 'if Poland wants to join?' I worried about 'the Balkanisation of Eastern Europe, particularly if/when the Soviet Union falls apart ... I'd like to see Gorbachev's job objectives.'

Three months after the wall fell, Nelson Mandela was released from prison in South Africa. Two months later, on 16 April 1990, he appeared at a celebratory concert at London's Wembley Stadium. Foolishly, I didn't buy a ticket.

Later, I would live for seven years in Berlin and explore every nook and cranny of a city where east and west were already becoming hard to tell apart. But I never stopped wishing I'd hopped on a plane in November 1989.

SOMETIMES, IF YOU keep your eyes open, revelatory experiences will come to you.

When in April 1992 our group of FCO Russian language students arrived in Moscow, our teachers quizzed us about 'the excursion'. They were contractually obliged to provide one, they said. Would we rather have a weekend in St Petersburg, as Leningrad had been renamed a few months earlier, or a four-day visit to Samarkand and Bukhara, in the newly independent Central Asian state of Uzbekistan?

We voted unanimously for Uzbekistan. I must confess that prior to that moment, I had not been absolutely clear whether Samarkand was a real place or not.

Travel was gruelling. 'The temperature on our Aeroflot flight started off very hot then fell to sub-zero temperatures, a pattern repeated on the return flight,' I wrote. 'There was nothing like cabin service, although on the return flight they did give us a bit of vile-looking sausage and stale bread, with a cup of tea.'

Yet the fact Uzbekistan had been cut off from the outside world for 70 years meant an unparalleled degree of culture had been preserved.

At a huge market in Samarkand, women without exception wore colourful national dress and all the men fantastical fur and felt hats. We watched a bare-chested man dive onto broken glass or lie on knives while people climbed on him. Mountains of fruit and vegetables, unobtainable in Moscow, rose all around. We visited mausoleums, madrassahs and the tombs of Timur – famous in the UK from Christopher Marlowe's 1587 play *Tamburlaine the Great* – and his grandson, the astronomer Ulugh Beg.

In Bukhara, wandering the back streets, I came across urchins playing by a baked mud wall. They addressed me in Uzbek; I tried out my Russian. They responded, then, noting my accent, came out with a bit of French, then English. I asked what language they spoke at home. Hebrew, they replied.

The ethnic diversity, history and culture of 1992 Uzbekistan was extraordinary. Yet it struck me that our teachers in Moscow had not considered an excursion to Central Asia much different from one to St Petersburg. The fact of Uzbekistan's separate statehood had not sunk in. When you saw the place in person, those changes seemed obvious. By the time I next visited, in 2012, Uzbekistan had abolished the Cyrillic alphabet and was being courted by China and Turkey. Many of the Russians, and the Jews, had left.

LEARNING IS EASIER if you eschew insouciance and maintain a sense of wonder.

In October 1987, shortly before I left Vienna to return to London, I attended the 'topping out' ceremony for the new British embassy. The hole for the foundations had been dug 36 weeks earlier; the construction team were proud of their achievement.

'One of the workers,' I wrote, 'a roofer with a great claw hammer hanging ostentatiously from his belt … read three poems, addressed to the building itself in the familiar Du form. The first opened with "Oh crude but diplomatic structure, you will stand for many years," followed by him drinking, and smashing his glass in the corner of the room. He then filled and emptied two further glasses for two more toasts.'

Returning to Vienna in 2016, I was surprised to see that the tradition of the Krampus, a kind of horned monster allegedly going back to pre-Christian times, had evolved from something occasionally glimpsed in remote mountain valleys into a nationwide touristic tradition. People love dressing up, and young men seem particularly to enjoy donning gigantic hairy headdresses, drinking beer and schnapps, brandishing flares, and trying to terrify onlookers – often, young women – by rushing, roaring, towards them in the dark.

Austria's pride in its exotic traditions is a key to understanding the country. Diplomats – and other travellers – should seek out such customs, treasure and study them.

Wisdom and public speaking

Cultivating your stock of wisdom includes exercising any skills and knowledge you may be lucky enough to have.

When I ceased full-time paid employment to look after the children in 2002, I attempted to redeploy my existing skills. My diaries are full of graphs and tables. They include lists of play-dates received (that is, our children invited to someone's house) and hosted in return, in an effort at reciprocity.

A chart sets out meals for each week from 9 October 2002 to 15 September 2003 as I sought to avoid repetition. Others list music practice, shopping and recipes, rotas for cat litter cleaning, revision for school exams and contents of the children's rucksacks for walking the Dales Way. I took over running the embassy children's library, which migrated into our attic bedroom. For the first time, I had a card saying 'writer'.

In February 2005 I was offered the chance to apply for a job back in London, on promotion. 'The only disadvantage', I wrote, 'was that it started now, or at least as soon as possible, and so would mean me going back to London within the next few weeks and living apart from the family for over a year. After much debate, we've just about decided that the prize is not worth the price, so I won't apply for it … I'll just have to hope that some other good jobs come up over the next year or so.'

Did I regret any of this? Not a bit. The adage that no one on their deathbed ever wished they'd spent less time with their children rang true. I learned a lot about writing, too: in the same letter, I recorded 'a commission from the *Boston Globe* to write a story about the Cologne Carnival', for which I bought my first digital camera.

FOCUSING ON YOUR strengths and weaknesses can also help you overcome your fears.

As director of Overseas Territories 2006–08 I attended the morning meetings of the PUS[8] – a regular gathering of top FCO officials to discuss issues of the moment.

They were the most intimidating events I ever attended.

The format of the meetings was one of studied informality. The PUS would sit behind a table, at which the most senior colleagues clustered. Behind them, a rough semi-circle of less stratospheric types assembled on a crescent of upright chairs. Further back, others perched on the arms of, or crouched in the recesses of, distant sofas.

The meeting started with set pieces: a summary by the foreign secretary's private secretary of the day's programme; a briefing from the head of news on media developments; a word from the PUS himself;[9] and perhaps an update from anyone dealing with a crisis. Then the PUS would invite each person around the semi-circle to speak. As your moment in the spotlight drew closer, every eye in the room would swivel your way.

In early meetings, confronted by senior peers hanging on whatever pearls of wisdom I might produce, I was so nervous I could barely choke out a few words. What could I say that was relevant? How could I showcase the vital work of the Overseas Territories Directorate? I imagined the big beasts of the Foreign Office leaving the room after the meeting, slapping their thighs with mirth, tears of laughter streaming from their eyes as they recalled my efforts.

I worked on it. I attended a course in public speaking. I made a point of reporting at every meeting one development preoccupying my team. It might be a cloud of toxic volcanic ash threatening the people of Montserrat; an overturned boat of Haitian migrants off the Turks and Caicos Islands; or a shortage of able-bodied adults to haul out the boats on Pitcairn. People seemed interested. I began to relish the opportunity to showcase our work. My phobia of the meetings evaporated.

Overcoming my fear of speaking in big meetings paralleled wider developments. As a junior official, like many people, I

---

[8] Permanent under-secretary – the most senior official in the department.

[9] At the time of writing, no woman has yet been PUS of the Foreign Office.

always found giving speeches terrifying.[10] The PUS's meeting was a breakthrough. When I became ambassador in Kyiv, I was speaking in public nearly every day. By the time I was ambassador in Vienna, I found myself giving other people advice on how to deliver speeches with maximum impact.

WHETHER THE LIFELONG learning recorded in this chapter adds up to full-blown wisdom is, at best, questionable. But I enjoyed all of it – and the experience formed me.

---

[10] 'The human brain starts working the moment you are born, and never stops until you stand up to speak in public' – George Jessel.

10

How to know people

Knowing people is a key skill for diplomacy and life. It is vital to understanding anything, anywhere. It is central to gaining influence. That means building empathy, getting up close, and interrogating stereotypes.

Rich and poor young Russians

In the Moscow bar, the drinks were cheap and the air was smoky. I spied an empty seat next to two young men.

"Sit down, please, welcome," said one. He reached out a hand. "My name is Satan."

When I arrived in Moscow in 1992 for language training, I believed my best chance of boosting my Russian was to shun my fellow Anglophone students. On the first night, I walked to Red Square, from our student dormitory at Park Kultury. The first thing I saw there was a bare-chested young man with a face wound, his body streaked with blood, shouting challenges at some uniformed police. Passers-by walked around him, shaking their heads.

The market reforms introduced in the early 1990s brought instability and chaos for ordinary Russians. Prices soared, living standards plummeted and jobs disappeared. Alcoholism offered a way out for some: in the winter of 1992–93 drunk men, lying insensible in the snow, accompanied by a friend or wife trying to prevent them from freezing to death, became commonplace. Rows of old people, trying to make ends meet, snaked outside metro stations, holding in their hands for sale a few household possessions, or reselling for a meagre profit scarce goods[1] they had queued for.

Yet the culture and traditions of Russia, much dating from before the 1917 Revolution, kept shining through – along with magnificent hospitality. In the smoky Moscow bar, 'Satan' and his companion greeted me as a long-lost brother. After another drink, they suggested we go and 'have a party'. I wondered whether this could be a cultivation attempt, concluded that no one could have known I would enter that bar and choose that seat, and went with them.

Our destination turned out to be Pushkin Square, where we sat on a bench next to an 1880 statue of the poet. Satan went to an old woman standing nearby with a shopping bag at her feet and returned with a couple of beers.[2]

We opened the beers and drank. Satan gestured towards the statue. "That is one of our great poets," he said. "Do you know his poem, 'My Memorial'? It is on the plinth." He began to recite the Russian text. I was impressed, then astounded, as this inebriated young bloke completed all five verses.

Later, my two new friends wandered off into the night. I never heard from them again. But our brief encounter was a timely reminder that even a 'down and out' country can have much to offer.

TWO OTHER YOUNG men helped me grasp how Russia was changing. I was visiting Daydream Island in Australia in the winter of 1993 when I heard someone speaking Russian. Josef and Pavel[3] were playing volleyball in the pool. I got chatting to them. They were there to buy a yacht, they said, and to sail it back to Vladivostok. If I was ever there, I should look them up. If they were surprised when I spoke Russian, told them I lived in Moscow and visited Vladivostok from time to time, they didn't show it.

Back in the early 1990s confident, rich young Russians were something of a novelty. Commercial enterprises were springing

---

[1] Known as 'deficit products', a Soviet phrase denoting rare or unobtainable items.

[2] At the time Russian beer, too, was a 'deficit product'.

[3] All names in this section changed.

up, but success was patchy. The fact that the elevator in our housing block was made by The Moscow Experimental Lift Company did not inspire confidence. Nor did the Russian Experimental Champagne sparkling wine brand.

The next time I visited Vladivostok, I phoned Josef. He said they'd bought the yacht, and suggested we go for a cruise around Russky Island, then in the news over a scandal involving the abuse of Russian naval cadets. I wasn't sure what to expect – the scale of the vessel, with a couple of luxury suites downstairs, surprised me. Pavel and their girlfriends Olga and Galina came, too.

After a few hours' cruising, Josef suggested we moor off Russky Island, and lunch on some fish and гребешки, a word I did not know. The autumn day was bright, and after a beer or two, I asked Josef what he did for a living. He worked in страхование, he said, insurance – one of those words, like бизнесмен, a businessman, which were becoming more widespread in Russia in 1994 but did not always mean the same in English as in Russian.

"What kind of things do you insure?" I asked.

"Well," he said, "suppose someone buys a мехсекция of fish –"

"What's a мехсекция?"

"A мехсекция?" Josef frowned at me, as if my Russian must be worse than he had thought. "A мехсекция is four railway wagons plus a refrigeration unit."

"Who would buy four railway wagons of fish?"

Josef sighed. "Someone buys a мехсекция of fish. The price is, say, half a million dollars. They collect the fish, and begin to sell them. But they do not pay the money they owe. I am the insurance. I go and have a talk with them, and they pay."

"Does Pavel help you?" I asked. Pavel was lounging nearby in an inflatable dinghy. He had curly blond hair, a bodybuilder's physique and a broken nose.

"Sometimes," Josef said. "Other times we work alone."

I decided not to ask any more questions. The sun was warm. Josef stripped to his swimming trunks, stuck a knife into his waistband, and dived into the sea. Pavel, Olga and Galina began to fish, with simple lines. Within 20 minutes Josef had found 20 гребешки, which turned out to be scallops. The others caught several fish.

We settled on the deck around a little camping stove, on which my Russian hosts proceeded to cook the fish and the scallops – the best I ever tasted. We washed it down with malt whisky, a gift I had brought with me, which we drank Russian-style, draining the glass with a toast. Everyone said the whisky was delicious.

Not for the first time, I was impressed by the ability of Russians to cobble together a nourishing and delicious meal from nowhere. More important, getting to know Josef and Pavel, and the day trip from Vladivostok, were a crash course in understanding the evolution of the Russian economy – not necessarily in a 100 per cent desirable direction.

I saw the two insurance executives again on a subsequent visit to Vladivostok. On that occasion, the hospitality offered, involving a deserted swimming pool complex and a sauna filled with young women, was clearly a blatant compromise attempt. But that is another story.

Interrogating stereotypes

Getting to know diverse people is a great way to recognise, and challenge, your stereotypes and preconceptions.

As director of Overseas Territories, I had regular contact with the US military and met some remarkable people.

Take Brigadier General Lyn D. Sherlock. No doubt the US Air Force has countless female ex-bomber pilots, but she was the first I'd met. Charged with leading a US delegation to discuss with UK counterparts the administration of the British Indian Ocean Territory during diplomatic talks in Washington DC, she radiated calm and authority. I found her charming and impressive.

An inspiring British military figure was a surgeon lieutenant commander from the Royal Navy who came to speak at an FCO leadership conference. Ramrod-straight in her dark blue uniform, Philippa Bennett held the audience of heads of mission from around the world spellbound as she recounted her experiences of leadership in the Royal Navy – including a where-is-this-going account of a late-night summons to her captain's cabin off the coast of Libya – and what others could learn from it. I am confident that half the ambassadors in the room would have signed up for the Navy on the spot after her speech, had they had the faintest chance of qualifying.

It is easy to allocate your military to a comfortable box of 'mercenary purveyors of death' or 'valiant protectors of our proud nation', depending on your political persuasion and the degree to which your country feels threatened.[4] If you interrogate yourself sufficiently, you may find yourself adopting easy stereotypes about all kinds of other institutions, or their employees – from the police to cab drivers and from bankers to, yes, diplomats.

Try and meet a few and see what they're actually like. Most institutions tend to contain a fully-fledged microcosm of society – including both good and bad bits.

GERMANY IS A country particularly prone to stereotyping, including in the UK and the US. Let's explore how contact with actual Germans may undermine some – but not all – of those stereotypes.

The idea that Germans are hard-working is, at the start of the 21st century, suspect. In fact, the country has organised itself to an outstanding degree in order to ensure that people do not have to work too hard. Germans work shorter hours than people in the US, the UK, or even France.[5] Never make an appointment with a German official on a Friday afternoon. If you believe German railways are paragons of efficiency, you haven't ridden Deutsche Bahn recently.

German punctuality is a myth that German diplomats work hard to dispel. In Kyiv from 2008–12 and in Vienna from 2016–19, I regularly attended meetings of European Union ambassadors where our German colleagues seemed to make it a point of honour to be the last to arrive. In personal dealings, by contrast, Germans – like Austrians – are fantastically punctual. If you give a dinner party starting at 8 p.m., German guests will arrive promptly five minutes earlier and mill outside until the hour strikes. Austrians dispense with the milling; I always sought to arrive 15 minutes early for any event I was hosting at the residence in Vienna, yet often arrived to find my guest(s) already there.[6]

---

4   Kipling's poem 'Tommy' explores the latter phenomenon.
5   Source: Our World in Data, 2017.
6   On one occasion, a distinguished author arrived for a reception a month early after a diary mix-up. I invited him in and we put the world to rights over several G&Ts.

In 1999 the German foreign ministry sent an invitation to embassies to join a group of young German diplomats on their annual skiing trip to the Swiss Alps. I was the only non-German who went. Others may have been deterred by the Spartan conditions: we travelled by overnight bus and I found myself sharing not only a room but a double bed with a friendly German diplomat called Uwe.[7]

On the slopes, the camaraderie, consultation and consensus were striking. As with the US Marines, no one was ever left behind. In groups of British skiers, faster and slower groups form; anyone dawdling may be left to fend for themselves. With my new German friends, we waited interminably for people to attend a call of nature, fix a ski binding, or simply catch up.

Skiing was followed by coffee and cakes at the hotel, a swim or sauna, and joint outings to fleshpots of Valbella-Lenzerheide such as the Fiasco Bar. The quest for consensus was ceaseless – both a reminder that some stereotypes are grounded in fact, and a lesson on working with my German hosts.

My favourite advice about Germans came from Sir Nigel Broomfield, British ambassador to Germany 1993–97. He once told me: "To make a German happy, you must offer him a *Konzept*. To drive him into ecstasy, you must offer him a *Gesamtkonzept*."[8]

PERHAPS THE ULTIMATE example of an institution on which everyone has an opinion with limited first-hand experience is the British royal family. Who hasn't cursed, or gushed, about Harry and Meghan?

In April 1986, Charles and Diana, then Prince and Princess of Wales, arrived in Vienna. The three-day visit took place when 'Diana-mania' was at its peak, focusing both on the Princess herself and her relationship with the heir to the throne.

---

[7] At least Uwe slept quietly. On another trip, I wrote: 'I shared a room with one G—, not a ball of fire and a snorer to boot.'

[8] A *Konzept* is, of course, a concept. Tellingly, there is no equivalent in English to *Gesamtkonzept* but it can be translated as an 'overall concept' or 'master plan'.

At the embassy, we spent months planning the three-day programme.[9] It included the royal couple arriving in Vienna on Concorde, along with dozens of models for a British fashion show, performances by the Philharmonia, a design exhibition featuring the first Dyson vacuum cleaners, a film festival, visits to the Vienna Boys' Choir, and so on. But the visit was dominated by the media.

The British royal press corps arrived on the same aircraft as the cast of the National Theatre's 'Love for Love',[10] along with John Haslam, assistant press secretary at Buckingham Palace. A tidal wave of journalists, photographers and camera crews from around the world swelled every pool and fixed position to breaking point – and beyond.

'The interests of the press', I wrote, 'are usually in being where they are supposed not to be.'

The result was a running battle to maintain some semblance of order between myself, Haslam and hundreds of media types. I wrote: 'My most common position seemed to be with my back to a mass of photographers, straining to prevent them surging forward as the Prince and (in particular) the Princess strolled by ... overheard from behind me as the Princess stood still for a few moments eighteen inches away: "It must be Christmas."'

On the first day of the visit, 14 April 1986, United States Air Force planes based in the UK bombed Libya, following acts of international terrorism attributed to Tripoli. The Austrian authorities tightened security, adding truck-loads of anti-terror units to the royal convoy.

My impression of Their Royal Highnesses was one of dogged professionalism at the eye of the whirlwind. Prince Charles, whom I was to see again on visits to Gallipoli in 2015 (along with Prince Harry) and Vienna in 2017, deployed a self-deprecatory humour in public, while being ready to slip the knife in with a lethal question – often about the environment – in private meetings with politicians.

The Princess of Wales showed a complete lack of pretension in her dealings with junior embassy officials (me), as when she declined offers to relocate an outdoor photo shoot with the

---

[9] Tip: visits organised at short notice are easier.

[10] I was thrilled to meet Tim Curry, star of *The Rocky Horror Picture Show*.

Vienna Boys' Choir indoors and walked out into the chilly drizzle.[11] Both found time to meet embassy staff at the end of their programme.

The diligence of senior members of the Royal Family compared with, say, government ministers, should not have surprised me. Before making judgements on people it's often helpful to have met them.

Nor should I have been surprised by the intensity of royal interaction with thousands of Austrians during their 1986 and 2017 programmes, or the lengths to which the Viennese would go to secure invitations to events. The professionally cynical Viennese turned out en masse and followed every second of the programme. Everything the visitors said or did was front-page news.

In 1986, Austrians were less bothered by the relationship between the royal couple than by a supposed romance between Prince Charles and the glamorous wife of the mayor of Vienna, Dagmar Koller. When Charles returned to Vienna in 2017 with the Duchess of Cornwall, the Austrian media debated at length whether he would remember Ms Koller after three decades, and rejoiced when they were once again perceived to have hit it off.

The impact of the 2017 visit was undiminished from that of 1986. Austria turned out in force, with a galaxy of top influencers – I met Dame Vivienne Westwood, was placed at a dinner next to Chancellor Christian Kern and had valuable face-time with President Van der Bellen and his team.

Royalty, and dynasties in general, embody multiple challenges and problems. But they can shine an extraordinary spotlight on what you are trying to achieve.

Immersion – and body language

The 'language immersion' is as intense a form of human interaction as a royal visit. The idea is to stay with a family for a month, speaking only the language you're learning, with four hours a day of tuition. It's not everyone's cup of tea, but you can learn a lot more than languages.

---

[11] A photographer caught me photobombing the picture as I hurried by in the background.

In October 1997, while head of Hong Kong Department, I visited the Diplomatic Service Language Centre to take my German C2 exam before my posting to Bonn as counsellor (EU and economic). I had a few minutes with my ancient German dictionary to prepare for the 'liaison interpreting' section: the subject was environmental land use and biodiversity. The word 'biodiversity' was not in the dictionary. I failed the exam.

Prior to resitting the exam in 1998, I went on German immersion in Cologne, and struck lucky. Gudrun, my hostess, was a Feng Shui master and head of a dynamic, fun family. 'I arrive punctually in Cologne and am met by Jörg', I wrote, in German, in my diary, 'who drives me home to meet Gudrun, Marie Christine (16), Jens Christian (14), Milli (13), Anna–Lea (7) plus dogs Sandy (Labrador-ish, blind?), Dick (barks, hates men), Lotte (tiny and sad), plus some smaller pets … Dinner tonight with all the children plus Inge, her two children (little Anna +?), JC's friend Andy plus Georg, AL's father.'

Family members took me swimming, or to the movies (*Deep Impact* in German). I visited the House of German History, in Bonn, with my German teacher, Petra. With my friend Rudi I saw a cabaret on a Rhine cruise: *Erfolgreich scheitern: Revolution im Rheinland* (*Revolution in the Rhineland: Fail Successfully*). Through an analogue bulletin board, I connected with Germans seeking conversation exchange: Catrin and Ulrike, too, showed me Cologne. All gave me a deep dive into 1998 Germany.

Eighteen years later, immersion in Istanbul plunged me into another rich learning environment.

The Foreign Office classifies languages according to difficulty. Class 1 languages such as Japanese and Mandarin require 22 months to reach C1 level. Class 3, such as Turkish, takes 14 months, Class 4, for example, Russian, 10.[12] My job as consul general in Istanbul was not, in Foreign Office lingo, a 'speaker slot', so I did not qualify for full-time language training. But I was keen to learn, and my line manager David Reddaway, ambassador

---

[12] Nine months when I learned Russian in 1991. This classification is disputed; for example, German (Class 6) is harder than French (also Class 6) although the latter is harder for Anglophones to pronounce.

in Ankara, agreed to my fitting in four weeks of immersion in Istanbul before I started work.[13]

I had started learning Turkish while ambassador in Kyiv. Over 127 hours of evenings and weekends, I did the then-innovative Rosetta Stone computer course twice. But I arrived in Istanbul in the searing heat of August 2012 with a cruder grasp of the language than is usual for immersion courses. A driver, instructed to speak only Turkish, took me to the suburb of Baltalimanı, where I moved in with Akın, a friendly young bloke, for four weeks. On my first night, phone battery flat, I lost my way in the sweltering, steep, unlit, wild-dog-infested backstreets and spent hours finding my way home.

Akın and over a hundred neighbours belonged to a single family from the Turkish Black Sea coast who had moved to the wooded slopes of the Bosphorus decades earlier. The sense of community was palpable. Conditions were simple:

'My room is ... a kind of lean-to added to an existing structure and is usually someone's office,' I wrote. 'There's a little bed and desk, but it is all rather full of stuff; and is hot and humid with windows that don't open and a flimsy door that does, with a fly screen. Because the room is a recent addition, I'm on the wrong side of a huge security door into the main house, with a security video camera surveying the room' [I threw a T-shirt over the camera]. 'So while everyone else sleeps behind heavily fortified doors, my room is exposed to any hypothetical intruders ... The main threat is from the omnipresent stray cats, and lots of little friendly lizards, one of which managed to find its way into my rucksack on the second morning and escaped, bemused, when I got out my computer at the language school.'

Akın was assiduous and friendly, making heroic efforts to engage me in conversation. One night he showed me a video of him singing in a Turkish glam-rock band in the Eurovision Song Contest. Another, we pored over an atlas discussing each country. We dined on stuffed vine leaves and drank herb tea from

---

[13] He suggested I might do the training in Konya, in Anatolia, rather than Istanbul, "to see another side of Turkey". Konya is, to put it mildly, a more ascetic city than Istanbul; I am not sure whether his proposal was blue-sky thinking or a practical joke.

the Grand Bazaar. My teachers Arzu and Emre took me to a mosque and a *cem evi* – a gathering place for the Alevi minority Muslim community. They also introduced me to *kokoreç*[14] and *şalgam suyu*.[15]

My poor Turkish left me in a fog of confusion. 'This week', I wrote, 'I learned that there will be a wedding party here on Saturday;[16] that the nickname of Akın's two-year-old niece, Fistik, means pistachio; that the tall, sad-looking woman who sometimes accompanies her is a Georgian nanny about to be deported; that the silent young man laying tiles is an Afghan who speaks no Turkish; and that the toothless road-sweeper in a skull-cap who greets Akın when we walk down the road is actually an uncle who has a big house nearby and likes to sweep the bit of road outside.'

My month in Baltalimanı was arduous but educational. Would I have liked air conditioning, a bigger desk, or reliable internet? Yes. But as in Cologne, I could not have asked for a better introduction to the Istanbullus, and to the metropolis on the Bosphorus where, as I noted, 'things dated from after 1453 are considered modern'.

ON 14 JUNE 2008, the day I arrived in Kyiv as British ambassador, a chat in several languages with a fellow passenger taught me important lessons about Ukraine – including that power is not always where you think.

My first official engagement that Saturday was to attend a Paul McCartney concert. McCartney, whom I met over the weekend and who struck me as a great bloke, played a splendid set in a teeming downpour to a crowd in Independence Square estimated at 350,000 people.

The crowd received the ex-Beatle rapturously, but the song that drove them wild was 'Back in the USSR', particularly its reference to the superior qualities of Ukrainian women.

---

[14] Lamb or goat intestines wrapped around seasoned offal.

[15] A salty, spicy turnip-juice mixture used to wash down *kokoreç*, or as a hangover cure.

[16] The party, to which my partner Gözde came expecting a rave-up, was in fact a *kına gecesi* or henna night, a women's gathering before a wedding.

I had experienced those qualities earlier that day. Waiting in the departure lounge at London's Heathrow Airport for my flight to Kyiv, a little nervous to be jetting off to my first ambassadorial job, I could not help noticing a tall, slender woman wearing short shorts and knee-length leather boots.

The words of 'Back in the USSR' came to my mind.

Boarding began, and I sat down in my preferred economy-class window seat towards the rear of the plane. The booted woman strolled down the aisle and sat down in the seat next to mine. My heart accelerated. Could a hostile power have engineered this? Surely the fact I had checked in the night before online, choosing my own seat, must render such a move impossible? Or could someone have hacked the British Airways booking app?

We got talking in Russian and English. She tried to teach me a few words of Ukrainian.

The Ukrainian woman was 24. She had grown up in Sevastopol, the home of the Soviet (and later Russian) Black Sea Fleet, in the south of the Crimean peninsula. One day, aged 19, she had met an American businessman from Phoenix, 28 years her senior. They had fallen in love, married and moved to Arizona. Sadly, five years later, their relationship had foundered and she had left him, taking with her only the green card, giving her permanent residence in the US, and the divorce settlement. Now she was studying English at a language school near Oxford Circus.

"You are studying English?" I said. "Did you not speak English before?"

"No," she said, "my English was very bad."

"How did you communicate when you first met him?" I said. "In Sevastopol?"

She paused, her dark eyes sparkling. Then she placed one hand on my arm and flashed a wicked grin. "Body language," she purred.

MEETING AN EXTRAORDINARY mix of people was one of the greatest privileges of my diplomatic career. Doing so not only helped me in my job of understanding and influencing countries but was richly, and repeatedly, rewarding.

11

How to be interrogated

A diplomat in the field may be thrust into the spotlight even at a junior level, facing media interrogations and tough exchanges with senior interlocutors. It's not always comfortable, but learning how to handle maximum pressure is invaluable.

Know your message

I gave my first Russian TV interview in August 1994. I and a colleague flew into Khabarovsk, near the Chinese border in Eastern Siberia, from Niigata in Japan, to minimise journey time on the eye-wateringly unsafe Russian airlines. After visiting local businesses and officials, being poisoned by *samogon* home-made vodka on a boat trip on the mighty Amur River and declining an offer to go bear hunting, we boarded the Trans-Siberian Railway for the 14-hour trip to Vladivostok.

In early 1990s Russia, the railway system was one of the few things that worked reliably. Our train rolled into the home of the Russian Pacific Fleet, newly opened to foreigners, dead on time. Bleary-eyed and unshaven, I descended from the carriage to find myself surrounded by journalists and TV cameras seeking Russian-language interviews.

I was delighted to oblige.

When junior, you should seize every opportunity for an interview. The more insignificant you are, and the further from HQ, the less chance screw-ups will have repercussions. More importantly, every interview is a chance to get your message across – in this case, 'the British embassy is here and keen to find out about Vladivostok'. Plus, interviews are a two-way street.

My dawn efforts at the station drew attention. A meeting with the controversial governor of the Far East Maritime Region, Yevgeny Nazdratenko, materialised. Up to that point, he had been 'unavailable'.

To HANDLE INTERROGATION by the media or other tough interlocutors you should train and practice, including in 'sandpit' situations where you can try out your skills in a relatively safe environment. But most of all, before opening your mouth, be clear about your goals, and what message you want to get across.

A trainer on a media course got this across brilliantly. He thrust a microphone in our faces and asked each of us, at speed, what we had had for breakfast.

At the end, he asked us if we'd communicated the points we wanted to make.

To go into an interview passively, waiting to see what the interviewer will ask, is a recipe for disaster.

BEING CLEAR ON key messages is invaluable in all kinds of sticky situations. In 1994 I visited Novosibirsk in Siberia. On arrival, I was ushered into a brilliantly lit room to meet a phalanx of senior politicians. TV cameras crowded in as Vladimir Nekhoroshkov, deputy governor of the Oblast, berated me for the lack of British engagement in the city. Other countries had sent major trade missions. Where were the British delegations? Why were we not organising investment by British companies? Novosibirsk did not need foreign money. Her enterprises were not begging for help, but wished to set up partnerships based on equality. Novosibirsk had 43 scientific institutes and a military-industrial complex dating from 1941; it teemed with potential. It was unfortunate that the embassy did not take the region seriously enough to send a higher-level representative than myself.

As first secretary (economic), my job was to report on the Russian economy and encourage efforts to reform it. I told Nekhoroshkov that British companies accused of reluctance to invest in Russia often complained that Russians – including some local authorities – kept their money in Switzerland and London instead of investing it locally. The job of persuading British firms to invest in Russia was primarily for the Russian authorities, some of whom were perceived to view foreign investment with suspicion and hostility. Novosibirsk was competing against cities worldwide, from China to South Carolina. Unless Russia provided legislative arrangements that worked and a sense that foreign investors were welcome, capital would go elsewhere.

Nekhoroshkov grinned and said he appreciated such frankness.

'The exchange on foreign investment in Russia', I later wrote, 'is typical of many we endure on our visits to the regions.'

Sometimes, as with the Élysée Treaty,[1] building relationships is a primary, and worthy, objective. On a visit to Irkutsk, at the junction of the Angara River and Lake Baykal, I asked to visit local enterprises and was shown around a pirate video factory. In the evening, our hosts invited us to a dinner where they offered to teach us the 'forty-seven Cossack toasts'. Toasting rituals have history in Russia, and I was keen to learn. Being an organised type, I made a note of each toast in my notebook.

After the eighth toast, my handwriting became illegible.

BEING CLEAR ON your objectives can also help deflect unreasonable or aggressive demands.

After the handover of Hong Kong to China in 1997, Beijing argued – as they had before the handover – that the UK had no business taking an interest in events in Chinese sovereign territory. In parallel, China sought to exert leverage through agents of influence in both Hong Kong and the UK. 'My sense from many Hong Kong senior officials', I wrote, 'was that they'd like us to continue to take an interest and speak up if things go badly; but they'd also like us to disappear altogether and leave them to sort things out with the Chinese.'

Soon after I became head of Hong Kong Department in 1997, I ran into Sir Anthony Meyer at an event in London. Meyer, a former soldier and diplomat, was famous mainly for being the first MP to run against Margaret Thatcher as a stalking horse candidate for leadership of the Conservative Party in November 1989. He lost, but his campaign signalled the beginning of the end for Thatcher, who was replaced by John Major a year later.

---

[1] See Chapter 7, 'How to handle politicians'.

"So, you are the head of the Hong Kong Department?" Sir Anthony peered at my name badge. "I think Ted Heath would be most interested to meet you," he said.

A couple of months later, I received from Sir Edward Heath, British prime minister from 1970 to 1974, an invitation to his house in Salisbury.

The invitation came at a time when I was on holiday in the west of England. Getting myself to Heath's home in Salisbury Cathedral Close, together with a jacket and tie appropriate for lunch with a former prime minister, was a challenge. When I approached the gate, armed anti-terrorist police loomed from the undergrowth. But once I had penetrated security, I found a sparkling assembly of guests including the chief constable of Wiltshire and the Spanish ambassador. Heath's house, Arundells, was magnificent. I admired the exquisite Chinese hand-painted wallpaper.

The purpose of the invitation did not become clear until after lunch. On a stroll in the garden, Heath buttonholed me. "What are you going to do about Robin Cook?" he said. Heath lambasted the then-foreign secretary's support for democratic institutions in Hong Kong and argued this would simply lead to the Chinese adopting anti-British positions.

Fortunately, despite the seniority of my host, I knew that his Beijing-friendly argument was the opposite of government policy. I took polite note of the ex-prime minister's unwise lobbying, but did not attempt to do anything about Robin Cook. I was never invited back.

SOMETIMES YOU MUST take a risk to get your message across. On my arrival as ambassador in Vienna, my press and public affairs team suggested I should have a hashtag, #keenonWien, to replace the #reasonstolikeIstanbul I had tweeted out over 600 times, usually with a picture, in Turkey. I went on to find more than 600 reasons to be keen on Vienna.

A second suggestion was an introductory video. I spoke decent German. Might I try a few phrases in regional dialects from around Austria? They duly filmed me introducing myself with "*Servus, ich bin Leigh*" ("Hello, I'm Leigh"), grappling with the famously difficult-to-pronounce Tyrolian word for a squirrel's tail, *Oachkatzlschwoaf*, and eating a *Käsekrainer*[2] from a kiosk. The video ended with me saying "*Olso, gemma und tamma wos!*" ("Right then. Let's get started!")

The video was not without risk. Filming me masticating a sausage and mangling the language opened me up to ridicule. Austria's biggest satirical show, *Wilkommen Österreich*, made fun of it. Yet the overwhelming reaction was positive, and the TV show's rebroadcast ensured huge coverage. With hindsight, it was as good an introduction to the country as I could have wished for.

DIPLOMATS AND THE media have a symbiotic relationship. Both hunger for information and enlightenment. Both, however much evidence may stack up to the contrary, are human beings.

In early 1990s Moscow, as we struggled to make sense of the chaos of communism collapsing, the ambassador held regular lunches with the UK press corps in the ex-sugar baron's mansion that served as residence and embassy on the Sofiyskaya Embankment opposite the Kremlin. At one such event, a series of speakers bemoaned the fact that the Communists, ejected from power in 1991, threatened to do well in upcoming elections. It took John Kampfner, then bureau chief of the *Daily Telegraph*, to point out that this was called democracy.

The worst press behaviour I ever witnessed, perhaps prophetically, came during the 1986 visit to Vienna of the Prince and Princess of Wales. I was responsible for handling the media, and rode my bicycle, black-tied, to the evening banquet at the City Hall. Despite my efforts, a fistfight broke out among photographers on a raised dais at the side of the room between those with good camera positions to capture 'Lady Di' and those at the back of the pack.

The worst scolding I ever received was from legendary journalist Hella Pick for failing to smuggle her into the ambassador's residence in Vienna to use his private phone. She also taught me how formidable a combination of charm, forcefulness and plain speaking can be.

---

[2] A hot sausage containing cubes of melted cheese that squirt out when you bite into it.

When to ignore advice

Occasionally, being off-message can be the best way to get the result you want. The trick is to know when.

In the 1980s, it was common practice in Europe to turn cows into cannibals. Farmers fed cattle protein supplements made from the carcasses of cows and sheep, including sick and injured animals. Why? Because it was cheaper than imported soya beans.

In 1986, a disease called bovine spongiform encephalopathy or BSE broke out in cattle in the UK and spread to other countries. BSE affects the brain: pitiful images emerged of cows unable to stand or control their limbs. In 1996, a new fatal brain disease emerged in humans, caught by eating BSE-infected beef. Variant Creutzfeldt-Jakob disease (vCJD) caused similar, disturbing symptoms in humans to BSE in cows, including dementia, and was invariably fatal.

In March 1996, the European Union banned exports of British beef. EU member states followed suit with their own bans. One of my jobs when I arrived in Germany in 1998 was to get the German ban lifted, because the UK had introduced measures to control BSE. The problem was that Germans have a quasi-religious zeal for food quality.[3] German beef farmers loved the ban, too.

The German federal government said they wanted to lift the ban, but it was up to Germany's *Länder*, or states. Most supported the ban. Experts told us that direct lobbying of *Länder*, which guarded their autonomy fiercely, would backfire. When ambassador Paul Lever met Kurt Biedenkopf, minister president of Saxony, a key *Land* supporting the ban, he was briefed not to raise the matter.

Lever did the opposite. Biedenkopf promised to look into it. Shortly afterwards, Saxony changed its position, creating a majority of *Länder* in favour of allowing imports, and Germany lifted its ban. By ignoring his briefing, being clear on his goals and deploying common sense, Lever hit the target.

BSE was an example of policy making amid uncertainty. Because of the long incubation periods of both BSE and vCJD and uncertainty about transmission mechanisms, no one knew

---

[3] The *Reinheitsgebot* or 'purity law', first adopted in Munich in 1487, still governs beer production in Germany.

if we faced thousands or even millions of human deaths. When British agriculture minister John Gummer sought to reassure the public that British beef was safe by feeding his four-year-old daughter a burger on TV, people were appalled.

In fact, worldwide deaths from vCJD up to 2021 totalled 232, of which 178 were in the UK.[4] The world may have got off lightly, although each case was tragic for those affected.

Back in the 1990s, I thought it would be aeons before restaurants in continental Europe, formerly big consumers of British beef, once again boasted that their meat was sourced from the UK. In fact, it returned rapidly to the menu. I never dreamed that within 20 years I would see a burger chain called *Rinderwahn* (mad cow disease) doing good business in Vienna – slogan 'Crazy about burgers'.

How can you work for those people?

What happens when your work goal is to promote something you disagree with? My friends harangued me for decades: 'How can you work for, and deploy the misleading/dishonest/abhorrent arguments of, such a lying/hypocritical/evil government?'

Following the Brexit referendum I, like other British ambassadors in the European Union and beyond, spent five years in Vienna trying to explain to bemused, baffled or apoplectic Austrians the UK government's latest moves.

It was clear from 23 June 2016 that politically neutral British civil servants and diplomats would work to implement government policy on Brexit – once politicians decided what it was. But two things made this difficult. The first was that polarised debate in the UK meant the two camps tended to treat each other not as political opponents but as enemies, idiots and traitors.[5] This made it harder for diplomats to argue government policies convincingly.

---

[4]   Source: National Library of Medicine, 2021.

[5]   The *Daily Mail*'s 'Enemies of the people' headline of 4 November 2016, attacking three judges for ruling that the consent of Parliament was needed for Brexit, was one example.

I once sat on a panel at a Vienna university alongside a German academic working in the UK. He described at length how Brexit doomed the British economy, and how Britons would soon be wandering the streets scavenging for food.[6] In response, I presented standard arguments about foreign investment in the UK, export successes and so on. He rounded on me. How could I, an intelligent person, trot out the British government line? Why did I not tell the truth, that Armageddon was just around the corner? What was wrong with me?

His intervention put me in a tough position. The easy answer would have been: 'Look, mate, I am a British civil servant. It is my duty to argue the government line, and I am surprised that you could expect me to do anything else.' But I couldn't say that, as it would imply that I didn't 100 per cent believe what I was saying. So, I gnashed my teeth and went on presenting encouraging statistics.

The second thing making it harder for British diplomats to argue the official line on Brexit was the tendency of the government to take actions open to legal challenge[7] such as the suspension of Parliament in 2019 – later found to be unlawful. Other things, such as signing up to a Northern Ireland Protocol that put a border straight down the Irish Sea, denying it would do any such thing, then threatening to overturn said protocol, inevitably caused eye-rolling among diplomats steeped in international law.[8]

I took two small actions to salve my conscience as I went in to bat, month after month, to argue the British government's case on Brexit. The first was to choose my words carefully. I would never say 'I think', much less 'I believe', before expressing any view which I personally did not share. Rather, I would use formulations such as 'the British government has said', 'the secretary of state believes', 'the prime minister is clear that' and so on. This may sound like semantics but I felt it was both professional and truthful. Within that context, I would argue the UK case passionately, in German, to good effect.

---

[6] Some might argue that this is exactly what has happened.

[7] This is putting it politely.

[8] Similar problems afflicted US diplomats as they fought to explain and justify the latest tweet from President Trump.

My second response involved neckwear. Years earlier, at the Cloisters Museum in New York, I had been inspired by the Unicorn Tapestries – an ancient artwork centred on the legendary creature. Unicorns, like other mythical beings, exist as much as you want to believe in them. I cherished my unicorn tie from the museum shop and wore it often in Vienna when appearing in public to argue the case for Brexit.

Some FCO colleagues could not stomach government policy. A friend who objected to the government's refusal to give the right of abode in the UK to British subjects in Hong Kong at the time of the handover in 1997 asked to be assigned to other duties. Elizabeth Wilmshurst, an FCO legal adviser, resigned in 2003 arguing that it would not be legal to invade Iraq without a second UN Security Council Resolution. In her letter of resignation she said an invasion would be 'detrimental to the international order and the rule of law'. History has pretty much proved her right.

Traditionally, foreign policy is less polarised than domestic policy. Diplomats have tended to disagree with government policy less often than home civil servants. Brexit may signal a new trend, as social media goads everyone to adopt strong views about everything.

WHAT IF YOU deliver your message, and people disagree violently? As so often, the novelist Anthony Trollope has the answer.

When I arrived in Turkey in 2012, half the country seemed to be on Twitter. My initial forays into the new medium had little impact. But my – scrupulously objective – images and comments from the Gezi Park protests in 2013 brought about that tipping point when thousands of people suddenly start following you.

It is a seductive and dangerous moment. As the Swiss ambassador in Kyiv once told me: "there must always be a risk that the quest for popularity will skew what you say".[9]

The reverse also applies: the more people notice what you say on social media, the greater the risk that they will attack you for it – or resort to trolling. I first became aware of this in Ukraine,

---

[9] He also said that Swiss government guidance for use of social media by diplomats was so voluminous as to deter any rational person from attempting it.

where each time my blog appeared in the online section of the *Kyiv Post*, an anonymous commentator would attack me in vile and personal terms. I later learned he was a person far away whom I had never met.

In Turkey, the response was on a different scale. In Ukraine, my blogs had politely raised questions about government policy as a matter of course. In Turkey, the Twitter debate was polarised and polemical; the slightest perceived criticism of anything risked triggering a torrent of abuse. My comments on the Gezi Park protests drew huge numbers of both positive and negative comments.

Later, when I tweeted about media freedom, I was deluged with hostile tweets, including death threats. Luckily, many people threatening me used language of a type no one had taught me in my Turkish lessons, muting its impact. But Turkish native speakers were horrified on my behalf, and for months my bodyguard arranged enhanced security.

Trolling has driven many people to abandon social media. My response has – so far – been informed by Trollope, who wrote about the problem long before Twitter and co. arrived on the scene.

In *Dr Wortle's School* (1879), newspapers attack Wortle, a headmaster, for allowing an unmarried couple to work at his school. Trollope describes Wortle's emotions: "'Never notice what may be written about you in a newspaper," he would have said. Such is the advice which a man always gives to his friend. But when the case comes to himself he finds it sometimes almost impossible to follow it. "What's the use? Who cares what the 'Broughton Gazette' says? Let it pass, and it will be forgotten in three days. If you stir the mud yourself, it will hang about you for months. It is just what they want you to do. ..." The Doctor had said this more than once to clerical friends who were burning with indignation at something that had been written about them. But now he was burning himself, and could hardly keep his fingers from pen and ink.'

The moral of the tale, that responding to attacks simply adds fuel to the fire, is as relevant now as it was in the 1870s. Summarised as 'shut up' rather than 'put up', it is sometimes known as the 'Streisand effect', after the US entertainer's 2003 attempts to suppress an aerial photo of her cliff-top mansion drew massive media attention. The gratuitous insults heaped on us on Twitter and elsewhere are the equivalent of Trollope's disobliging newspaper commentaries.

TRAINING, PRACTICE AND being clear about your message and goals all help handle tough interrogations and interlocutors. But knowing when to ignore people whose agenda is simply to disagree with you is the hardest thing to learn.

12

How to keep your feet on the ground

Russia's war on Ukraine, the climate crisis, conflict in the Middle East and febrile domestic politics can make it feel as if the world is going to hell in a handbasket. How to stay balanced and calm?

Diplomats, grappling with intractable problems as they move from country to country, have as much trouble as anyone staying grounded and focused. It helps if you are comfortable in your own skin, recognise your fallibility and have principles to underpin your decisions.

Staying grounded

The privatisation of the National Freight Corporation in 1979–80 gave me an early masterclass in politics and in staying grounded – and not just through the cut and thrust of parliamentary debate around one of the Thatcher government's first privatisations.

On one occasion, a meeting of the Public Bill Committee to debate the detail of the legislation took place in a magnificent neogothic committee room of the House of Commons. When we broke for tea, I stood at an equally magnificent, if old-fashioned, urinal next to Labour MP Frank Dobson.

He grinned at me. "It's all piss and wind," he said. "It's all piss and wind."

This was the only conversation I ever had with Frank Dobson. So, I do not know if he regularly described the machinations of Parliament in this acerbic manner. But his comment was a valuable corrective to any tendency by a young civil servant to ascribe excessive importance to his work.

Dobson's gritty wisdom came to my mind years later when I had the privilege of meeting another stalwart of the British establishment. Roger Glover, long-time bass guitarist for rock-band loudness record-holders[1] Deep Purple, invited me backstage after a concert in Kyiv. The legendary musician had been rocking since 1969, yet – like most of the band – seemed startlingly normal.

"What's the secret?" I asked him as we disposed of a beer or two. "How do you stay sane, and grounded, under the pressure of being a global megastar?"

"Well," he replied, "you should never take yourself too seriously." This struck me as admirable advice.

FRIENDS ARE VITAL to help keep your feet on the ground. Diplomats moving constantly between countries must, arguably, work even harder to maintain friendships than those who live mostly in one place. In December 2005, shortly before I joined the Overseas Territories Department (OTD) of the FCO in London, the Civil Partnership Act came into effect in the UK. It gave same-sex couples the rights and responsibilities of marriage.[2] In June 2006, gay friends invited me to their moving and elegant civil partnership ceremony in Islington, followed by a slap-up lunch at the River Café in Hammersmith.

At the time, I was visiting the UK from Berlin. My new boss in London heard I was in town. She kindly invited me to come and meet members of my new team in OTD at their weekly afternoon tea.

I prioritised my friends and enjoyed a fabulous, boozy lunch. I reached the FCO halfway through the tea. To my alarm, my boss invited me to make a short speech introducing myself. I did my best, but felt as though anyone coming within a couple of metres would realise I had just consumed countless gin and tonics.

Was I coherent on my first appearance in my new job? I never had any feedback to the contrary. And I felt I had stuck to my principles.

---

[1]   *Guinness Book of Records 1975.*

[2]   Officially recognised same-sex marriages became possible in the UK only in March 2014.

When to admit you're wrong

In an uncertain world, being prepared to admit you're wrong, or unsure, can be liberating –and not only for politicians.

On 17 June 1981, I attended a Tag der Deutschen Einheit (Day of German Unity) concert at the Philips Halle in Düsseldorf. Four bands played, including Düsseldorf's own DAF (standing for Deutsch Amerikanische Freundschaft or German–American Friendship) and Fehlfarben.

The evening was raucous and violent: when punks invaded the stage, I joined them.

When it comes to weird Dadaist nihilist punk, the Germans excel. A band called German–American Friendship, singing songs about political violence on a holiday to mark the Day of German Unity? You couldn't make it up.

In 1981, I found the very concept of German unity absurd. Five years later, I shook my head at the optimism of activists demonstrating at the Conference on Security and Cooperation in Vienna for the independence of the Baltic states. In 1991, I pitied the naivete of my Moscow colleagues for arguing the UK should open embassies in every republic of the former Soviet Union.

None of us should feel too certain of our predictive powers – especially about the future.

ANYONE CAN BE wrong. The trick, when confronted by evidence, is to learn rather than deny.

In the spring of 1992, as my class at the Foreign Office Language Centre grappled with grammar en route to our C1 Russian exam, two native speakers joined us for conversation.

One introduced himself as Andrei Smirnov, a Soviet naval interpreter. Suave and witty, he spoke English as though born and bred in Oxfordshire. His party piece was to recite 'Heather Ale', an epic poem by Robert Louis Stevenson, in English and then in Russian. Clearly, rote learning and the study of phonetics in the Soviet education system produced world–class results.

We all agreed Smirnov must be a Russian spy.

The second native speaker to grace our class in London was an Armenian playwright. Seasoned, charming and self-deprecating, he told us none of his first eight plays had been produced, but he had found success with his ninth. He had subsequently staged his eighth; then his seventh; and so on, working backwards. "The critics", he said, "praised the increasing maturity of my style."

He told us his first journey outside the Warsaw Pact had been to West Berlin. "I went into a café at Bahnhof Zoo," he said, "and ordered a beer and a sausage. It was delicious. I looked around me. Other people were eating, too! From full plates! When I gazed out of the window, the workers on the building site were going about their business with no evidence of oppression, coercion or starvation. In that moment, I understood that everything I had been told about the West was a lie."

Know your prejudices

Knowing yourself should include interrogating your own prejudices. That includes the extent to which you unthinkingly support – or criticise – your own country.

Like most Brits, I had barely heard of the Falkland Islands when news broke in London on 2 April 1982 that Argentine forces had captured them. For the first 24 hours, events in the South Atlantic felt remote. Then, on Saturday 3 April, Parliament held a debate so extraordinary that I recorded it on a cassette tape.

Prime Minister Thatcher announced that 'a large task force' would head south the following Monday, in parallel with diplomatic efforts to recover the islands. The leader of the opposition, pacifist, republican and opponent of nuclear weapons Michael Foot, said in reply: 'Even though the position and circumstances of the people who live in the Falkland Islands are uppermost in our minds – it would be outrageous if that were not the case – there is the longer-term interest to ensure that foul and brutal aggression does not succeed in our world.'

Foul and brutal aggression! Had Michael Foot just agreed with the PM? Something historic was happening.

The military campaign seemed to move at a snail's pace, compared with today's 24-hour news cycle. 'Read in the newspapers about how we Brits bombed Port Stanley a day or two back,' I wrote. It was the first time I had experienced the sense of being misled by our own side. Ministry of Defence spokesman Ian McDonald, famed for his monotone delivery, gave briefings which it later emerged were often inaccurate – such as claims that long-distance raids by Vulcan bombers had crippled Port Stanley Airport. Aerial photos later showed most of the bombs had missed their target.

When clashes began at sea and losses on both sides mounted, I was startled by how the conflict wreaked havoc on my emotions. One day I returned from work to find a housemate watching television. "They've sunk *The Sheffield*!" he wailed. I had never considered myself particularly patriotic, but the mood swept me up, along with much of the rest of the nation – and Michael Foot.

Were we wedded to enlightened principles of resisting aggression? Or was it something more primitive – a collective mass reflex such as swept the country after the death of Diana, Princess of Wales in August 1997? Whatever the reason, I found myself longing for 'us' to win against 'them'.

The Falklands Conflict was a reminder of how easily a thirst for war can be generated – all the more so in an age where social media can whip up a mob at the drop of a hat.

WE'RE ALL PRONE to chauvinism. For my first French exchange, in 1971, I travelled by overnight bus from Manchester to London, then by train and ferry to Paris. My German exchange to Uerdingen, in 1972, included a memorable first bratwurst in a subway at Cologne station.

On these trips, I and my fellow teenagers fell prey to the novice traveller's malady of seeking to compare one's own country favourably with wherever one is visiting. 'In Britain, we don't have ID cards,' we would brag. 'Here, we can buy cigarettes from a vending machine any time we like,' our German friends would respond, crushingly.

Many of us carry the spores of this illness into adulthood. Diplomats, despite their supposed sophistication, are not immune. As a diplomat of country X, it is your job to present evidence, couched in a self-effacing way, to support the thesis that X nestles securely towards the top of the pyramid of the world's most fabulous nations. Any expat may reasonably present such arguments. But beware that morphing into reflex criticism of the new country in which you reside.

Eavesdrop on late-night chat in embassy bars or dinner parties from Austria to Zimbabwe and you will hear foreign nationals bemoaning the inefficiency, bureaucracy and inadequate work ethic of their hosts.

Even nations renowned for rationality can be afflicted. A Danish friend of mine could not stop talking about the superior quality and boundless variety of milk in her native country. A Swedish diplomat, watching an England-France match in a German pub, prayed the French would win. "I had a posting in London," she said. "The Brits are so arrogant!"

The root cause of the 'my dog's better than yours' delusion is the insecurity felt by anyone trying to make themselves at home on foreign shores where everything from making a doctor's appointment to opening a bank account feels pernickety and alien. In some cases, insecurity may be fuelled by a nagging suspicion that the institutions, tailoring, cuisine, *joie de vivre*, weather or cheese of the host country may in fact be better than those back home.

I do not condemn those suffering from such tragic delusions. Anyone not unsettled by the challenges of a foreign culture is either arrogant or dead. But diplomats and other travellers should examine themselves for symptoms and bear in mind that statistically speaking, the chance of you happening to be born in the best country on Earth are small.

THE REVERSE PROBLEM is the pernicious belief that everything in your own country is abysmal. This can affect any of us, but particularly afflicts those who have made a new home abroad. It sometimes takes a foreigner to point out the merits of your homeland.

After the fall of the Berlin Wall, I took part in a series of visits by British counter-terrorism experts to build CT cooperation with the countries of the former Warsaw Pact. Many were keen to talk: between spring 1990 and summer 1991 we visited Prague, Warsaw, Budapest and Sofia.

On our first visit to Prague, then still the capital of Czechoslovakia, changing times were tangible. 'Wandering around the Interior Ministry in Prague', I wrote, 'seeing a scruffy long-haired bloke in a kaftan and earrings and a leather-clad cigar-smoking woman conferring in the corridor, I realised this was the minister and his private secretary.' Our hosts put us up, two to a room, in a run-down government guest house: I shared with a senior member of a British government agency. We wondered whether the room would be bugged and remained silent just in case.

I was surprised by the keenness among the governments we visited to work with the Brits. On our second visit to Warsaw, I asked a local contact: why us?

"It's simple." The Pole grinned. "Obviously, for historical reasons, we don't want to train with the Russians. Or the Germans. The US make everything so complicated. The French just are complicated. Who else is there? Working with the British is a no-brainer."

(Reverse) conspiracy theories

An extension of excessive self-criticism is what I call *reverse conspiracy theorising*. This, too, is to be avoided if you want to maintain your equilibrium.

On my first visit to the Berlin Wall Museum in April 2000 I got into an argument with a bloke at the information centre. The building of the wall, he said, like the 1956 Soviet invasion of Hungary, had not been the responsibility of the Soviet Union but was the fault of the United States. Timely intervention by the US, he said, could have stopped both. The CIA must have had a secret agenda to encourage the building of the wall. I demurred, baffled.

One of the grounds for classic conspiracy theories is people's fear of chaos. Rather than accept that *que sera sera*, they seek a hidden hand or dark forces behind events. There is no evidence.[3] But attributing blame to a sinister conspiracy gives them comfort that they have an inside track on what is really going on.

Reverse conspiracy theorising is when, in response to cataclysms such as the building of the Berlin Wall, people focus not on the perpetrators of the atrocity, but on asking 'What did we do wrong?' When Russia invaded Ukraine in February 2022, I did many interviews. Some asked why Putin was doing

---

[3]   Otherwise, they wouldn't be conspiracy theories.

such a thing. But the most common question was: 'What could we have done to prevent this?' or even 'Is this our fault?' I was reminded of tragic cases of children who blame themselves for their parents' divorce.

Of course, both sides share some responsibility for most disputes. But the main culprits are usually obvious. The CIA overthrew the democratically elected Mosaddegh government in Iran in 1953. The Soviet Union invaded Hungary in 1956. The East German government built the wall in 1961. Russia invaded Ukraine in 2022. It may be interesting for future academics to explore what other countries could have done differently. It may give us a spurious sense of being more in control of events to lambast our own side for failing to stop whatever catastrophe has occurred. But in most cases, the more urgent question is *what can and should we do now to combat or reverse whatever bad things are happening?*

In case you are so far from being grounded as to subscribe to conspiracy theories, consider the Welsh Secret Service.

When I arrived in Turkey in 2012 I found what was in many ways an ultra-modern country. Digital government services put the UK to shame. Mega-factories churned out electronics branded with European, Korean and Japanese household names. Gleaming new airports and motorways seemed to open daily. Turkey's economy had surged from 2002 to 2011, reaching 11.2 per cent annual growth. In 2013, Mancunian economist Jim O'Neill, who had invented the acronym BRICs to describe Brazil, Russia, India and China as future growth poles, talked of the MINT economies – Mexico, Indonesia, Nigeria and Turkey – as the next big thing.

Against this background, I was puzzled to find Turks passionate (and self-avowed) conspiracy theorists. Serious people argued that everything from the 2013 Gezi Park protests to currency movements were the result of anti-Turkish plotting by shadowy dark forces. The arguments were often contradictory. Secularists claimed outsiders were not criticising police action against the Gezi protestors because they saw Turkey's 'mild Islamism' as a model for the region. Pious types argued that 'the West' was slamming police actions because it hoped the protests would overthrow the pro-Islamic authorities.

Against this background, I met a wise journalist in Istanbul. 'Had lunch with one Gareth Jenkins, a long-time Turkey-watcher who is the world authority on Turkish conspiracy theories,' I wrote. 'He told me when people accused him of being a spy, he'd say he worked for the Welsh Secret Service. When people said they'd never heard of it, he told them that showed its tradecraft.'

The comment by Jenkins highlights a paradoxical feature of conspiracy theories: *the greater the absence of evidence for the existence of a conspiracy, the more certain those who believe in it become that it exists.* Such logic makes the Welsh Secret Service the most powerful intelligence agency on Earth. Operating from their secret Snowdonia base, eschewing websites, parliamentary oversight or acknowledgement, they strike fear into the enemies of the principality.

Conspiracy theories are not restricted to any political culture, as events in the United States and elsewhere have shown. But there are reasons why such thinking floats to the surface. Most important, history is full of genuine conspiracies – often enacted against weaker or disempowered political entities by stronger ones. People in countries that historically have been bossed by bigger powers are more likely to think that whatever happens must be the result of hidden action by dark powers. The tendency of some countries to behave in ways perceived as arrogant amplifies such beliefs.[4]

Personally, I like the idea of dark powers and hidden parallel universes. Who has not watched *A Midsummer Night's Dream* and wondered at a world where our actions are controlled and manipulated by mischievous fairies? But it is worth bearing in mind that many conspiracy theories have their roots in history, inequality and powerlessness.

EMPATHY, HUMILITY AND principles can help us all navigate through complex lives and impossible choices. Recognising that you, too, are fallible can also help.

---

[4] For example, autocracies are often better than democracies at feting dignitaries from smaller nations. Vladimir Putin found time to meet Lassina Zerbo, the Burkinabé executive secretary of the Comprehensive Nuclear-Test-Ban Treaty Organization, in Moscow, at a time when we could not persuade even junior ministers in London to see him. These things are not forgotten.

13

How to craft a career

Most of us fancy a fascinating, fun, rewarding career, but how to achieve this is not always obvious. You can make a good start by setting yourself clear goals, being proactive in seeking to attain them and getting on with the job.

Being proactive

In balancing conflicting objectives, I often prioritised the rest of my life over my career.

In 1988 I was interviewed for a job as private secretary to the minister for Europe.

"Got any questions?" the minister said.

"I'm going to Lundy Island for New Year," I said. "What if a crisis blows up?"

"You'll just have to come back," he said.

"We'd have to charter a helicopter," I said.

In the UK, the archaic term 'private secretary' means the boss of a minister's outer, or private, office. Some people prefer the French *chef de cabinet*, or the elastic US term 'chief of staff', because they sound more important.[1]

---

[1] Titles for British public servants are wilfully confusing, including permanent under-secretary (PUS), the most senior civil servant in a department; deputy under-secretary (DUS) for the next tier down; and assistant under-secretary (AUS) under that.

Becoming a private secretary is a stepping stone to stardom throughout the civil service, including the Foreign Office.[2] The position gives you a helicopter view of policy formation, contact with senior officials, and first-hand experience of ministers in action – or inaction, as the case may be.

In 1991, FCO HR thought I was ripe for private office. I was not so sure. I wanted to write novels. What if ministerial demands obstructed my creative endeavours?

My first interview was with Europe Minister Francis Maude, a Thatcherite who never quite made it to the first rank of politics. He was not impressed when I set out my plans for a New Year holiday on an island in the Atlantic Ocean. Did I embroider the island's remoteness? Perhaps I did.

Undaunted, HR put my name on the shortlist to become private secretary to Maude's successor, Tristan Garel-Jones, even when I did not bid. Again, I did not shine in the interview. The successful candidate went on to have an illustrious career. 'Quite happy, in retrospect,' I wrote two years later, 'the novel is finished and the next one is under way.'

Might my career have soared if I had seized wholeheartedly the opportunity to become a private secretary? Possibly. But like my later decision to take four years' parental leave, it enhanced my quality of life and relationships. And the career could have been worse.

AN EXAMPLE OF career proactivity was transferring to the Foreign Office. In 1979, in the Department of Transport, I would look out of my 17th-floor office at the sea of windows in the neighbouring tower. 'If I have a good career,' I mused, 'I shall be sitting in another of those windows in 30 years' time.'

The FCO offered a more diverse geography. In January 1997, for example, I researched jobs coming up when I finished in Hong Kong Department. One incumbent head of mission of a job I scoped out told me: 'Knowing the King is your main

---

[2] Vinay Talwar's 2021 internal study *What Success Looks Like? A Study of Senior White Men in the Foreign and Commonwealth Office*, designed to explore how to improve diversity in the upper reaches of the organisation, found that 65 per cent of the study cohort had held private office jobs.

job. Semi-god. So likes non-sycophantic people. Entirely oral culture. You're out constantly. Must be ready to spend time hanging about.' Other jobs I explored were in New Delhi, The Hague, Rome, Lisbon, Kuala Lumpur, Rangoon, Bonn, Paris, Tokyo, Maseru, Prague, Brasilia, Montreal, Havana, Montevideo and Vilnius.

Notwithstanding my efforts to go to Africa or South America, by June 1997 I was writing to my brother 'We now know we are going to Bonn.'

But it could have been anywhere on Earth.

A PROACTIVE APPROACH to your career may also increase your chance of happiness in other areas.

In 1995–98, working on the handover of Hong Kong, I regularly flew between London and Hong Kong or Beijing in business class. The job was intense. Before flying, I relished the prospect of a long flight with no disturbances.

Once on board, however, I felt a mild panic at the rich mix of activities on offer, from perusing the fresh new airline copy of the *Financial Times* to listening to music, chatting to a fellow passenger, or reading my briefing papers. It was like a microcosm of trying to figure out how best to use our available life-span.

What if we watch a movie and it's crap? We miss the chance to talk to the interesting-looking neighbour, changing our lives forever. What if we address our neighbour and they won't stop talking, so we miss the chance to read our book? How about gazing at the moonlit cloudscapes from the aircraft window – a wonder we should never take for granted?

I found it helped to have an idea before boarding of how I planned to spend time on the flight and to try to stick to it, allowing flexibility for better alternatives if they arose.

The same, arguably, is true both of careers, and of life in general.

Early Christians argued about salvation by faith, or by works – a distinction picked up by Izaak Walton in *The Compleat Angler*, written in 1653. 'I shall tell you, that in ancient times a debate hath risen, and it remains yet unresolved, whether the happiness of man in this world doth consist more in contemplation or action?'

The ancient Greeks explored the issue in the character Tithonus. When Eos, Titan of the dawn, kidnapped Tithonus from the royal house of Troy to be her lover, she asked Zeus to make him immortal *but forgot to ask for eternal youth*. Tithonus lived for ever but became older and older, in misery. I picture him as a wizened cricket, writhing on a bare shelf in a cell. Clearer life goals might have helped him, too.

So HOW DO you decide your next move?

When, in 2002, my wife and I swapped jobs – she becoming counsellor (EU and economic) in the embassy, I taking over primary childcare responsibilities for four years – it presented me with unexpected choices.

The children would be at school during the day. Should I get a part-time job? Write? I drew up notes to help decide. 'It would be good to do something else entirely,' I wrote. 'Advantages of not working: stop competing. Explore alternative life. Get to know children better. Costs: probably bad for career. Could be boring. Less money ... Do I enjoy the Monday–Friday routine? No. See not working as opportunity, not period to be endured.'

I decided to write, noting also: 'If writing isn't working, consider other jobs.'

In fact, writing did work. The *Financial Times* liked my articles, and commissioned more. The novels I wrote secured me a literary agent. Spending more time with the children turned out to be the best thing I ever did.

For many, the idea of formally analysing an important life decision – whether to have a child, say, or which house to buy – may seem crazy. For some, gut feeling works best. For me, spending weeks evaluating what to do next helped me feel sure I had made the best choice.

How to match people to jobs

Matching people to jobs in diplomacy is as difficult as in any other line of work. When I joined the Foreign Office in 1983, we were given our next posting, often apparently at random, by an all-powerful HR department.

Later, an element of choice crept in: you filled in a form giving a preference for a continent and a type of work. Then, a devolved interview-based jobs market came in.[3] You, as 'hiring manager', recruited people to work for you, within a personnel-devised framework designed to ensure fairness and consistency.

The problem was the tension between the needs of individual hiring managers and the organisation as a whole. What if I, in Berlin, recruited Smith, who HR felt needed experience in Sub-Saharan Africa, or to use her Japanese skills? What if, after the 2020 merger of FCO and the Department for International Development, key officers from both organisations needed rewarding jobs – or encouragement to depart the new Foreign, Commonwealth and Development Office for pastures new? Eventually, the pendulum swung back towards a more directive role for HR.

My efforts to return to the FCO in 2005–06 after four years of looking after the children came in the heyday of the devolved jobs market.

'I have not got the Director EU job, not much to my surprise,' I wrote. 'Less pleasingly, I didn't make the short-list (i.e. I've not been invited to interview). Will now apply for the next job, Director Global Issues and Economics (*sic*). If I don't get an interview for that, it will be an indication of how tough my reinsertion into the FCO will be.'

I didn't get an interview for director global issues and economics, either.

British diplomats liked the devolved jobs market as relatively fair and transparent. Whether a more directive approach from HR would have helped me find a job sooner in 2006 is impossible to say. But in the end, I got lucky – both in deciding to take a four-year career break and in finding a great job – as director of Overseas Territories – at the end of it.

WHAT ABOUT COMPUTERISING the matching of diplomats to desks? In 1984 I was asked to write a report exploring the possibilities.

In the 1980s, FCO personnel experts hoped computers would create a fair and objective system of postings and promotions.

---

[3]   Interviews for FCO jobs only became possible with the advent of global video-conferencing – a good example of technology changing an organisation.

Enter into the system details of each staff member – languages, experience, training, economic aptitude, numeracy and so forth – plus the specifications of each job, and the computer would spit out the ideal candidate.

It didn't work. Which data should be entered? How should it be weighted? What categories, or qualities, should be included? How much latitude should one allow for timing, preference or family circumstances?

What if candidate Evans, proposed by the computer as perfect for the first secretary slot in Paris, was, to anyone who had ever met Evans, laughably inappropriate; whereas Brown, unaccountably overlooked by the algorithm, was tailor-made to take Paris by storm? What if the ambassador in Paris disliked Evans and Brown but fancied the look of Patel?

Twenty-five years after my report on statistics I sat on a board assigning candidates to senior Foreign Office jobs. One candidate for a demanding role was H—, a person unknown to me. We had before us hundreds of pages of scrupulously objective data prepared by the personnel department, analysing the suitability of each candidate.

Personnel raised doubts about H—. He was deficient, they said, in vital skills, including leadership, supporting the development of his team and completing staff appraisals on time. Yet the majority of the board, who knew H— personally, said he was dynamic, driven and rich in regional expertise. They appointed him. He went on to have a distinguished career.

Austria takes a different approach to top jobs. "We assume that anyone who has reached the appropriate grade is capable of being an ambassador," a senior diplomat told me. "When the next round of appointments falls due, our aim is to draw up a slate of candidates that is politically balanced.[4] Then we put it to ministers for agreement."

The US appoints, as ambassadors to more agreeable capitals, individuals whose primary qualification is that they have contributed large sums to the campaign of the successful presidential candidate. Few have diplomatic experience, although

---

[4] Austria has one of the highest membership rates of political parties in Europe, including many government employees.

some have had fathers or grandfathers serving as ambassadors. Yet in many cases they do a great job – particularly in cultivating top people, a priority for any ambassador.

Despite these different systems, British, Austrian or US ambassadors are not, arguably, conspicuously better or worse than each other.[5] As for my report on statistics and computers, I submitted it on time with dozens of recommendations – including that whoever operated the personnel computer should be numerate.

I never heard of that report again.

How to recruit diplomats

How do you become a diplomat in the first place? When I joined the FCO in 1983, I went on a course in Brussels to learn about the functions of the European Community. I discovered that different countries appointed diplomats in diverse ways.

France often recruited graduates who had completed the two-year multidisciplinary study course of the National School of Administration (ENA) in Paris. Even to enter ENA, students had to sit a competitive exam, often preceded by years of study at another top institution such as Sciences Po or the École normale supérieure.

Wannabe German diplomats tended to start by studying law. Entrants had to be fluent in English, plus French or another UN language. If successful in the multi-stage selection process, candidates joined a 'crew' of diplomats for two years of full-time training including history, rhetoric and diplomatic practice. Each year's crew tended to bond, forming networks for their future careers.

The selection procedure for British diplomats focused on skills, rather than knowledge. Candidates for the 'fast stream' could have studied any subject at university. Little formal training took place: once recruited, diplomats started work, typically with a couple of short postings in the UK, with a focus on on-the-job learning.

---

[5] The US system occasionally appoints notable weirdos, but so do other systems.

Subsequent experience showed that despite these varied paths, French, German and British diplomats did not differ conspicuously from each other. When they came together to tackle joint challenges, they appreciated each other's qualities, even if they did not agree. Diplomats from the three countries respect each other and work together well.

It is often tempting to think that 'the way we do things around here' is the best, or only, way to complete a task. In fact, as in recruiting diplomats, a broad range of approaches may work – or it may not make much difference how you do it.

Core career skills

The ability to get things done – no matter what the task – is a core skill in any profession.

In 1986, the British embassy in Vienna received an odd request.

The explosion at the Chernobyl nuclear power station on 26 April that year in what is today Ukraine had led Austria to ban all sales of fresh vegetables, empty the sandpits in playgrounds, and warn against letting children play outside. Austria had a greater proportion of its area (10.3 per cent) contaminated with radionuclides than any other country except Belarus.

A few weeks later the embassy was asked to 'provide a 1 ft × 1 ft area of soil (including the grass) to a depth of 1 to 2 inches ... the sample should include soil as well as root mat ... it is important that the grass has not been cut since 26 April 1986.'

We were to place the sample in a plastic bag, and return it to the Atomic Energy Research Establishment (AERE) in Harwell. The purpose was to measure the radioactivity in the soil.

The instructions were not classified, but we were not encouraged to draw attention to our actions. My boss Tony Morgan and I drove to the suburbs in his Volvo and found what we hoped was a suitable area of soil ('in an area well exposed and not sheltered by buildings and trees'). The sun blazed down from a clear sky as I stuck the spade into the ground.

"Are we contaminating ourselves, doing this?" I asked him.

"Let's hope not," he said.

We felt like grave robbers in a 19th-century novel.

What use the AERE made of our soil sample we never discovered. It is in the nature of diplomatic work that you send carefully crafted reports and analyses back to your capital and receive the same level of response you might get if you printed and burned your efforts on a pyre in the garden. Our curious soil collection of May 1986 was no different.

ANOTHER KEY TO career progression is effective delegation. In 1991 I bought a book called *Don't Do. Delegate!* I read it with interest, but kept it out of sight of my junior colleagues.

On the night of 4 September that year, I was in bed at home when the FCO resident clerk called me to say that left-wing Ecuadorian guerrillas had seized the British embassy in Quito. What should we do?

I called the embassy and spoke to the ambassador. Yes, he said, a number of men had invaded the building. The local armed forces were negotiating. He rang off, somewhat preoccupied.

As head of operations in SCD, I was supposed to run crises of this type. But was it a crisis? The ambassador had sounded distracted rather than alarmed. I phoned my boss for a second opinion.

Hilary Synnott had been a naval officer and submariner before joining the Foreign Office. He was unimpressed to be called at 3 a.m. "You handle it," he said. "Call me if there's a problem. I'll get some sleep."

I was stunned. Most FCO senior staff faced with a potential crisis would whirl into action, assuming command and issuing orders to everyone in sight. Instead, Hilary had dumped all the responsibility on me. I spent an uncomfortable few hours calling Quito, and the FCO, to try and find out what was happening, before going into work, where Hilary – well slept – asked me to update him. It turned out that most of the guerrillas had left the embassy; the remainder left the next day.

Synnott later became high commissioner in Pakistan and regional co-ordinator of the Coalition Provisional Authority in Southern Iraq from 2003 to 2004. He taught me more about delegation and crisis management in those few hours in 1991 than I learned in the rest of my career – or from reading my book about delegation.

Bosses should beware thinking that because they are the most senior in an organisation, they are the best at doing every task within it, or, worse, that they are the only person capable of doing those tasks. Your team members learn fastest when you give them maximum responsibility. That gives bosses a chance to focus on strategy. And bosses function best when they've had some sleep.

Diptels, chargé(e)s and handovers

A specialised area of writing vital to a Foreign Office career is the diplomatic telegram.

When, in her statement to the House of Commons about the invasion of the Falkland Islands on 3 April 1982, Prime Minister Margaret Thatcher said 'Yesterday morning we sent a telegram,' laughter rippled around the House as people pictured someone pottering down to the post office.

Diplomatic telegrams, known in the UK in the age of the internet as 'diptels'[6] and in the US as cables, represent a formal communication between a diplomatic mission and HQ. A diptel from the Foreign Office is, in the British system, issued in the name of the foreign secretary and from a mission, in the name of the ambassador – even though the individual may not have actually seen the text.

At a Cabinet Office coordination meeting on EU policy that I attended in 1988, a Treasury official confronted Sir David Hannay, the rather grand UK permanent representative to the European Community, with a policy telegram from his mission in Brussels that contradicted something Hannay had just said. "Who wrote this nonsense?" Hannay said, scanning the text. "It is signed by someone called Hannay," the Treasury official replied.

I first signed off diplomatic telegrams as deputy head of Hong Kong Department, when my boss, Sherard Cowper-Coles, was

---

[6] I was part of the team that designed the new diptel format when it became possible to send them directly from your desk, rather than via a comms hub. I argued for strict limits on length and a standard structure. The format has endured; the best diptels, distilling into 600 words an issue, why it matters and what should be done about it, are things of beauty.

away. The sense of responsibility for hitting 'send' was profound: was the quality of the product adequate? Did it reflect the views of the foreign secretary? Such responsibility is one of the joys of diplomatic life. Maintaining both quality and a sense of ownership in an era where technology encourages micro-management is a challenge with which diplomats continue to grapple.[7]

When a head of mission[8] physically leaves the country, it is customary for the second in command to become the chargé(e) d'affaires, often shortened to chargé(e). In larger missions, if both the HOM and the deputy are away, some more lowly person assumes the role. This happened to me a month after I arrived in Bonn in July 1998. It was the first time my name had graced a diplomatic telegram. The text read:

SUBJECT: CHARGE OF MISSION

1. Robert Cooper left Germany this morning on transfer to London. I have assumed charge.

TURNER

The next summer I was chargé again. 'Unfortunately (or not),' I wrote, 'we had a couple of quite good crises, most notably some excitement on BSE, which saw me instructed to fly to Berlin for the day to lobby the Minister of Health, Frau Fischer.' I felt nervous as I was ushered, for the first time as chargé on an official call, representing the Government of the United Kingdom of Great Britain and Northern Ireland, into the presence of Frau Fischer. She turned out to be younger than me and jolly company. I got down to business with my lobbying brief – in German – and it became just another working day.

---

[7]   Before I left what had become the FCDO, when Dominic Raab was foreign secretary, the guide to writing a 'submission' – policy advice to a minister – had expanded to over 70 detailed pages. When I joined in 1983, no guidance was thought necessary.

[8]   Abbreviated to HOM. An ambassador or head of a multilateral mission. In the Commonwealth may also be a high commissioner, i.e. ambassador to a Commonwealth country.

Diplomats may find the responsibilities of being a chargé(e), or even an ambassador, thrust on them at an early age.[9] It is a privilege.

WHAT ABOUT SIGNING OFF? I have always sought to leave behind a good impression when finishing a job.

British heads of mission usually leave before their successors arrive. At other levels, you may have a few days learning the ropes from your predecessor before she, or he, moves on. Most people hope their successors will not be so brilliant as to make their own tenure seem ineffectual, or so clueless as to suggest the job was unimportant.

Handover notes – where a diplomat leaves words of wisdom for a successor – have a patchy tradition. I loved the discipline of distilling years of work into a few pages. I would often start writing my notes a year or more before leaving, adding sections as annual rituals such as 11 November[10] came round, or particularly enjoyable or gruesome events reminded me of other key aspects of the job. Sensitive items such as key personalities and staffing I would pass on orally.

Only rarely was I the beneficiary of a handover note when I started a new job. But I was grateful to one predecessor who gave me both barrels on the unutterable ghastliness, as she saw it, of certain key contacts. Another improved my quality of life by devoting several paragraphs to the quirky plumbing of the residence. A third left me an unfinished 75-page guide on how to do the job exactly as he had done it. Some of my successors thanked me effusively for my handover notes; others remained silent.

As for the handover in Berlin – where I took over the job of running the house and looking after the children, while my

---

[9]   The youngest ambassador in recent times was Jules Chappell, who became ambassador to Guatemala, El Salvador and Honduras in 2009 at the age of 31.

[10]   Traditionally, British ambassadors serving overseas lead Remembrance Sunday events, remembering those killed in conflict, on the second Sunday in November or on 11 November itself – the day of the armistice at the end of the First World War.

predecessor took over my job as counsellor (EU and economic) at the British embassy – we never got in each other's hair. The only people who criticised my cooking – notably the fennel and orange ratatouille – were the children.

I DO NOT CLAIM to have had an exceptional diplomatic career. But a degree of proactivity and planning, and being flexible about goals when required, helped me feel that I had got out of the job all that I could reasonably have expected – while enjoying myself to the maximum.

14

How to be an ambassador

This chapter focuses on the role of ambassador: a job so intriguing and, arguably, aspirational that it has routinely been applied to hotels, apartment buildings, and even automobiles[1] of somewhat varying degrees of elegance. Many of the following lessons apply to leadership positions in any organisation. Others may be helpful for those seeking to be invited to, or to gatecrash, diplomatic functions. But I have also included a few anecdotes specific to ambassadorial roles.

One of the hardest things about being an ambassador is keeping your feet on the ground. Generations of brilliant diplomats have preceded you. Everyone assumes you must be wise, sophisticated and all-knowing. You do not, on the whole, want to disabuse them of this.

In fact, for ambassadors, the people are the task – both inside and outside the embassy.

Focus on people

Every ambassador wants to form load-bearing relationships with as many host country stakeholders as possible. By knowing everyone *before* a crisis blows up and you need their help, you can turbocharge your diplomatic impact.

In March 2020, as COVID-19 cases exploded, Austrian ski hubs such as Ischgl, where snow fans congregated from around the world, became hotspots for the virus. The lockdown that

---

[1] Including the Nash Ambassador (US), the Austin Ambassador (UK) and most famously the Hindustan Ambassador (India).

followed ended the ski season prematurely. Austrian local authorities, terrified of being accused of spreading the virus, refused to let hundreds of British ski instructors and chalet staff return home, leaving them trapped in closed resorts.

No embassy in Vienna could get its people out. We became increasingly concerned about the health and wellbeing of our stranded citizens. In the tense, panicky atmosphere as COVID-19 exploded, high-level lobbying did not seem to help.

Then I remembered a junior official in the Ministry of Health I had chatted to in the margins of a meeting with the minister. As the pandemic raged, I called him up. He was harassed but helpful, and directed me to key decision makers in the western provinces of Vorarlberg and Tirol. We hammered out a way forward. Days later, we were able to get buses into the resorts to ferry hundreds of our people home. Other countries followed suit.

None of this would have happened if I hadn't met – and remembered – the helpful Ministry of Health official. I later invited him to lunch to thank him.

THE SECOND KEY category of people an ambassador must comprehend, cultivate and gruntle is his or her own team. Recruiting and developing the best staff possible is crucial, because they will do most of the work.[2] For a head of mission, the key staff are the deputy head of mission (DHM) and personal assistant (PA). Drivers and bodyguards (if applicable) come close behind.

When I recounted to my DHM in Kyiv, Judith Farnworth, some ghastly calamity or impending cataclysm, she would often reply, in the way of a mother to a fearful child, "Do you want me to make it go away?" Some might find this patronising. For me, it struck precisely the right note. A good DHM, who runs the embassy and shields the ambo from all but the key decisions, is a gift from heaven. I also had outstanding DHMs in Istanbul and Vienna.

The ideal PA will discreetly identify and deflect problems before they reach you. They have that mystic blend of fierceness and friendliness that ensures people always feel welcome to walk

---

[2]   Unless you are in a one-person micro-mission.

into your office – unless you don't want them to. They will also be on terms of intimacy with a host of homologues in ministerial cabinets, protocol departments and other embassies, who can make things happen when the chips are down.

Drivers and bodyguards are among the people an ambassador spends most time with. I have seen senior figures treat their chauffeurs or close protection officers with contempt or indifference. This is insane. Both are essential to their principal's safety and wellbeing. Both can, literally, open doors. Their mood is key to the atmosphere of the mission. They deserve to be treated well.

In fact, that is true of all the staff in an embassy. A diplomatic mission, more than most organisations, is almost invariably something of an outpost. Many diplomatic staff are far from home; for locally employed officers, working in what amounts to a foreign diplomatic enclave is a legal and social challenge. While it is the ambassador's job to set the tone and to lead the mission, any member of staff can put them on a pedestal – or land them in the mire.

When size matters

In diplomacy, size matters. The practice of competing powers trying to build the most impressive embassy reached a crescendo in 19th-century Constantinople. The first British presence in the city had been built in 1802 for Thomas Bruce, Seventh Earl of Elgin[3]– the first diplomatic building overseas to be owned by the British government. Elgin's requirements, sent to London, included 'mahogany dining tables of a full breadth for eighty people' and four tons of nails. It burned down in 1831.

Its successor, Pera House, opened in 1847. It was beset from the outset by scandal over its scale and cost. Following a further fire in 1870, *The Times* reported rumours that the building had been destroyed. The humour is biting:

'Thus will have perished one of the most pretentious and costly buildings that have ever been erected for the service of the British

---

[3] Most famous for his controversial procurement of the Parthenon sculptures.

nation ... Many a sovereign has not a grander house over his head ... It was not beautiful; people were told that it looked well at a distance, but we never found anyone who had been far enough off to admire it.'

Other countries including Italy, France, Germany, Russia and Japan built fabulous palaces in the Ottoman capital to demonstrate their power and influence. All are still there. But in 1923, following the Turkish War of Independence, Ankara became the capital of Turkey – partly because it was less vulnerable to attack than Istanbul. New embassies rose there, transforming those in Istanbul into potential white elephants.

At the time of writing, Istanbul is a throbbing, wealthy metropolis. Its role as a hub for the region, reinforced by a new airport and the growth of Turkish Airlines, has again filled Pera House with activity; when I left in 2016, we had around two hundred and fifty staff. The legendary chandeliers in the ballroom regularly illuminated business engagements with Turkey's commercial capital.

Other ex-embassies in the city stood dusty and forlorn.

THE UK AMBASSADOR's residence in Vienna embodies the British imperial grandeur of 1875, the year it opened. Following the 1938 Anschluss, the National Socialist Flying Corps occupied it. After 1945, British authorities debated for years whether to repair the bomb-damaged building or demolish it.

In 1950, a Ministry of Works architect, Zwi Sirotkin, visited Vienna. He recommended the residence be repurchased and refurbished. He also recommended buying a bomb-damaged plot next door to build new embassy offices.

At the time, British officials occupied a requisitioned space nearby at Reisnerstraße 40. But no one took forward the plan to build new offices on the bomb-damaged plot. Instead, the ambassador's wife, Lady Caccia, began the task of 'levelling the ground and filling in craters, etc' to transform the space into a garden for the residence. For decades, the proposed office project languished. When I arrived in Vienna in 1984, the embassy was still at Reisnerstraße 40 and the residence enjoyed a gigantic, beautiful garden.

But the fate of the greenery had been sealed. On 7 March 1983, the Public Accounts Committee[4] interviewed the FCO permanent under-secretary, Sir Antony Acland. The committee argued that the Vienna residence was oversized, given Austria's modest importance. The PUS replied smoothly that this was for historic reasons: the building had been constructed in the days of the Habsburg Empire.

John Maxton MP, a Scottish Labour Party politician, intervened. 'Would you not agree that the Austro-Hungarian Empire disappeared in 1918?' he asked. Sir Antony could only reply, 'Yes.'

Mr A. Montague Alfred of the Property Services Agency sat alongside Sir Antony. He sought to support the PUS by noting that the PSA had long recommended that the garden 'should be built upon for offices'.

The ambassador when I arrived in Vienna, Michael Alexander, fought to stop the new project. He even employed a photographer to take pictures of the splendours of the garden featuring himself, his wife and their dog. But the die was cast. Construction work on the new embassy began in 1986; it opened in 1989.

SOME BRITISH ENVOYS, like those in Paris, Washington or Vienna, occupy accommodation that is almost preposterously grand. But not every embassy or residence fuels the ambassador's delusions of grandeur. Those in cities with a shorter diplomatic history may range from modest (the 'tiny but nice enough' flat where I stayed with my kind colleague Carolyn Browne in Astana in 2014) to dismal.

My residence in Kyiv was planned by an oligarch based on a villa she had seen in Florida, and abandoned half-built when she ran out of cash. The design included a double-height reception room, spanned by a first-floor bridge, cutting the building in half. By residence standards, it was a good but not exceptional set-up. 'Sunday evening and I'm having a celebratory beer to mark the fact that I think I've fixed the heating,' I wrote one night in December.

---

4   A cross-party group of MPs.

I found hosting ceaseless official events in my home draining. To survive, I would leave evening receptions in the residence after a couple of hours, and retreat to my private lounge. But the central reception room made it impossible to pass from one end of the building to the other without being seen. So, I would descend to the basement, pass under the reception, climb the back stair to my bedroom and wait – often in bed – until the last guest had left.

Residences and human infrastructure

A residence is like an airport security arch. When I worked on counter-terrorism, the UK would sometimes try to improve aviation security somewhere in the world by purchasing an expensive piece of kit designed to stop terrorists carrying weapons and explosives onto aircraft. But without experts for maintenance and operation, it simply gathered dust.

Similarly, the key to making a residence work is not an ambassador with a scintillating personality or sociable nature, although those help. Rather, it is a team that know the building and how to use it. In countless capitals, I saw grand, fading residences, little used – a millstone around the ambassador's neck rather than a diplomatic asset.

A residence manager (in old-speak: butler) sounds a bit weird to non-diplomats. But someone like the legendary Antonio Navarro in Vienna,[5] who could deliver without onerous ambassadorial input a quick lunch, a dinner for 12, or a reception for 150 while guiding you in how to make the biggest impact, is priceless – particularly if guests depart marvelling at the experience. An ambassador faced with a gruelling work schedule plus hosting regular lunchtime and evening meetings in a huge, complex building will learn to worship the ground that a good residence manager walks on.

If that person also exudes charm and people skills, they become diplomatic assets of the highest order in their own right. The fact that famed chimpanzee expert and environmental activist Jane Goodall visited the Vienna residence regularly during my

---

[5] Tragically for future British ambassadors in Vienna, Antonio retired in 2023.

time there had nothing to do with me but everything to do with Antonio.

It was a good reminder, if one were needed, that I might be the ambassador, but the residence was never really my house.

A BRITISH AMBASSADOR in a Mediterranean country gave me a tip as I headed to Kyiv. "People expect the British ambassador to be a big man or woman in town," he said. "Someone everyone knows, and who knows everyone. Make use of it."

This was excellent advice. An ambassador has unparalleled opportunities to cultivate people of influence. Your job is to develop a load-bearing, two-way flow of information. First, you want to learn from contacts everything about the country you are in, or the organisation at which you represent your country (such as the United Nations). Second, you will expound to them the policies and other wonders of the country you represent, in order both to inform and to influence them.

Languages can help. 'On Thursday, having had lunch with Prime Minister Azarov on Wednesday', I wrote from Kyiv, 'I had lunch with Yekhanurov, the former Defence Minister. Having spoken Russian to Azarov I spoke Ukrainian with Yekhanurov, so felt very multilingual. Neither of them understood a word I said, probably.'

This two-way flow applies whether your interlocutor is a university professor, a musician, a politician, another ambassador, the family you are staying with on a language course, or a class of schoolchildren or soldiers you have gone to visit.

In some countries of the former Soviet Union or former Yugoslavia, ambassadors have more pulling power than in longer-established capitals. In Paris, London, Berlin or Washington, locals see ambassadors as what they are: glorified civil servants. For ambassadors of medium-sized countries in London to get a meeting with a cabinet minister is an achievement. In Bishkek or Ljubljana, they will have greater access.

In Kyiv, for example, I got to know fairly well both Prime Minister Yulia Tymoshenko and her successor Mykola Azarov, as well as Presidents Yushchenko (helped by my efforts to speak Ukrainian) and Yanukovych. I put my table-tennis table to good use, placing it in my entrance hallway and inviting guests for a quick game before lunch.

One oligarch, a senior politician, agreed to play with alacrity, having told me within minutes of arriving that his personal fortune was $2 billion. The game grew competitive, and we draped our jackets on a chair. Afterwards, he narrowed his eyes as I went to retrieve my garment. "Be careful you don't take mine," he said, "it cost ten thousand dollars."

Another oligarch came to sit with me on the terrace. Sipping an aperitif, we gazed out over a sea of apartment blocks. "Just think," my lunch guest said. "There could be a sniper in any one of those windows with his weapon trained on us right this moment." That terrace was never the same again.

A third businessman, perhaps seeking to impress me, told me about his wine cellars. The one in Kyiv, he said, had 20,000 bottles. The one in Donetsk, 30,000. I asked him which wines he liked most. "None," he said, "I don't drink."

Flair, branding and the QBP

An ambassador should exhibit flair – in a suitably self-effacing way – to underscore both the excellence of the country that has sent him or her, and the qualities of his or her team.

One fine example of such flair came when the British Embassy in Berlin reopened in September 1999 after a 60-year hiatus and the transfer of its operations from Bonn. The ambassador, Paul Lever, drafted its first diplomatic telegram as follows:

UNCLASSIFIED

FM BERLIN, TELNO 001 OF 030900Z SEP 99

SUBJECT: SIR N HENDERSON'S EN CLAIR[6] TELEGRAM NO. 552 OF 3 SEPTEMBER, 1939: REPRESENTATION OF THE UNITED KINGDOM IN GERMANY.

1. The required assurances referred to in TUR[7] were, sadly, not received: the subsequent course of events has been well documented.

---

[6] Unenciphered.

[7] Telegram Under Reference, i.e. the report referred to in the title.

2. But 60 years to the day later the British
Embassy to Germany has re-established itself
in Berlin.

LEVER

The 'required assurances' referred to a flurry of contacts on 3 September 1939, following Germany's invasion of Poland two days earlier. At 12.25 a.m. and at 5 a.m.[8] the Foreign Office sent telegrams to the British ambassador, Sir Nevile Henderson, instructing him to seek a meeting with Joachim von Ribbentrop, the German foreign minister, to say that unless the British government received assurances by 11 a.m. that German aggression in Poland had ceased, Britain and Germany would be at war. No such assurance was forthcoming.

It is a tradition in issuing diplomatic telegrams to refer to related reporting. The aim is to try and convince recipients, particularly your capital, that your mission is producing a seamless, holistic set of analysis. But rarely has there been such an elegant reference to an earlier diplomatic telegram as the above, picking up on an instruction received precisely 60 years earlier.

The reopened Berlin mission initially operated out of the former British embassy to East Germany at Unter den Linden 32–34. The pre-war embassy in the Wilhelmstraße had been damaged by wartime bombing. The East German authorities tore it down; its site became part of the Berlin Wall's death strip. But the UK retained title to the site. Her Majesty the Queen opened the new embassy in July 2000.

No MATTER HOW much flair an ambassador may exhibit, it's hard – as in any multinational organisation – to make sure HQ notices your qualities when you're on the other side of the world. A steely-eyed ex-ambassador gave me great advice as we discussed my forthcoming posting to Kyiv in 2008. "When you're an ambassador," she said, "you're miles from London. You have to do something that people identify with you – build a brand, if you like."

---

[8] Source: Tara Finn, 'Diplomatic countdown to war'.

When I started in Kyiv, I was too busy to think much about branding. But in 2009, I began to wonder 'Is that it?' I enjoyed being an ambassador. But I wanted to reach the next level. "For what are you known in the Foreign Office?" my coach asked. "What do you like doing most? You need to combine that with diplomacy, so it becomes part of your brand."

It turned out that what I liked doing most was writing. I began a blog.

In 2009, diplomatic blogging was in its infancy. My efforts, published in English and Ukrainian on the nascent Foreign Office blogging site, had modest impact. Then a Ukrainian-language newspaper in London, *Ukrainska Dumka*, asked if they could reprint it. There followed *Delo*, a Russian-language business weekly in Kyiv, and the English-language *Kyiv Post*. Then *Ukrainska Pravda*, Ukraine's biggest blogging site, began publishing my posts in Ukrainian, often generating much debate.

In the following years my blogging, on everything from freedom of speech to Down's syndrome, British films and music, Chernobyl, visa policy and reform of the Ukrainian gas industry, became central to my work.

From 2009 to 2021, 498 of my posts went up on the Foreign Office site.[9] In 2011, I started with Twitter, and in 2015 Instagram. By the time I retired, I had perhaps built something of the brand that my wise colleague had urged. I also learned another key lesson: that you perform best when you're doing what you love most.

IF PEOPLE ARE the task, some people are more central to ambassadors' lives than others. In Kyiv, I encountered for the first time that group of individuals who crave invitations to national day celebrations at embassies – in the case of the UK until 2022, the annual Queen's Birthday Party or QBP.[10] Long-retired Brits

---

[9]   By the time I retired, blogs had somewhat fallen out of fashion in the FCDO. But good people continued to write them.

[10]   It is characteristic of the constitutional confusion of the UK that it has no national day. British diplomatic missions, needing something to celebrate, hold 'King's Birthday Parties' on or around the King's official birthday on the third Saturday in June. Queen Elizabeth's official birthday was a week earlier.

told me in tears that their invitation must have been lost in the post. Others took direct action: a Ukrainian gentleman sporting thick glasses and a tuxedo turned up at every Kyiv national day, without an invitation, presenting himself as a distinguished professor and friend of the ambassador. He penetrated security at nearly all of them.

For most diplomats, the craving makes no sense. Who would want to come and stand for hours in a garden or crowded reception room with a bunch of strangers?

The reasons are belonging, status, fun and mystique.

People want to attend national days to feel they belong. Some countries hold two parties: one for their nationals, one for contacts. The UK system is ruthlessly utilitarian, and focuses on contacts, leaving some local Brits disgruntled.

Many non-diplomats see embassy events as high status. I am reminded of Groucho Marx's oft-quoted words: 'I refuse to join any club that would have me as a member.' But it's not daft; until the 19th century many diplomats were aristocrats[11] and the association of embassies with power and influence gives them an enduring allure.

A supposed association with spies and skulduggery further fuels the mystique of embassies. What are they doing behind those walls? Plotting? A national day seems to offer a peek into a forbidden and mysterious world.

Such celebrations offer, to put it politely, varying amounts of fun. A few have magnificent food, world-class cocktails and fascinating attendees. But many feature long speeches, cringe-making folkloric entertainment and interminable greeting lines. I sometimes took visiting friends and relatives to national days; they came away slack-jawed with horror at what I had to endure.

There is no relationship between the status of a country and the quality of national days. Some powerful countries feature bog-standard snacks and cheap drinks in plastic cups. South American and Caribbean nations display an above-average tendency towards mojitos and dancing. Much depends on a head of mission who cares about the event.

---

[11] Still the case for some countries.

Dear would-be guests: if you want to be invited to a future King's Birthday Party or national day event, the single best thing you can do is to have work contacts with the embassy. Organisers long for useful, dynamic people to invite. But your contacts must be regular. That second secretary you used to know? She left four years ago, and her successor, never having met you, struck your name off the list. You must be both useful and current or, like a retired ambassador, memories of you will slowly fade away.

15

How to make diplomacy reflect our changing world

Diplomatic practice may seem conservative. But in many areas, diplomacy is mutating – to keep pace with a world in transformation.

Women and diplomacy

Margaret Thatcher became prime minister in May 1979. Reviled and worshipped by sparring political tribes, she changed the UK – while herself reflecting wider changes in society – and diplomacy.

I first saw Britain's first female prime minister in the flesh when working on European Community issues in the 1980s. Mrs Thatcher met German Chancellor Helmut Kohl in London to discuss the 'future financing' of the Community – one of my subjects. As the largest and second largest net contributors, Germany and the UK in theory had a common interest in reforming the chaotic budget process. Having contributed to a briefing for the meeting, I went along afterwards to see how things had gone.

In the 1980s, security in Whitehall was relatively relaxed. I left the Foreign Office through a back door – long since sealed – onto Downing Street, and entered No. 11, where Thatcher and Kohl were giving a press conference.

The room, packed with mostly male journalists, bristled with tension: the two big beasts of the European Community were renowned for loathing one another. I clicked the door shut behind me. Margaret Thatcher looked up and fixed me with a stern gaze.

Although I was no fan of Thatcher, the instant of communication between the two of us rocked me back. She was probably irritated that someone had entered the press conference so late. But in acknowledging my existence for a few moments – a trick of top politicians – she made me see her as a human being. That in turn made me conscious that throughout her career, she had put up with a lot of men in suits.

I often met Mrs Thatcher when I was director of Overseas Territories from 2006 to 2008. The Falkland Islanders venerated her for having saved them, as they saw it, following the Argentine invasion in 1982. They often invited her to events in London. Widowed, frail and suffering from dementia, she cut a melancholy figure, lost in a fog of confusion yet visibly cheered by the adulation of her most ardent fans. I felt sorry for her.

Researching this book, I came across a photograph of Mrs Thatcher at the December 1987 Brussels European Council. The picture shows the 12 heads of state and government in the European Community of the time, plus the 12 foreign ministers, European Commission head and so on.

Mrs Thatcher is the only woman in the room.

In 1984 I was asked to explore why so many female new entrants were exiting the FCO.

I had joined the Diplomatic Service in 1983 alongside 20 others. Our group included 21 different degree subjects, 11 non-Oxbridge graduates (historically an above-average proportion and seen as a step towards diversity) and 11 women (ditto).

Within a year, nearly all of the women had resigned. I interviewed them about their reasons for leaving. One or two said they found the male-dominated, public-school vibe of the FCO alienating. But most said the main problem had been the reluctance of male partners to accompany them on an overseas posting.

Implementing equal opportunities for diplomats has never been a linear process. In the UK, the 1933 Schuster Committee report considered the admission of women to the Diplomatic and Consular Services and recommended they remain excluded. Evidence from heads of mission published in the report gives a flavour of male sentiment at the time:

'To put it bluntly, the clever woman would not be liked and the attractive woman would not be taken seriously' – Sir H.W. Kennard, Berne[1]

'The interests of the public service would be better served by endeavouring to secure a more virile type of official than by embarking on the experiment of admitting women' – Sir Patrick Ramsay, Athens

'It is unthinkable that a diplomatic or consular officer should produce babies and at the same time do her work properly' – Sydney Waterlow, Sofia

Although female diplomats were admitted in 1946, married women were barred from diplomacy until 1972. The first woman was appointed head of mission the following year; the first married woman in 1987. By 2008 the UK had 18 female HOMs; by 2012, 38. But critics argued they were often appointed to less important or desirable posts.

In 2018 the Foreign Office installed a 'Mirror Challenge'. Based on an idea from Mary Beard, professor of classics at Cambridge University, it featured pictures of the first women to hold 13 of the 26 top jobs, and mirrors for the remaining 13. The idea was to encourage women and other underrepresented groups to imagine themselves in those senior positions and create an expectation that their pictures would soon replace the mirrors.

By early 2024, 10 of the 13 mirrors representing jobs never done by a woman had turned: Abuja, Berlin, Paris, Tokyo, Washington, Ankara, Brasilia, Islamabad, New Delhi and the legal adviser in London. Around a third of all UK heads of mission were female. Only the mirrors for Riyadh, the UK mission to the EU and the permanent secretary remained. This did not mean 'job done', but it did mark progress in getting the Foreign Office to reflect society.

Families

Both women and men still face problems combining modern families and diplomacy.

---

[1] Quotes taken from 'Women and the Foreign Office', FCO Historians, 2018. Recommended.

The policy of posting diplomats to distant corners of the globe for years at a time originated when all diplomats were men, few women had careers, and no one thought twice about packing children off to boarding school for much of their childhoods. One may debate the damage inflicted on children, adults and relationships, but until the late 20th century, the system ground on.

Now that diplomats are as likely to be women as men, both partners tend to have careers, and many people consider boarding schools the work of the devil, the system is creaking. Some countries do not allow the partners of foreign diplomats to work; many do not recognise foreign professional qualifications. What happens to the diplomat posted to Beijing whose other half is a history professor at a great university, the cardiac surgeon in Washington whose partner is sent off to represent his country in N'Djamena, or the teacher who doesn't want to give up her career to accompany her partner to Osaka?

The advent of budget airlines in the 1990s helped ease the crisis for diplomatic families divided by smaller distances. When I was in Moscow from 1992 to 1995, flights back to London were costly and rare. Fifteen years later, a British ambassador there complained to me that his staff flew back to the UK so often ("even for parties at the weekend") that they had insufficient exposure to Russia properly to understand the country.

The challenges facing diplomats navigating far-flung geographies are a sub-set of those afflicting all families. More parents are in paid employment. Fewer people live and work where they grew up. But diplomats have a particular requirement to live and work overseas, and to move regularly.

Foreign ministry HR departments have striven to adapt. Innovations include job sharing between husband-and-wife ambassadors and 'commuter packages' for diplomats to fly home regularly rather than relocating whole families. Home, or 'nomad' working enables couples to live together wherever their employers may be. But not all diplomacy can be done remotely. Distant, tougher postings have become harder to fill.[2]

---

[2]   I myself turned down invitations to apply for jobs as head of the Helmand Provincial Reconstruction Team in Lashkar Gah, Afghanistan, or as ambassador to Sudan. Distances and postings affected my relationships, too.

When asked whether I recommend a diplomatic career, I tend to qualify an affirmative answer by pointing out that it's challenging for family life.

Many people still yearn for adventure at the utmost ends of the Earth. But squaring the circle of relationships, families and work looks likely to remain a constant struggle.

All this underlines the value of not putting all your eggs in one basket of work. Management guru John Hunt, speaking at a London Business School course I attended in 1996, put it well. Statistically speaking, he said, only one of the twenty people in the room would reach the pinnacle of the FCO. "The rest of you, indeed all of you," he said, "should have something else in your life that gives you intense satisfaction, in addition to your careers."

This was good advice.

Top nations: past, present and future

In a changing world, 11 September 2001 highlighted challenges to post–1945 US hegemony. I was in my office in Berlin when a colleague put his head around the door to tell me two planes had crashed into the World Trade Center in New York.

In the following hours, as we viewed awful images of fireballs, falling bodies and collapsing buildings, confusion reigned.

The report of the National Commission on Terrorist Attacks Upon the United States, also known as the *9/11 Commission Report*, is a gripping read. It details both the planning of the terrorists and the response.

That day another fireball, of chaos, engulfed the US authorities. No one knew what was happening, or how to respond. Anyone who believes that governments have total command of information, or that they operate smoothly in a crisis,[3] should read the *9/11 Commission Report.*

The internet was in its infancy – Facebook was founded only in 2004, Twitter in 2006. Yet rumours soon swirled about supposed fiendish plots by the US or Israeli governments to fake the whole event. This was partly conspiracy theorising by

---

[3] Many political thrillers – although not mine – depict governments as far more in control of events, and information, than is actually the case.

people yearning to see a hidden hand behind something horrific and incomprehensible. Many could not believe the US was as vulnerable as 9/11 suggested. But reflex anti-Americanism played a part, too.

In Germany, a wave of pro-US sentiment swept the country. I attended a rally at the Brandenburg Gate where politicians united in condemning the attacks. Everyone agreed that hijacking passenger aircraft and flying them into skyscrapers was wrong.

But the sympathy did not last. As the so-called War on Terror swung into gear, followed by the 2003 invasion of Iraq, suspicion of US motives and actions blipped back to normal – a default position for much of humankind.

Where does anti-Americanism come from? The top source is top nationhood. The parodic English history book *1066 and All That*, published in 1930, says that after the First World War, 'America was thus clearly Top Nation, and history came to a .'[4] It is natural for citizens of other countries to resent whoever is the top nation.

What about past top nations? In countries such as Iran and Turkey, where the UK formerly had an outsized footprint, people often believe London continues to play an exaggerated role in world affairs. A young opponent of Iran's theocratic regime, in exile in Berlin in 2001, told me "If you lift up the turban of a mullah in Iran, you will find stamped on his head the words 'Made in England'." Turkish has a saying 'If two fish are fighting in the Euphrates, an Englishman has passed by.'

Future top nations are also judged by tougher standards than others. As China's economic and military might bring it closer to top nation status, the rest of the world is paying more critical attention to its domestic and international policies, from Xinjiang to the South China Sea.

---

[4]   US political scientist Francis Fukuyama echoed this sentiment when he argued 69 years later that the dissolution of the Soviet Union meant 'the end of history'. I don't know if he had read *1066 and All That*.

Top nationhood also affects diplomatic practice. As UK permanent representative to the UN in Vienna from 2016 to 2021 I was often frustrated that the glacial appointments process for US ambassadors meant Washington's influence was absent from the negotiating table for months or even years after a change of president. The envoys eventually appointed were usually experts and fine company. But consultation and building alliances – essential to UN diplomacy – were not always as automatic an instinct to them as might have been ideal.

The UK, too, after historic periods of top nationhood, is less inclined to consultation and compromise than many. This was a factor in Brexit. A policy endorsed by 28 nations carries more weight than that of a single country. But many British politicians found the constant rounds of EU meetings with 27 partners, all of whom somehow felt entitled to hold and argue different positions, tedious and frustrating. How much easier it would be to decide policy on one's own and clear one's diary a bit!

History will judge how that worked out.

WHEN DO – OR SHOULD – powerful nations intervene in the affairs of others? Countries that have suffered colonialism – most countries, in other words – often query the logic of military intervention by Western powers. Others, seeing unchecked suffering or cruelty raging somewhere, ask 'Why doesn't someone do something?'

When I was consul-general in Istanbul, people would ask me why US or UK interventions were so unpredictable. The UK went to war following Iraq's 1990 invasion of Kuwait, or Argentina's of the Falklands in 1982, they would say. It acted to relieve the Ethiopian famine of 1984. What about chemical attacks in Syria in 2013, or the 1994 Rwandan genocide, or 1990s atrocities in the Balkans? The lack of consistency, they argued, must mean unacknowledged factors at play – oil, racism, indifference toward Muslim suffering, or a secret strategic plan.

It was a hard question to answer.

First things first: no brilliant global strategic plan exists. If a secret cabal of *über* oligarchs or politicians – or, according to conspiracy theorists, shape-shifting lizards – is running the world, they do it in a way so mysterious that I have never seen sight or sound of it during a lifetime as a fully indoctrinated[5] diplomat and civil servant.

Rather, decisions on whether to intervene are based on a stew of politics, chance, a dollop of national interest and principle – but less than you'd expect – and, above all, a large portion of doability.

Politics and chance go together. How much do voters care about something happening far away? Do they identify with the victims? When someone attacks your family in your house, you care a lot. Less so if it is someone further down the street, whom you don't know, or in the next town, or whom you actively dislike – and so on. If the media pick up a story and bring it into your front room, as with the Ethiopian famine in 1984, you will be more likely to pressure your government to do something.

Another element of chance is 'shit happens'. In 1991, a coup in Somalia fuelled anarchy and starvation. In 1992, US forces deployed to Mogadishu to support UN famine relief, delivering supplies to wide acclaim. In 1993, US forces became more engaged in military operations – still with UN backing – culminating in the infamous Battle of Mogadishu in October 1993 between US forces and local militias. That led to the withdrawal of the entire UN force, probably not to the benefit of the Somali population in later years. The entire intervention can be seen as the antithesis of a great power having a plan and achieving it.

Politics and chance regularly trump national interest and principle. When Russia invaded Crimea and eastern Ukraine in 2014, it breached core principles of international law and threatened to upend the entire post-1945 order of countries respecting one another's boundaries, with potentially catastrophic consequences – as we saw in 2022. Yet few European governments reacted. Politics meant many leaders did not want a row with Russia, whose oil and gas were enriching countless

---

[5]   Being briefed on highly classified material is known in the UK as 'indoctrination' – a term with a flavour of brainwashing. Rather than refer to actual classifications – some of which are themselves classified – diplomats sometimes talk about 'secret squirrel' material, meaning anything with a stratospherically high security marking.

well-connected interests. Ukrainian suffering did not capture the public imagination. It all seemed distant and obscure.[6]

Doability means precisely that. If a permanent member of the UN Security Council, with a veto, opposes action, the United Nations cannot act. Is the capital of the country, or the affected region, within easy reach of military forces? Does the country have powerful friends, or an active diaspora? Any of these factors may mean that even where the objective case for intervention seems overwhelming, nothing happens – or vice-versa.

On the whole, the growing hesitation of powerful countries to intervene in far-off (or nearby) lands is a good thing. So is the fact that such interventions are subject to increasingly stringent scrutiny. Barring an improbable global outbreak of common sense, however, future interventions are probably inevitable. So, too, is the certainty that they will take place inconsistently, and be criticised by much of the world.

NOWHERE IS THE clash between past top nationhood and 21st-century status starker than in the King Charles Street HQ of the Foreign, Commonwealth and Development Office. At an entrance, a statue of a Gurkha stands to attention, bayonet fixed. On a wall, a bare-breasted African offers up riches to a scantily-clad White woman on a rock above her, flanked by a lion, as a booty-laden ship sets sail. In the former India Office, straight-backed Sikhs pay homage to the Unknown Soldier in a cathedral lit by slanting shafts of sunlight. By the foreign secretary's office, Vikings storm ashore to ravish a kneeling woman in a work titled *The Seafarers Claim Britain as Their Bride*.

The decor of King Charles Street is beyond politically incorrect or, as we used to say, ideologically unsound. If an incensed conceptual artist had set out to construct an immersive sculpture to satirise Britain's history of colonial exploitation, they could not have come up with a more spectacular artwork than the entire Foreign Office main building.

---

6   British Prime Minister Neville Chamberlain in 1938 referred to the conflict between Nazi Germany and Czechoslovakia as 'a quarrel in a far away country, between people of whom we know nothing'.

The Office, as its residents call it, knows its accommodation is atavistic. The Goetze murals of allegorical historical scenes outside the foreign secretary's office were unpopular even before they were completed in 1921. Countless consultations have been launched to make the toe-curling décor more representative of today's United Kingdom. But all have foundered on planning controls (King Charles Street is a Grade 1 listed building) and political equivocation over post-imperial guilt – or the lack of it.

Leaving aside aesthetic and political arguments, the core question is: does a building influence the thinking, or the mentality, of those within it? The answer can only be a resounding 'yes'. This was one reason why, in the 1960s, the government decided to demolish the building as part of plans to disperse Whitehall ministries across London.

What impact would rehousing the Foreign Office in, say, a modernist 1960s office block at Elephant and Castle have had on the thinking of mandarins and ministers? Tangible evidence of the UK's contemporary status as an economically challenged, medium-sized power would have confronted them 24/7. Instead, in the sumptuous corridors of King Charles Street, symbols of Britain's erstwhile status as a world-bestriding colossus are omnipresent. We can debate whether this encourages ambition – or delusions of grandeur.

Personally, I'd keep the building. With hindsight, demolition would have been an act of vandalism. But like the Soviet-era statues of Lenin and Stalin that used to adorn town squares across eastern Europe, most of the artwork in the Foreign Office belongs, set in a historical context, in a museum.

Reforming the Foreign Office

As the Foreign Office has struggled with modernising its accommodation, so too has it grappled to reform itself.

Any organisation spread over hundreds of countries is hard to change. Diplomats are sent to a country with all their worldly goods. Hard-to-integrate-into-new-schools children or sacrificing-their-careers spouses may move with them. Jobs with language training mean identifying candidates years in advance. Cutting jobs (in FO lingo, 'slots') is disruptive, and often takes place only at the end of a posting. By then, the review has been forgotten and urgent new tasks have arisen requiring extra staff.

In the year 2000, ministers in London decided that British missions in the countries of the European Union were too expensive. Surely, they argued, with so much work being done at the EU level, we could slash diplomatic representation? 'Life at work … dominated by the "Review of EU Bilateral Embassies",' I wrote from Berlin, '[an] exercise that has left everyone feeling aggrieved and insecure.' In 2007, the catchily titled 'More Foreign, Less Office' review transferred staff from Europe to Asia, the Middle East, Africa and Russia.

The reforms came full circle when, after the vote to leave the European Union in 2016, the FCO deployed *more* staff to EU posts to deal with the additional tasks Brexit would generate. Many are still there.

TECHNOLOGY, TOO, HAS transformed diplomacy, with mixed results.

As recently as the 1980s, an official would draft policy advice, often dictated or written in manuscript and typed up by a typist, then put a paper copy of that advice up through senior officials to ministers. Those higher up the chain might add comments in manuscript, or by appending a typed sheet. The ability to distribute side-copies[7] was limited by the need to distribute them manually. Recipients of side-copies would intervene only if they disagreed violently with what was proposed. These primitive practices meant orders of magnitude less information circulated, demanding the attention of busy officials, than now.

Times changed. My first job description in the Foreign Office, in 1983, included 'supervising the storage and updating of material on the departmental word processor'.

I did not use emails regularly at work until 1998, when I moved to the economic section of the British embassy in Bonn. Around that time, a friend at the London Business School told me she had been astonished when someone in the next room sent her an email, instead of coming to speak to her. The political section of

---

[7] Copies addressed to copy-addressees, i.e. those, other than the action addressee, who the originator felt needed to see it.

the Bonn embassy declined to be connected to emails, arguing that they did not need them.

Both turned out to be prescient.

When I returned to the Foreign Office after four years of parental leave in 2006, I found email chaos. Paper filing systems had been abandoned without a working replacement.[8] You could send documents to ten, one hundred or one thousand people at the stroke of a key. People had little time to do anything except process email traffic – much of it irrelevant – and attend meetings.

The fallacy that everyone with a stake in a decision should be consulted – *no matter how numerous they are, or how tangential their interest* – bred paralysis. It also confused ownership of policy, making decisions worse. As mobile electronic devices proliferated, people felt always on call and overwhelmed. Efforts to regain control with instant messaging or video conferencing had limited impact. A permanent sense of crisis permeated government departments.

Diplomacy, and diplomatic excellence, persist. But information overload handicaps both.

The future of diplomacy

Diplomacy in the Western world has had a torrid few years. China's swelling power, failures across the Middle East, and Russia's descent into authoritarianism fuel a sense that foreign ministries in Washington, London, Berlin and Paris have lost the plot.

In the UK, hammer blows have rained down on the Foreign Office. Following the 2016 referendum, the job of implementing Brexit was given to the new Department for Exiting the European Union. DExEU in turn was abolished, its job supposedly done, in 2020. Responsibility for EU policy returned to what became the Foreign, Commonwealth and Development Office with the merger of the FCO with the Department for International Development (DFID) in September 2020. Concurrently, the government slashed the UK's overseas aid budget from 0.7 per cent to 0.5 per cent of gross national income.

---

[8] Still the case.

The merger between FCO and DFID, coinciding with Brexit and a global COVID-19 pandemic that forced diplomats worldwide to work from home for months, paralysed what was left of the decision-making machinery of both departments. The chief achievement of the merger, other than administrative chaos, was to incense those employees of the 'legacy' FCO and 'legacy' DFID who saw the fusion as value destroying and the aid cut as a betrayal.

Wags argued that no hostile power in their wildest dreams could have hoped to create such a combination of measures to handicap British foreign policy in promoting the security and prosperity of the United Kingdom as Brexit and the FCDO merger.

The challenges facing diplomacy are not restricted to the UK. Better communications have robbed foreign services worldwide of their gatekeeper function. In the 1980s, the Foreign Office had a monopoly on classified traffic with overseas missions. Now, the smartphone of every government official includes global encrypted video conferencing. Their opposite numbers around the world will often speak English with a British or US accent.

YET RUMOURS OF the death of diplomacy are exaggerated. As noted in the prologue, diplomacy has been in turmoil at least since the advent of the telegraph in the 1840s. Twenty-first-century diplomats must take the best lessons from centuries of diplomatic practice, blend experience and wisdom with modern technology and skills, and continue to advise their political masters on how to understand foreigners – or, in British terminology, 'overseas'.

Compared with the stuffy, sedate and homogeneous Foreign Office I joined in 1983, the organisation I left in 2021 was agile, diverse and inquisitive. Like all foreign ministries, it faces challenges, but with strong leadership and clear strategic goals[9] it can regain its mojo and continue to prove its enduring relevance.

For all who think we are living in the worst of times, I commend the 1946 sci-fi novella 'Vintage Season' by H. Kuttner and C.L. Moore. In this dark tale, a man discovers that what he

---

[9] Not more than three, please – see 'Top tips for diplomats and ambassadors' (Epilogue).

believes is a period of unprecedented awfulness will be seen in the future as the start of a great new era.

It doesn't end well for him, though.

Just as the international environment shows no sign of becoming easier to navigate, the requirement for expertise in distant places, policies and peoples will persist for years, decades and lifetimes to come. Diplomats must train and adapt to new circumstances and challenges, but a deep understanding of people and what makes them tick will never go out of fashion.

Epilogue:
Top tips for diplomats and ambassadors

How can we summarise a diplomatic life and its lessons – for diplomats or anyone else?

I have been blessed with a career of variety and challenge. Not every diplomatic day sparkles. But most jobs are what you make of them. I was struck by the wisdom of journalist Lyse Doucet when she appeared on the radio programme *Desert Island Discs*: "I have constantly bathed in a sense of gratitude," she said. "Be curious, explore the island, live your best life every day."

Being a diplomat entails joys and travails. Constant moves strain friendships and families. You have to align with the values of your employer more than in most jobs. But you do have a degree of choice; and as Audrey Hepburn sang in *Breakfast at Tiffany's*, 'There's such a lot of world to see'.

I am inclined to view with caution those who advocate 'taking your whole self to work'. Rather, a private hinterland is desirable, and keeps you sane. Study the fine advice of Mr Wemmick in *Great Expectations* by Charles Dickens, about work and home – the latter, in his case, the 'Castle', a simple but eccentric abode where he lives with his father, 'the Aged': 'The office is one thing, and private life is another. When I go into the office, I leave the Castle behind me, and when I come into the Castle, I leave the office behind me.'

To sum up, I have drawn up my top tips for diplomats, and for ambassadors. Most people, including me, find it hard to remember a list of more than three goals or objectives, so I've kept it short. Non-diplomat readers may decide to what extent these rules apply to their own chosen job or occupation.

Three tips on being a diplomat

1. Be expert, whether in languages, cultures, geographies or other skills, such as economics. Use that expertise to build wisdom and judgement.
2. Focus on people. Knowing them, understanding them and building relationships of influence with them is your core task.
3. Be long term. Deliberate, discuss and debate before you decide. The pace of social media makes this hard – but don't forget that the ancient Egyptians and Chinese found life hectic, too. Talleyrand's advice of *pas trop de zèle* still holds true.

Three tips on being an ambassador

1. Being an ambassador is a unique privilege. People expect you to be brilliant and knowledgeable because you stand on the shoulders of giants. Take a deep breath, stand tall, be wise, and justify those expectations.
2. Your job is to have opinions about your country or area of responsibility. You must make the hardest judgement calls when the going gets tough, or when your political masters need your advice. Get it right by being a good diplomat (see above).
3. Identify and focus on the work you find most absorbing. You perform best when you're doing what you love. People will notice the difference.

When I retired I had mixed feelings about, for example, removing from my wallet the 'First 15 minutes crisis leader checklist' that had nestled there – all too often disturbed – for the past 13 years as a head of mission. I was sorry to leave behind so many brilliant and inspirational colleagues. But I was pleased to have more time for my writing. I realised, as I walked one day through Vienna, that the best way to live longer is to use to the full the life you're living right now.

Thanks for reading.

Leigh Turner
London, 2024

Bibliography

Rebuilding the British embassy in Istanbul, pp xii, 199–200
Berridge, G.R. (2009) *The Times*, 7 June 1870, quoted in *British Diplomacy in Turkey, 1583 to the Present: A Study in the Evolution of the Resident Embassy*, Leiden: Martinus Nijhoff Publishers.

Proposals for institutional reforms of the Foreign Office, p xv footnote 4
Fletcher, T., Malik, M. and Sedwill, M. (2024) *The World in 2040: Renewing the UK's Approach to International Affairs*, London: UCL Policy Lab.

Modern architecture, pp 1, 2
Bradley, S. and Pevsner, N. (2003) *London 6: Westminster*, Pevsner Architectural Guides: Buildings of England, New Haven, CT: Yale University Press.

FT favourite city survey, p 17
Heathcote, E. (2011) 'Liveable, lovable – and lauded', *Financial Times*, 27 May.

2016 Turkey coup attempt, p 23
Pitel, L. (2016) 'Diplomats danced as putsch began, Laura Pitel reports from a summer party in Istanbul interrupted by a military coup d'etat', *Mail on Sunday*, 17 May.

Brussels satire book, p 49
Menasse, R. (2019) *The Capital*, London: MacLehose Press.

Population forecasting, p 68 footnote 19
Vollset, S.E. et al (2020) 'Fertility, mortality, migration, and population scenarios for 195 countries and territories from 2017 to 2100: a forecasting analysis for the Global Burden of Disease Study', *The Lancet*, 17 October, vol 396, no 10258.

Peng, X. (2022) 'China's population is about to shrink for the first time since the great famine struck 60 years ago. Here's what that means for the world', World Economic Forum, 26 July.

Peng, X. (2024) 'China's population shrinks again and could more than halve – here's what that means', The Conversation, 18 January.

Russia population forecast, p 80
Vollset, S.E. et al (2020) (as previously listed).

Denstone College, p 92 footnote 7
Fraser, M., Gilfillan, D., Hall, N., Holt, R., Mateer, N., Preece, R., Siddall, C., Swales, M., Woolley, J. and Dowsett, D. (1983) Denstone expedition to Inaccessible Island. Denstone College. (https://doi.org/10.17863/CAM.31580)

White Papers, p 91 footnote 5
Foreign and Commonwealth Affairs (1999) *Partnership for Progress and Prosperity: Britain and the Overseas Territories*, Cm 4264, London: The Stationery Office.

Foreign and Commonwealth Office (2012) *The Overseas Territories: Security, Success and Sustainability*, Cm 8374, London: The Stationery Office.

Alan Clark, p 101
Clark, A. (2003) *Diaries: In Power 1983–1992*, London: Phoenix.

'Iraq Dossier', p 107
Report [No.10] (2003) 'Iraq – Its Infrastructure of Concealment, Deception and Intimidation', January. (https://web.archive.org/web/20040619112534/http://www.number-10.gov.uk/files/pdf/iraq.pdf)

Transparency International, p 110 footnote 11
www.transparency.org/en/cpi/2023

Hans Rosling, p 130 footnote 22

Rosling, H. (2019) *Factfulness: Ten Reasons We're Wrong About The World – And Why Things Are Better Than You Think*, London: Sceptre.

Background on diplomat Charles Stewart, pp 122–3

Rowell, C. and Burchard, W. (2017) 'The British Embassy at Palais Starhemberg: furniture from the Congress of Vienna at Mount Stewart', *Furniture History*, vol 53, pp 191–223.

Boris Pasternak, p 141 footnote 4

Finn, P. and Couvée, P. (2014) *The Zhivago Affair: The Kremlin, the CIA, and the Battle Over a Forbidden Book*, New York: Pantheon.

Our World in Data, p 156 footnote 5

In 2017, the average worker in the US worked 1,757 hours per year; in the UK, 1,670 hours; in France, 1,514 hours; and in Germany a mere 1,354 hours. (https://ourworldindata.org/grapher/annual-working-hours-per-worker)

Variant CJD, p 170 footnote 4

Ritchie, D.L., Peden, A.H. and Barria, M.A. (2021) Variant CJD: reflections a quarter of a century on, *Pathogens*, 10(11), 1413.

Effective delegation, p 192

Jenks, J.M. and Kelly, J.M. (1987) *Don't Do. Delegate! Secret Power of Successful Management*, London: Kogan Page.

Tara Finn, p 205 footnote 8

Finn, T. (2019) 'Diplomatic countdown to war', Foreign Office Historians, 3 September. (https://history.blog.gov.uk/2019/09/03/diplomatic-countdown-to-war)

Admission of women to the Foreign Office, p 211 footnote 1

FCO Historians (2018) 'Women and the Foreign Office: a history', *History Notes*, Issue 20. (www.gov.uk/government/publications/women-and-the-foreign-office)

'Vintage Season', p 221
Kuttner, H. and Moore, C.L. [originally published under the joint pseudonym 'Lawrence O'Donnell'] ([1946] 2009) 'Vintage Season', in B. Bova (ed.) *The Science Fiction Hall of Fame, Volume Two A*, New York: St Martin's Press.

Index

Belarus 7, 75, 136
Bellwin, Lord 103–5
Bennett, Philippa 155
Berlin 11
  East 144, 145
  reopening of British embassy in
    10–11, 204–5
  West 143–5, 178
Berlin Wall 74, 118, 145, 182
  fall of 54, 146, 180
Bermuda 87, 96–8
Biedenkopf, Kurt 169
Blair, Tony 25, 107, 108
blogging, diplomatic 26, 173, 206
body language 163
bodyguards 32, 199
Bonn 10, 11, 194, 204
borders and state power 53–4
Botswana 131
brand, building a 205–6
Brazil 129, 139, 182
Brexit 42–52, 220–1
  Article 50 letter 47
  British citizens' rights 50
  Chequers Plan 46
  collective death wish 47
  Department for Exiting the
    European Union (DExEU) 220
  difficulties in arguing government
    line on 47–8, 170–2
  expats and 19, 48
  failures of political leaders 48
  government actions open to legal
    challenge 171
  impact on conducting foreign policy
    51–2, 221
  justification and neckwear 172
  Northern Ireland Protocol 19, 171
  origins 42–4
  referendum 46–7, 50, 52
  top nationhood a factor in 215
  trying to explain 19, 47–8, 170–2
British Antarctic Survey (BAS) 88,
  90, 98
British Antarctic Territory 14, 25, 98
British Broadcasting Corporation 36,
  56
  World Service 131–2

British Indian Ocean Territory (BIOT)
  14, 88, 89, 92–3, 155
Brize Norton, RAF 14, 39–40
Broomfield, Sir Nigel 157
Brzezinski, Zbigniew 16
BSE (bovine spongiform
  encephalopathy) 169–70
Buchenwald concentration camp
  145–6
Budapest 54
Budapest Memorandum 75–6, 82

C

Caccia, Lady Anne Katherine 200
Cameron, David 50, 52
Campbell, Alastair 24–5
car sizes 97–8
career breaks 12–13, 149, 187, 188,
  195–6
Cawley, Alison 3
censorship of literature 141–2
Central Asia 18, 80, 147–8
Chalker, Lynda 5
chargé(e) d'affaires 194–5
Charles, Prince of Wales 157–8, 168
Charles Stewart Conversations 122–3
Chatham House Rule 123
chemical and biological warfare
  (CBW) 35, 36
Chequers Plan 46
Chernobyl disaster 191–2
China
  Cultural Revolution 70–1
  economic reform 67
  handover of Hong Kong to 9–10,
    68–70
    policy after handover 166
  Hong Kong security law 71–2
  instability 70–2
  leaders' fear of democracy 67–70,
    71, 72
  moving closer to top nation status
    214
  poverty rate 67
  Shanghai Museum 67–8
Chubais, Anatoly 112
Civil Partnership Act (2005) 176

U

UK Independence Party 52
Ukraine
  Association Agreement with EU
    77
  'Big Treaty' with Russia 76
  Chernobyl disaster 191–2
  cutting of gas supplies to 109
  Deep and Comprehensive Free
    Trade Area (DCFTA) 77
  Donetsk 73, 75, 81, 204
  Holodomor 81
  independence referendum 16, 75
  language 17, 78, 203
    learning 16–17
  moving closer to EU 16, 76–7
  nuclear weapons 75–6, 82–3
  oligarchs 204
  Partition Treaty on the Status and
    Conditions of the Black Sea
    Fleet 76
  Putin's fear of a successful,
    democratic 66, 72, 74
  religion and diplomacy 28–30
  Strategic Missile Forces Museum
    82–3
  Ukrainians 73, 74, 79, 81, 162,
    163
  see also Crimea; Kyiv;
    Russia–Ukraine war
Ukrainian International Airlines
  flight 752 84
United Nations (UN) 107, 120,
  129–30, 215, 217
  forces in Somalia 216
  languages 139–40
  Office on Drugs and Crime 19
United States (US)
  9/11 Commission Report 213
  22nd Amendment 105
  appointments to top diplomatic jobs
    189–90, 215
  hitchhiking xv–xvi, 142
  intervention in Somalia 216
  shooting down of Iran Air flight 655
    84
  top nation status 213–14, 215, 216
Uzbekistan 80, 147–8

V

Vereker, John 97
video, introductory 167–8
Vienna 3–5, 19–20
  "capital of spies" 118
  Charles Stewart Conversations
    122–3
  Hunt's visit to 114
  Johnson's visit to 44–5, 74n1, 118
  lunch with Kneissl and her team
    114–15
  police 4–5
  royal visits to 157–9, 168
  UK ambassador's residence 200–1,
    202–3
  wild boar in Lainzer Tiergarten
    25–6
Vienna Convention on Diplomatic
  Relations 117
'Vintage Season' (sci-fi novella) 221–2
Visegrád Group 112
Vladivostok 153, 154–5

W

Waldheim, Kurt 4, 122
Wall, Stephen 6, 42
Walton, Izzak 186
Washington DC 33, 201, 203
Waterlow, Sydney 211
weapons of mass destruction (WMD)
  107
Welsh Secret Service 182–3
'whataboutism' 84
wild boar attack 25–6
Wilde, Oscar 132
Wilmshurst, Elizabeth 172
women and diplomacy 209–11

Y, Z

Yanukovych, Viktor 16, 76, 77,
  125–6, 203
Yekhanurov, Yurly 203
Yeltsin, Boris xiii, xiv, 21, 57, 58, 64,
  113
Yushchenko, Viktor 16, 29, 81, 203
Zerbo, Lasina 183n4